Robert Miles
Marc Bertonasco

CALIFORNIA STATE UNIVERSITY, SACRAMENTO

Prose Style for the Modern Writer

PRENTICE-HALL, INC.
Englewood Cliffs, New Jersey 07632

Library of Congress Cataloging in Publication Data

MILES, ROBERT (date)
   Prose style for the modern writer.

   Bibliography: p.
   Includes index.
      1. English language—Style.   I. Bertonasco, Marc F.,
(date), joint author.   II. Title.
PE1421.M52   808'.042   76-44391
ISBN   0-13-731521-X

PRENTICE-HALL SERIES IN ENGLISH COMPOSITION
James C. Raymond, Series Editor

Printed in the United States of America

10   9   8   7

Prentice-Hall International, Inc., *London*
Prentice-Hall of Australia Pty. Limited, *Sydney*
Prentice-Hall of Canada, Ltd., *Toronto*
Prentice-Hall of India Private Limited, *New Delhi*
Prentice-Hall of Japan, Inc., *Tokyo*
Prentice-Hall of Southeast Asia Pte. Ltd., *Singapore*
Whitehall Books Limited, *Wellington, New Zealand*

Contents

iii

III ADVANCED PRINCIPLES OF STYLE

Preface

This text presents the basic principles of expository and argumentative style. Much of what we say might have been applied to descriptive and narrative prose as well, but we have confined ourselves to discussing the kind of prose that most writers find most useful —the prose of the college essay, the business report, the magazine article, and so on.

Our primary audience is the college student. The text can be used by students at varying levels of sophistication, those taking a senior seminar in prose style as well as those just getting started in freshman composition. This flexibility comes from the way in which the text has been organized. Sections I and II deal with simpler points of style; section III turns to complexities. Thus an introductory course can concentrate on sections I and II, with only occasional glimpses into III, while an advanced course can survey I and II but give most of its attention to III.

We have consistently put pedagogical concerns above scholarly ones. We have aimed to produce a practical guide for apprentice writers, not a contribution to the scholarship of linguistics or stylistics. We have not tried to break new ground but merely to summarize the best available advice regarding prose style, in a form that would be clear and useful to writers-in-the-making. One result is that we tend to be conservative in our references to grammar. We use the terminology of traditional grammar rather than newer grammars because—in our own classes, at least—those students who know any grammatical terms at all tend to know the traditional ones. In any case, we keep grammatical terminology to a minimum; we never present the terms without adding examples; and when we must define the terms, we offer simple working definitions rather than the thorough but complicated ones that might have been more pleasing to purists.

Our emphasis on pedagogy rather than scholarship has caused us to oversimplify not only with regard to grammar but also in matters of style. Apprentice writers, we believe, need simple, clear-cut advice; but in matters of style, simplicity is won only at the cost of oversimplification. In order to be clear and useful, we have had to ignore innumerable complexities. If we had strained to be fully accurate, our text would have become an enormous tome filled with elaborate explanations of minor points irrelevant to the problems actually faced by apprentice writers. The pages would have been littered with "furthermore's," "however's," and "on the other hand's," a multitude of exceptions and qualifications and theoretical hypotheses that would have prevented even the most eager apprentices from sifting out the advice they need at this stage in their development.

Classroom discussions can remind students that the principles of style set forth in these pages are not absolute truths achieved through mystical union with the divine, but merely provisional rules for apprentices, to be treated more and more skeptically as the apprentices advance toward a mature mastery of their craft. (Students ready to move beyond the level of sophistication represented by the present text can do so by consulting the books listed on pages 241-42.)

One feature of the text that especially pleases us is its abundance of illustrative passages, most of which come from the writings of distinguished contemporary stylists. Another is its abundance of exercises. Admittedly, some of the exercises do no more than ask the student to repair faulty sentences—a less-than-exciting activity that we nevertheless find indispensable in our own classes when we seek to explain certain principles of style. Most of our exercises, however, will enable students to create sentences, or short passages, that are at least partly their own. Perhaps the exercise supplies some raw material—a syntactical pattern, a subject matter, or even some of the words to be used—but the student converts the raw material into sentences.

One such exercise is *sentence imitation,* a favorite device in the rhetorical traditions of the ancient world and the Renaissance, and one that still proves effective in helping students to master unfamiliar syntactical patterns and figures of speech. We also ask the student to do a great deal of *sentence combining.* This is another exercise with a long tradition; but given the impetus provided by new research and a new name, it has achieved a new popularity. And rightly so. It has its dangers: it can entice students into producing cumbersome sentences filled with dangling or loosely connected modifiers. But under the guidance of an instructor alert to these dangers, sentence combining can help even the most tin-eared of students to sense the fluency, versatility and subtlety of emphasis of which their sentences might become capable.

We also offer exercises similar to those devised by Benjamin Franklin, who hoped that with their aid he "might possibly in time come to be a tolerable English writer." In the early pages of his autobiography Franklin explains how he improved his own prose by systematically ruining the prose of his betters, especially Addison. Having found a particularly impressive passage in *The Spectator,* Franklin would render it fragmentary and discontinuous. After setting it aside for a day or two, he would rewrite it in an effort to restore its original excellence. Then he would compare his final version with the original prose by Addison, and "sometimes had the pleasure of fancying that in certain particulars of small import I had been lucky enough to improve the method or the language." We present a great many exercises based on Franklin's example. We mutilate—or ask the student to mutilate—passages by such accomplished writers as Bernard Shaw, George Orwell, James Baldwin, Dwight Macdonald, and Germaine Greer. Then the student is asked to revise the mutilated version and compare his results with the original prose by Shaw, Orwell, or whoever. Thus the student accomplishes two purposes at once. Not only does he practice one or another principle of style; he also examines quite closely the style of an outstanding writer and discovers something about how that style achieves its particular kind of eloquence.

We are grateful to the many people who helped us prepare this text. First of all, we received valuable advice from a number of reviewers: Gerald Allard (Cosumnes River Community College), Harry Brent (Rutgers University), Frank J. D'Angelo (Arizona State University), Michael Dryden (Foothills High School, North Highlands, California), Ronald E. Freeman (University of California, Los Angeles), Michael Genung (California State University, Sacramento), Michael Heinz (an editor for the *Sacramento Bee*), William Karns (Cosumnes River Community College), Richard L. Larson (Lehman College), John Munsill (California State University, Sacramento), Ellen W. Nold (Stanford University), Christopher R. Reaske (Junior College of Albany), Donald Sturtevant (California State University, Sacramento), Gary Tate (Texas Christian University), and Jerome Winterman (Cosumnes River Community College). And we owe special thanks to James C. Raymond (University of Alabama), who reviewed several drafts of the book and offered excellent advice about matters both large and small, ranging from theories of style to niceties of wording.

The people at Prentice-Hall have been extremely helpful. Bill Oliver believed in our project when it was little more than a prospectus, and since then he has provided expert assistance at each stage of its evolution. And Barbara Kanski, our production editor, has skillfully supervised all the activities by which a manuscript is converted into a book.

Finally, we wish to thank the many students who have worked with the following lessons and exercises, in one form or another, during the past fifteen years. Their fascination with prose style has sustained and intensified our own fascination. We dedicate this book to our students.

ROBERT MILES
MARC BERTONASCO

Introduction

We all enjoy an eloquent style. We enjoy it whether it appears in the naughty quips of an Oscar Wilde ("The only way to get rid of a temptation is to yield to it") or the moralistic rumblings of a Samuel Johnson ("As I know more of mankind, I expect less of them").

Eloquence can sometimes win an election. According to the pollsters, the turning point in the Kennedy-Nixon campaign of 1960 was the series of debates in which John Kennedy won the confidence of millions of voters, not just because of what he said but also because of *how* he said it. He showed his sense of style again in his Inaugural Address, one line of which is still frequently quoted: "Ask not what your country can do for you. Ask what you can do for your country." This challenge may have had some influence on the droves of people who soon afterward joined the Peace Corps or the civil rights movement. But suppose Kennedy had expressed his challenge in a different way. Would he have aroused any enthusiasm with *this* kind of style?

One should not pose questions as to what services one's country might be able to perform for one's own benefit. A more appropriate course of action would be for one to consider in what ways one might be able to make some contribution to the improvement of the national situation.

1

Those spineless sentences wouldn't have convinced anyone to do anything.

Eloquence is valuable not only to public figures such as Kennedy but to people in all sorts of occupations—a student writing a paper, a journalist writing for a newspaper or magazine, a parent complaining about an incompetent teacher, an insurance agent explaining a policy, an employee recommending a change in company procedures, an environmentalist arguing a case before a county planning commission. . . . If "eloquence pills" were made available, millions of buyers would flock to the drug stores.

Many people seem to feel that a pill, or some kind of magic, is the only way to achieve eloquence. But what they really need is an antidote to a certain kind of nonsense they've swallowed. Here are the articles of this false faith. (1) Style is a Mystery. (2) Either you're gifted with an eloquent style or you aren't. (3) If you don't have one, you can't hope to get one. The grain of truth in this creed is that, obviously, some people have more talent than others. The dangerous falsehood in it is the claim that eloquence can't be learned—that no amount of training can change a mediocre style into an effective one. How ridiculous. Even a talented writer has to do a great deal of hard training if he [1] wants to convert his talent into a reliable skill. Bernard Shaw advised an aspiring young drama critic to do what Shaw himself had done: "The one certain thing is you must write, write, write every day for several years if you are to become a master workman in your profession." Like any other craft, writing requires an apprenticeship. We think of William Cobbett and Somerset Maugham copying out and analyzing long passages from Swift; Ben Franklin devising stylistic exercises from the essays of Addison and Steele; Abe Lincoln poring over texts in rhetoric and copying down passages of superior prose ("He read all the books he could lay his hands on," his stepmother said. "When he came across a passage that struck him, he would write it down on boards if he had no paper and keep it there till he did get paper; then he would rewrite it, look at it, repeat it"). And we think of Malcolm X, in prison, writing out words and definitions, a page or two every day, until he had worked his way through an entire dictionary. Talent makes a difference, but so do practice and perseverance.

And writers who don't aspire to become master stylists, but merely competent ones, don't need any inborn talent. All they need is ordinary

[1] Or she. Here and hereafter the masculine pronoun, when used in this kind of locution, is meant to refer to both sexes. We have tried several methods of avoiding this use of the masculine pronoun, but all our solutions have created new and more onerous problems: a profusion of clumsy and unclear sentences filled with roundabout phrasing, too many plurals, and too much passive voice.

intelligence, an ordinary command of the language, and a capacity for hard work. With these modest materials they can develop a clear, persuasive style, and perhaps even a style marked by grace, vigor, and individuality.

I

Words

1

Levels
of Style

This book could not possibly deal with all kinds of styles. Consider the enormous variety it would have to contend with—the styles of George Orwell, Eldridge Cleaver, Germaine Greer, John Stuart Mill, Jane Austen, Jerry Rubin, Plato, Nietzsche, Mao Tse-tung, Richard Milhouse Nixon (both public and taped), newspaper gossip columns, street signs, cereal boxes, feminine hygiene commercials. . . . Obviously we must simplify. And one way of doing so is to divide all styles into three main types: High, Middle, and Low.

Middle Style will serve perfectly well for most of your writing. It is the style in which most of the world's writing gets done. But Middle Style is best defined by telling what it is *not* before pinning down what it *is*. Hence we will start by talking mostly about High Style and Low.

HIGH STYLE AND HARD WORDS

The High Style aims at loftiness and grandeur. Today's readers are likely to find it too ornate and ceremonious for all but a few occasions, but at certain periods in the past it was used more freely. Here, from two centuries ago, is High Style at its highest—Samuel Johnson ruminating on the dangers of the imagination:

> To indulge the power of fiction and send imagination out upon the
> wing is often the sport of those who delight too much in silent specu-

7

lation. When we are alone we are not always busy: the labor of ex-cogitation is too violent to last long, the ardor of inquiry will sometimes give way to idleness or satiety. He who has nothing external that can divert him must find pleasure in his own thoughts, and must conceive himself what he is not, for who is pleased with what he is? He then expatiates in boundless futurity, and culls from all imaginable conditions that which for the present moment he should most desire, amuses his desires with impossible enjoyments, and confers upon his pride unattainable dominion. The mind dances from scene to scene, unites all pleasures in all combinations, and riots in delights which nature and fortune, with all their bounty, cannot bestow.[1]

As you can see, the High Style differs sharply from the style of ordinary conversation. Usually it differs by virtue of its solemnity, its resounding rhythms, and the elaborate structure of its sentences. And sometimes, as in the passage by Johnson, it differs in the sophistication of its wording. How often would ordinary conversation contain such phrases as "to indulge the power of fiction" or "silent speculation" or "the ardor of inquiry," not to mention "the labor of excogitation" or "expatiates in boundless futurity"?

If we pause to compare High Style with Middle, we find that Middle Style doesn't aim for loftiness or grandeur, but for clarity and simplicity. It comes closer to sounding like conversation. And therefore it relies mainly on familiar wording, the kind of wording recommended by the most respected commentators on modern prose—H. W. Fowler, for instance, as well as George Orwell, Bertrand Russell, and, more recently, Sir Ernest Gowers: "Use familiar words rather than the far-fetched, if they express your meaning equally well; for the familiar are more likely to be readily understood." [2] This doesn't mean that you must use *only* the shortest, most familiar words. To do so would keep you from taking advantage of the abundance of synonyms in our language. If you limited yourself to the short, familiar word *think*, you would deprive yourself of a wealth of alternatives: *reflect, speculate, contemplate, deliberate, ruminate, meditate, ponder,* and *conjecture,* to name just a few. If one of these longer, less familiar words is exactly suited to the meaning and rhythm of your sentence, if its nuances are precisely the ones you wish to convey, then by all means use it. But if *think* (or *consider* or *believe*) can "express your meaning equally well," then why not use the more familiar word?

Is this advice superfluous? Would the ordinary writer use familiar words anyway? Not necessarily. Too many writers think they sound

---

[1] *Rasselas*, Chapter 44.

[2] Sir Ernest Gowers, *The Complete Plain Words* (Baltimore: Penguin Books, 1963), p. 81.

more proficient and profound when they lard their prose with fancy-sounding words. Thus we find a businessman writing:

> We believe that, notwithstanding the many uncertainties in the out-look, an effort of foresight and preparedness will prove helpful in overcoming the problems that will arise and in promoting that expansion of trade and enterprise at home and abroad which is indispensable to the attainment and maintenance of healthy economic conditions.[3]

A psychologist writes:

> The classification of individuals relative to one another and with reference to the possession of a particular mental ability or group of abilities is, therefore, necessarily based upon their relative ability to express in some intelligible and unmistakable fashion their mental power and qualities.[4]

And an educationist (a teacher of teachers) writes:

> Another consequence of abandoning the postulate of consensus on role definition that deserves exploration lies in the implications it has for explaining different behaviors of incumbents of the same postion. Most students concerned with role phenomena, assuming consensus on role definition, have tried to account for the variability in behavior by invoking such variables as different motivations, attitudes, or personality characteristics. Our research experience suggests that different expectations held for incumbents' behavior and attributes are crucial for an understanding of their different behaviors and characteristics. Theoretical formulations which attempt to explain different behaviors of incumbents of the same position cannot be based on concepts in which the postulate of role consensus is involved.[5]

We have arranged these passage by degrees of clarity, starting with the unclear and ending with the unintelligible.

Student writers sometimes indulge in the same false grandiloquence. They rarely go as far as people with Ph.D.'s, but they set out in the same wrong direction. They too often suppose that the best way to

[3] Quoted by Ivor Brown, *A Word in Your Ear and Just Another Word* (New York: E. P. Dutton, 1963), pp. 8–9.

[4] Quoted by P. B. Ballard, *Thought and Language* (College Park, Maryland: McGrath, 1970), p. 178.

[5] Neal Gross *et al.*, *Explorations in Role Analysis* (New York: John Wiley, 1958), p. 321. Quoted by James D. Koerner, *The Miseducation of American Teachers* (Baltimore: Penguin, 1965), pp. 290–91. You would enjoy the entire last chapter of Koerner's book: "English or Educanto?" (pp. 282–96).

improve their style is to flaunt unusual words lifted from a thesaurus, a dictionary of synonyms, or a self-help book promising a more powerful vocabulary in 30 days. And they wind up sounding like a weak imitation of Samuel Johnson. In an effort to sound impressive, they write *prognosticate* instead of *predict, ratiocinate* instead of *think logically, salubrious* instead of *healthful, visage* instead of *face, feral* instead of *wild, edifice* instead of *building, aperture* instead of *opening,* and *bellicose* instead of *warlike* or *aggressive.*

Sometimes, too, such writers will be eager to use *vogue words.* A vogue word is one that becomes so popular that it is used too freely and with too little regard for its meaning. The writers who use such words seem to be more concerned with sounding impressive than with expressing their thoughts clearly and precisely. *Existentialist* has been a vogue word of remarkable staying power, chiefly among people who have never read any existentialist philosophers or theologians. *To implement* (meaning simply *to carry out* or *put into practice*) may prove even more tenacious, since it has entrenched itself in the bureaucracies of government, business, and education. Other vogue words of the moment are *chauvinism, ecology, relevant, escalation, charismatic, organic, dichotomy, archetypal, input,* and *self-actualization.*

The writer who works too hard at sounding impressive is also likely to use a great many *foreign expressions.* Surely he is entitled to those words so firmly established in standard English that they no longer have to appear in italics—such terms as "bona fide," "bourgeois," "laissez faire," and "status quo." But what about foreign expressions still on the fringes of English—*angst, weltschmertz, zeitgeist, deus ex machina,* and *success d'estime?* "Never use a foreign phrase," Orwell wisely said, "if you can think of an everyday English equivalent"—and you usually can.[6]

Another temptation to the writer who yearns to sound fancy is *jargon.* To be sure, every trade needs its jargon, its collection of technical terms. Physicists need *proton* and *electron;* auto repairmen need *carburetor* and *voltage regulator;* weather forecasters need a word to encompass all rain, snow, sleet, and hail—hence *precipitation.* Teachers use an abundance of jargon: *advanced placement, exceptional students, individualized learning, child-centered curriculum, learning package, open* and *closed classroom, homogeneous* and *heterogeneous* and *ability grouping,* and so on. Now, if such words enable a specialist to write for other spe-

[6] Excerpted from "Politics and the English Language" in *Shooting An Elephant and Other Essays* by George Orwell; copyright, 1945, 1946, 1949, 1950, by Sonia Brownell Orwell; copyright 1973, 1974 by Sonia Orwell. Reprinted by permission of Harcourt Brace Jovanovich, Inc. and A. M. Heath & Co. Ltd., London. George Orwell, "Politics and the English Language," *Collected Essays, Journalism and Letters* (New York: Harcourt, Brace and World, 1968), IV, 139.

cialists more clearly and concisely than he otherwise could, we would certainly not deprive him of his jargon; but even then we would urge him to use as little of it as possible. And when he writes for a general audience, an audience of lay people, we would insist that he stick to the Middle Style. He can do so by observing two commonsense rules. First, he should keep the jargon to a minimum, replacing it with everyday English unless he would thus become painfully wordy. Second, if he must use a jargon term, he should define it clearly.

Persistent violation of these rules has created the gibberish known as "sociologese." Some sociologists write very well—Charles Horton Cooley, Robert and Helen Lynd, and Peter Berger, for example. But others write like this:

> The typical, dominant speech-mode of the middle class is one where speech becomes an object of perceptual activity, and a "theoretical attitude" is developed towards the structural possibilities of sentence organization. This speech-mode facilitates the verbal elaboration of subjective intent, sensitivity to the implications of separateness and difference, and points to the possibilities inherent in a complex conceptual hierarchy for the organization of experience. [The lower working classes] are limited to a form of language use which, though allowing for a vast range of possibilities, provides a speech form which discourages the speaker from verbally elaborating subjective intent, and progressively orients the user to descriptive rather than abstract concepts.[7]

Why would anyone write like this? One motive may be the already-mentioned desire to sound profound. Another may be a desire to sound scientific and thus to partake of the enormous prestige now attached to science. The same reader who complains about finding such moderately difficult words as *taciturn* or *aggrandize* in a newspaper editorial will bow down in reverence before words with a scientific flavor—*symbiosis, kinetograph*, or, from the passage above, *an object of perceptual activity* and *a complex conceptual hierarchy for the organization of experience*. Another motive behind sociologese may be simply a desire for self-preservation. Bertrand Russell, after scolding sociologists for their excessive use of jargon, added that sociologists who write plain English might be in danger of losing their jobs.[8] Can this be true? We do know that students under certain professors—particularly in departments of sociology and psychology—are encouraged to use plenty of jargon lest

---

[7] Quoted by H. W. Fowler, *A Dictionary of Modern English Usage*, 2nd edition, revised by Sir Ernest Gowers (New York: Oxford University Press, 1965), p. 570.

[8] "How I Write," *Portraits from Memory* (New York: Simon and Schuster, 1956), p. 213.

they sound "amateurish" or "popular." If you find yourself studying under such a person, you might try asking him to read these pages, or the Bertrand Russell essay, or Malcolm Cowley's aptly titled "Sociological Habit Patterns in Linguistic Transmogrification" (*The Reporter*, 20 September 1956), or Fowler's *Modern English Usage,* especially the entries for "Abstractitis," "Formal Words," "Love of the Long Word," and "Sociologese."

LOW STYLE AND COLLOQUIAL LANGUAGE

High Style, as we have seen, sometimes uses unfamiliar words and thus becomes difficult for the general reader. The wording of Low Style, however, is neither unusual nor difficult. It tends to be as plain and ordinary as the wording of casual conversation. For some purposes this style is perfectly appropriate: notes to the milkman or baby-sitter, letters to friends, and perhaps letters, or even articles, for a campus newspaper. And occasionally—in the hands of a Shakespeare or a Mark Twain—the Low Style can achieve the eloquence of great literature. But for most purposes the Low Style sounds too much like casual talk. It can too easily suggest that the writer has uttered his thoughts just as quickly and indiscriminately as he would at a bull session or a beer party.

What are the characteristics of the Low Style? Most of them appear in the following excerpt from a young man's letter to a college newspaper:

> I'm fed up with the way gals get treated in the latest flicks. For one thing, there aren't many of them around anymore. The best flicks you see these days are mostly about guys: *Patton, Godfather, Deliverance, Papillon, The Sting.* And when women do get a piece of the action, they're either whores like the woman played by Linda Lovelace or bitches like Mrs. Robinson in *The Graduate* or stupid masochists like the woman who gets raped in *Straw Dogs.* Oh sure, once in a while you see a woman you can dig, like Billie Holiday in *Lady Sings the Blues,* but that's a pretty unusual thing. You'll hear people laugh at the female stereotypes in the flicks of the forties and fifties, but women were at least important in a lot of those old flicks, and besides, the stereotypes were sort of interesting.

One mark of Low Style is *colloquial diction.* Although such diction fits perfectly well into casual conversation, the Middle Style uses it sparingly, precisely because it sounds so much like casual talk. In speaking with friends we say, "I'm *fed up* with waiting around," or "That *gal* has *a lot of* courage"; but most dictionaries with usage labels would mark those terms *colloquial* or *informal* as a warning against injudicious use in the Middle Style. Middle Style uses such terms cautiously and infrequently to avoid sounding too much like Low, as it certainly would if it used as many colloquialisms, in as small a space, as we find in the letter about films. There we find *fed up, gals, anymore* (instead of the properly divided *any more*), *guys, a piece of the action, oh sure, pretty* (meaning *rather*), *a lot of,* and *sort of* (meaning *rather* or *somewhat*). We also find three *get's. Get,* though not usually labeled *colloquial,* does impart some colloquial flavor, especially when three *get's* show up in so short a passage.

The passage also contains *slang*—specifically, *flick, bitches,* and *dig.* Slang words are colloquialisms so extreme that they must be used even more cautiously and less frequently. But they are not outlawed from the Middle Style altogether. The right slang in the right place can add just the right touch of humor, realism, or local color. Here the slang adds a touch of humor:

> Henry Miller, by his own account, is never less than superb, in life, in art, in bed. Not since the memoirs of Frank Harris has there been such a record of success in the sack.
>
> Gore Vidal [9]

Sack is slang for *bed,* but here the slang seems quite appropriate.

Another frequent mark of the Low Style is the liberal use of *first- and second-person pronouns.* The letter about films contains one *I* and four *you's.* Middle Style varies considerably in its use of such pronouns. Middle Style on the verge of High uses them infrequently except in autobiography. Middle Style on the verge of Low uses them freely. The same is true of *contractions,* four of which appear in our sample passage. Contractions are rare when Middle Style approaches High, frequent when it approaches Low. If you fear that your Middle Style is sinking too close to Low, you might be wise to replace your contractions with spelled-out words. When in doubt, leave the contraction out.

This principle applies not only to contractions but also to the other Low-Style wording we have examined: first- and second-person pronouns, slang words, and colloquialisms in general. Be alert for these as you review your first draft, and if they threaten to make your Middle Style sound too much like Low, replace them with wording of greater formality. Professional writers have to review their prose in the same way. Edmund Wilson said that at one time he "tried injecting some current slang into my purely critical writing, but I found that this was likely to jar and that I later had to take it out." [10]

As we have said, however, the kinds of Low-Style diction examined up to this point *do* legitimately show up from time to time in the Middle Style, especially when the writer is an old hand at spicing Middle with sprinklings of High and Low. But two other traits likely to appear in the Low Style should *never* appear in Middle. One is *imprecision and lack of clarity.* The Middle Style regards clarity as a cardinal virtue, whereas Low Style is likely to go on sinful sprees of imprecision and obscurity. Note the gross lapses in precision in the passage about films. One such lapse occurs in the third sentence. The colon after *guys* suggests we are about to get a list of "guys" portrayed in recent films, and indeed the list could be read that way until we reach *Deliverance,* which is obviously not a "guy." A more puzzling bit of imprecision occurs in the very first sentence, in the phrase "the way gals get treated." Does *gals* mean actresses or female characters? Does *get treated* refer to professional treatment, artistic treatment, physical treatment, or what? The sentence could mean anything from "I don't like the fact that actresses have been getting unimportant roles in recent films" to "I disapprove of the violence toward women—the beatings and rapes—in recent films." The writer's actual meaning becomes clear only when we reach the fourth sentence.

Middle Style, at its best, shuns one other kind of wording that often appears in Low Style: *hackneyed expressions,* or *clichés.* These expressions, after many years of service, have lost all freshness and force. Stylistically they are dead, and they deserve to be buried—for the purposes of Middle Style, at least. In casual conversation, or in prose that resembles such conversation, you are free to use clichés rather than pausing to think up new expressions; but in writing Middle Style, though prefabricated phrases will persistently leap into your mind, you should resist the urge to use them. They are always inelegant; they are usually insipid; and they are sometimes downright ludicrous. Here are some of the worst:

busy as a bee	in the twinkling of an eye
sober as a judge	like a bolt from the blue
blushing bride	with kid gloves
white as a sheet	hook, line, and sinker
with flying colors	packed like sardines
diamond in the rough	on pins and needles

These would so obviously mar your Middle Style that you would prob-

[10] *A Piece of My Mind* (New York: Doubleday Anchor, 1958), p. 157.

ably not be tempted to use them. Other clichés, however, are more seductive because less blatantly offensive:

right there and then	cover a multitude of sins
as clear as daylight	when all is said and done
a sight for sore eyes	get back on an even keel
crushing defeat	the finer things in life
with a vengeance	a new lease on life
in high gear (*or* low)	heave a sigh of relief

Delete all clichés from your Middle Style, then, even if your only alternatives are undistinguished everyday expressions. Write "the law" rather than "the long arm of the law," "rigid rules" rather than "hard and fast rules," "in unmistakable terms" rather than "in no uncertain terms," and "last" rather than "last but not least." Better a plain phrase than a dead one.

THE MIDDLE STYLE

Middle Style occasionally borrows from High and Low —a few erudite words from the one, a few lively colloquialisms from the other. But mostly it uses words peculiar to neither extreme, words familiar to the general reader but not colloquial. It conveys the image of a writer who is intelligent but not pretentious, well educated but not pedantic, and able to relax without becoming slack or slovenly.

But there is no single Middle Style. The Middle Style has room for much diversity. In one essay it might be slightly above Low; in another it might be just under High; in another it might stick to the very middle of Middle. How can you tell which kind of Middle Style to use? Generally you can rely on two considerations. (1) The more serious your message, the higher your style. (2) The more educated and sophisticated your audience, the higher your style. An illustration will clarify these criteria. Suppose a businesswoman, having spent six months in the Philippines, writes up her experiences for three different purposes and three different audiences. A popular travel magazine has asked her to write an article for tourists—an assessment of hotel accomodations, restaurants, sights to see, and so forth. For this purpose she might well use a relaxed, informal style, a Middle Style with liberal infusions of Low—contractions, slang, first- and second-person pronouns, and so on. But when her corporation asks her to report on business conditions in the Philippines, she will probably chasten her style somewhat, replacing most traces of colloquial language with phrases of greater formality. And when a prestigious foreign-affairs journal invites her to analyze the

Philippine political situation, her Middle Style is likely to reach up toward High, avoiding colloquialisms almost altogether and employing a diction both exact and elegant.

Let's look more closely at the several varieties of the Middle Style. First, by revising the passage about films, we can achieve a Middle Style not far removed from Low:

> I don't like the way women have been presented in recent films. For one thing, women don't get many important roles. Men are the important ones in the best films: *Patton, The Godfather, Deliverance, Papillon, The Sting,* and so on. And women who do get important roles are either sluttish like the woman played by Linda Lovelace, bitchy like Mrs. Robinson in *The Graduate,* or stupid and masochistic like the woman who gets raped in *Straw Dogs.* Occasionally you see a woman you can like, such as Billie Holiday in *Lady Sings the Blues,* but that's a rare exception. You hear people laugh at the female stereotypes in the films of the forties and fifties; but at least women were important in those old films, and at least the stereotypes were interesting.

In general the wording has become more precise and less colloquial. But several vestiges of Low Style remain—an *I,* three *you's,* two *don't's,* a *that's,* three *get's,* and a *bitchy.*

That casual a Middle Style might qualify for a popular film magazine or an essay for an informal college course in film, but for most purposes the writer would probably elevate his style a few degrees by eliminating a few more symptoms of Low:

> In recent films the depiction of women has been incomplete and inaccurate. First of all, women rarely appear in important roles. Men have dominated the best films: *Patton, The Godfather, Deliverance, Papillon, The Sting,* and so on. And the women who do get important roles are generally either sluttish like the woman played by Linda Lovelace, pampered and selfish like Mrs. Robinson in *The Graduate,* or stupid and subservient like the woman who gets raped in *Straw Dogs.* Rarely do you see as likable a woman as Billie Holiday in *Lady Sings the Blues.* People laugh at the female stereotypes in the films of the forties and fifties; but at least women were important in those films, and at least the stereotypes were interesting.

This falls somewhere in the middle of the Middle Style. Only a few signs of the Low Style remain—two *get's* and one *you.* *Bitchy* has given way to *pampered and selfish,* and the wordy phrase *are the important ones* (in the third sentence) has been replaced by the more formal *have dominated.* On the other hand, the passage has little resemblance to the High Style. Even the most bookish words in the passage—*subservient* and *stereotype*—are not likely to puzzle the ordinary reader unless he reads very little indeed. (By the way, we changed *masochistic* to *subservient* not because *masochistic* sounded too High or Low but because it seemed the wrong word for the woman in *Straw Dogs.*)

The following passage, an excerpt from a graduate dissertation, reaches up to a slightly higher level of style—a Middle Style on the verge of High.

> In Shakespeare's later plays the attention shifts to the *private* character of public personages. In *Hamlet,* for example, Claudius is not deficient as a ruler; he handles public matters effectively and deals competently with Fortinbras and Norway. But in social and domestic relations he is evil. It is here that the canker of corruption has its origin. Claudius has gained the throne by a "foul and most unnatural murder," that of his own brother. Then, almost immediately, he marries the wife of the murdered man and converts the "royal bed of Denmark" into a "couch for luxury and damned incest." And soon he converts the other members of the court—all except Hamlet and Horatio—into pawns in his games of evil.

The tone is formal, and suitably so, since the passage comes from a serious essay intended for a scholarly audience; but even the most erudite words in this prose—*personage, domestic,* and *canker*—are not esoteric.

Having decided which level of the Middle Style is suited to a given piece of writing, you should stay close to that level. Perhaps you can mix in a few expressions from above or below, but only if you watch out for clashes in tone. A student writer not yet sensitive to the varying tones of various levels of style put together the following collection of incongruities:

> Thus we observe that nineteenth-century parents were not likely to pamper their kids. The parents never flinched from the imposition of harsh discipline, and if the kids didn't like it that was just too bad. The inflicting of corporal castigation was deemed a parental prerogative and obligation through a noncupative social agreement.

This is like showing up at a party wearing a tuxedo jacket and bluejeans. Within three sentences the writer ranges from the colloquialism of *kids* and *just too bad* to the formality of *castigation* and the esotericism of *noncupative.* We can unify the tone by removing the discordant highs and lows:

> Thus we see that the typical nineteenth-century parent was not likely to pamper his children. He never flinched from imposing harsh discipline, even if his children objected, argued, or cried. Society generally agreed that corporal punishment was both his right and his duty.

Admittedly, some professional writers can achieve brilliant effects through their sudden shifts in level of diction. H. L. Mencken, Gore Vidal, Eldridge Cleaver, Germaine Greer—any of these accomplished essayists can move, within a single paragraph, from a lofty High Style to the easy clarity of Middle or the racy slang of Low. But such tactics require perfect control. Any apprentice who tries them must keep in mind the danger that his leaps between levels might cause strange collisions in tone, not as startling perhaps as the collision between *kids* and *noncupative*, but bizarre enough to disfigure his style.

Exercises

I. The passage by Samuel Johnson on pages 7–8 is a good example of the High Style. Translate that passage into some variety of Middle Style. Use any kind of Middle Style you please—one that comes close to High Style or Low, or one that sits squarely in the middle of Middle.

II. The following passage is written in the Low Style. Rewrite the passage to convert the Low Style into Middle. You can keep a few Low-Style expressions if they don't seem out of place in your Middle-Style revision; but for the most part replace slang, colloquialisms, clichés, etc., with Middle-Style wording.

> He's been putting away so much food and booze that he's made a bum of himself. He stuffs his face with doughnuts and coffee, pasta and potatoes, cheap hot dogs and vending-machine cherry pies, and, every day, snort after snort of gin. Then he wonders why he's fat as a pig, weak as a baby, and slow as molasses in January when it comes to doing any thinking. A couple of years ago he used to spend his nights laughing it up with his old buddies or maybe even giving the once-over to a pretty high-type book, but now he plunks himself in his armchair and goes off into a kind of stumblebum dream with his eyes open. He takes a gander at cowboys or cops on the boob-tub until those little black-and-white people on TV call it a night and the screen goes all gray.

III. This next passage is an offensive mixture of Low, Middle, and High Styles. Rewrite the passage to give it a consistent Middle Style. Substitute Middle wording for any expressions that seem too Low or too High.

> Americans used to be kind of slobbish, not exactly what you'd call aseptic. I mean as recently as four score years ago, most men didn't give a damn about many of the postulates of antisepsis and decorum that're now taken as gospel truth by just about everybody and his

brother. Your run-of-the-mill middle-class slob didn't put any stock in undergoing manual ablutions before partaking of grub; he didn't submerge his weary limbs in *aqua pura* more than once each hebdomad; he didn't brush his dentition until the gunk that got stuck in there became a real pain in the neck; he had no recalcitrance toward slurping his java or soup from a saucer; and he didn't care a hell of a lot if he missed the living-room spittoon when he expectorated the liquified residue from his chaw of tobacco.

IV. The following passage from Germaine Greer's *The Female Eunuch* is another mixture of Low, Middle, and High Styles. The style is basically Middle, but contains unmistakable infusions of Low and High. Do you find the mixture offensive? Or do you find that Greer has woven the strands of Low, Middle, and High into an attractive pattern?

(1) List the words or expressions that sound High. (2) List those that sound Low. (3) Write a short evaluation of Greer's use of High- and Low-Style diction—perhaps one paragraph on High and another on Low.

The passage describes and criticizes the ideal of feminine beauty that modern men and women are expected to worship, even though that kind of beauty may exist nowhere but in the make-believe world of magazine covers and television commercials.

Her essential quality is castratedness. She absolutely must be young, her body hairless, her flesh buoyant, and *she must not have a sexual organ.* No musculature must distort the smoothness of the lines of her body, although she may be painfully slender or warmly cuddly.
5 Her expression must betray no hint of humor, curiosity or intelligence, although it may signify hauteur to an extent that is actually absurd, or smoldering lust, very feebly signified by drooping eyes and a sullen mouth (for the stereotype's lust equals irrational submission), or, most commonly, vivacity and idiot happiness. Seeing that the world
10 despoils itself for this creature's benefit, she must be happy; the entire structure would topple if she were not. So the image of woman appears plastered on every surface imaginable, smiling interminably. An apple pie evokes a glance of tender beatitude, a washing machine causes hilarity, a cheap box of chocolates brings
15 forth meltingly joyous gratitude, a Coke is the cause of a rictus of unutterable brilliance, even a new stick-on bandage is saluted by a smirk of satisfaction. A real woman licks her lips and opens her mouth and flashes her teeth when photographers appear: *she* must arrive at the premiere of her husband's film in a paroxysm of delight,
20 or his success might be murmured about. The occupational hazard of being a Playboy Bunny is the aching facial muscles brought on by the obligatory smiles.

So what is the beef? Maybe I couldn't make it. Maybe I don't

have a pretty smile, good teeth, nice tits, long legs, a cheeky arse,
25   a sexy voice. Maybe I don't know how to handle men and increase my
market value, so that the rewards due to the feminine will accrue to
me. Then again, maybe I'm sick of the masquerade. I'm sick of pretending eternal youth. I'm sick of belying my own intelligence, my
own will, my own sex. I'm sick of peering at the world through false
30   eyelashes, so everything I see is mixed with a shadow of bought
hairs; I'm sick of weighting my head with a dead mane, unable to
move my neck freely, terrified of rain, of wind, of dancing too vigorously in case I sweat into my lacquered curls. I'm sick of the Powder
Room. I'm sick of pretending that some fatuous male's self-important
35   pronouncements are the objects of my undivided attention, I'm sick
of going to films and plays when someone else wants to, and sick
of having no opinions of my own about either. I'm sick of being a
transvestite. I refuse to be a female impersonator. I am a woman,
not a castrate.[11]

V. Consider the stylistic level of an essay you wrote at some time
in the past. Write out your answers to the following questions.

1. Your essay almost certainly uses a Middle Style, but perhaps it
contains expressions that sound like High Style or Low. Write a list
of the words and phrases that sound High, another of those that
sound Low.

2. Did your Middle Style reach up toward High? Did it reach down
toward Low? Did it stick to the middle of Middle? Describe the
stylistic level at which the essay was written.

3. Was that stylistic level appropriate for the essay? In answering,
take into account both subject and audience.

VI. From the essay you reviewed for exercise V, choose a paragraph—or roughly 200 words—to rewrite at a different level of style. If
your prose tended to stay in the low or middle range of the Middle
Style, rewrite the passage at a higher level, aiming for a High Style or
a Middle Style on the verge of High. If the passage was originally quite
formal—if it used a High or high-Middle Style—rewrite it at a lower level,
perhaps using a Middle Style that hovers just above Low.

[11] Germaine Greer, *The Female Eunuch* (New York: McGraw-Hill, 1971),
pp. 52–53. (London: MacGibbon & Kee Ltd.)

2

Connotations

Connotations are the subtle shades of meaning that make the difference between one synonym and another. *Dense vegetation* and *jungle* are synonyms because they have the same denotation: they could refer to the same geographical location. But their connotations differ sharply. *Dense vegetation* is almost devoid of connotations; it sounds impersonal enough to appear in a scientific journal. But *jungle* evokes images of leopards, boa constrictors, oppressive heat and humidity, and bright colors—reds, greens, and yellows—alternating with malevolent darkness. Compare the effect of "His mind is like dense vegetation" with that of "His mind is like a jungle."

Any thesaurus or dictionary of synonyms will illustrate the importance of connotations. Suppose you are writing a letter of complaint about your child's third-grade teacher, who has taught the child nothing except to twitch and tremble at the thought of going to school. You consult the thesaurus for some help in characterizing the teacher's way of acting toward your child, and you find a variety of synonymous verbs to choose from:

> alarm, appall, browbeat, bully, consternate, cow, daunt, deter, discourage, dismay, disquiet, frighten, hector, intimidate, menace, overawe, panic, petrify, scare, shock, stampede, startle, terrify, terrorize, threaten

Most of these, you decide, do not accurately express the teacher's behavior. *Alarm, shock,* and *startle* connote an action that occurs only once and instills only a momentary fear. *Menace* connotes a threat of physical violence. *Panic* and *stampede* connote uncontrollable terror. But while *panic* and *stampede* are too strong in their connotations, *deter, discourage, dismay,* and some others are much too mild.

In this fashion you consider the impact of the various synonyms, searching for a few words, or perhaps just one word, whose connotations will convey exactly how the teacher has acted. *Frighten* might do the job, except that *frighten* doesn't place the blame solely on the teacher. A teacher can *frighten* a child without intending to do so, whereas this teacher not only frightens her students deliberately but enjoys watching them squirm. Well, then, can you use the word *bully?* Possibly—but to say that the teacher *bullies* the child does not suggest the fear that she instills. *Intimidates* is a better word. It suggests both the bullying and the fear. And perhaps *terrorize* is also appropriate. True, it arouses thoughts of kidnappings, bombings, machine guns, and the like; but perhaps only so extreme a word can suggest how vulnerable a child feels when his classroom is controlled by a sadist. You finally decide that all four of those synonyms will come in handy in your letter of complaint. *Frighten* and *bully* will serve your purpose fairly well; *intimidate* will serve even better; and perhaps you can use *terrorize* for special empahsis.

Or suppose you are writing about the last years of Sigmund Freud, the years in which he lost most of his old friends, suffered excruciating pains from cancer of the mouth, and yet persevered with his studies and produced such important works as *Civilization and Its Discontents, Moses and Monotheism,* and the *New Introductory Lectures on Psychoanalysis.* You write, "During all this time he remained courageous and stubborn." But instantly you recognize that *stubborn* is not the right word. It connotes stupid intransigence, not the gallant tenacity you had hoped to convey. You consult your thesaurus under the heading for *stubborn,* and there you discover a wide assortment of synonyms:

> adamant, balky, contrary, determined, dogged, dogmatic, firm, immovable, indomitable, inexorable, inflexible, insistent, intractable, intransigent, mulish, obdurate, obstinate, persevering, persistent, pigheaded, refractory, resolute, rigid, stiff, strong-willed, tenacious, unbending, uncompromising, unrelenting, unshakable, unyielding, willful

Which of these would best fit into the sentence, "During all this time he remained courageous and _____"? Your decision would depend partly on what you wanted to emphasize in the sentences that followed. If you intended to focus on Freud's persistence in his work, you might choose *persevering* or *resolute.* If you wished to emphasize his refusal to surrender to sorrow and pain, you might choose *unyielding* or even *indomitable.*

Or perhaps you would select, with good reason, some other word from that list of synonyms. This business of weighing connotations must finally, to some extent, be a matter of personal taste; and tastes will differ. What's important is that you keep asking yourself, "How will this word affect my readers? Will it convey precisely the connotations that I wish to convey?" If the first word that comes to mind doesn't quite suit your meaning, you can open your thesaurus and look for synonyms. Your dictionary can help too, but only in a limited way. It becomes invaluable when you have doubts as to the denotative meaning of a word; but though it will often suggest the connotations, it usually will not do the job adequately: no dictionary is large enough, or sufficiently up-to-date, to record every connotation of every word in our variegated and ever-changing language. In weighing the connotations of a word, you must rely mostly on your own discernment—on the sensitivity you have developed toward that word from hearing it in conversation and seeing it in print.

And if you stay constantly alert to connotations, your words will usually convey the very meaning you had hoped to convey. Occasionally you will let an ill-chosen word sneak into your prose, as even the best writers do; but you will not be likely to call Freud *stubborn* or *inflexible* or *pigheaded* when you mean something closer to *unyielding,* and you will not say, "The teacher has *disquieted* my son" when you mean to accuse her of *bullying, frightening, intimidating,* and even *terrorizing* the child.

Exercises

I. Each of the following passages contains a number of blank spaces. Which of the words listed below the passage would be most appropriate in those spaces?

1. The citizens of Darwin, Australia, paid no attention to the cyclone warning, for storms in that region almost always (1)_____ from Darwin. Hence they were unprepared for the (2)_____ winds of up to 125 miles an hour which (3)_____ the wooden houses of Darwin like matchboxes, leaving the city in a shambles. A pilot flying over the (4)_____ city compared it to "Hiroshima after they dropped the A-bomb." (This passage is derived from "The Death of Darwin," *Newsweek,* January 6, 1975.)

   1. veered away, retreated, slipped away, stole away
   2. knotted, spherical, swirling, circling
   3. warped, splintered, bruised, squeezed
   4. decimated, devastated, harmed, plundered

2. Aristotle Onassis, a man of (1) _____ wealth, recently died, leaving his wife a princely fortune and a collection of highly (2) _____ paintings. Jeanne Dixon, a celebrated American soothsayer, has confidently predicted that Onassis' widow (the former Jacqueline Kennedy) will marry for a third time. Jeanne Dixon has frequently been (3)_____ the fate of the Kennedys ever since that time twelve years ago when, she says, she foresaw the assassination of President John Kennedy and tried to (4)_____ him.

1. apocryphal, fabled, fabulous, mythical
2. valuable, unequaled, unique, bizarre
3. responsible for, involved in, implicated in, tangled up with *associated with*
4. admonish, notify, threaten, warn

3. Clayton struggled to pay attention to our family conversation, but he was too (1)_____worries about his tax return. Occasionally he tried to mask his withdrawal by smiling gently at Grandmother. So (2)_____ was his smile that it fooled her into thinking he had forgotten his troubles; but no one else was (3)_____ by his transparent (4)_____.

1. fascinated by, derailed by, enthralled by, preoccupied with
2. jubilant, cheerful, ecstatic, ludicrous
3. deceived, defrauded, gulled, hoaxed
4. maneuver, plot, project, swindle *play*

4. Science has slowly, by almost (1)_____ degrees, established itself in our culture, so that now many Americans have the same (2) _____ science that their Puritan (3)_____ had (toward, in, to) religion. But although science has become a major intellectual (4) _____ in our civilization, a number of Americans still hold (5) _____ to religious beliefs.

1. insignificant, invisible, imperceptible, imperceptive
2. fidelity toward, faithfulness toward, faith in, attachment to
3. ancestors, originators, parents, family tree
4. energy, strength, dominance, force
5. pigheaded, tenaciously, willfully, obstinately

5. In his search for enlightenment, the Buddha devoted seven years to (1)_____ and self-mortification. Although he sacrificed his health to (2)_____ himself from the things of this world, he still failed to (3)_____ enlightenment. But nothing could shake his (4) _____.

1. asceticism, asperity, hardship, masochism
2. distract, excise, divert, detach

3. catch, achieve, capture, grasp
4. rigidity, determination, stubbornness, inflexibility

II. Examine an essay you wrote in the recent past. Pick out five words that might have been better chosen, words whose connotations do not quite convey the meaning you had intended. Replace those words with more accurate synonyms. If necessary, revise phrases or entire sentences.

3

Clarity

We have already emphasized the need for clarity in writing. Now we will examine that need more closely.

We grant that clarity is not supremely important in all kinds of writing. In much poetry, and in certain kinds of prose, other values may have to come first—conciseness, forcefulness of rhythm, richness of metaphor, or subtlety of suggestion. Here is an instance of effective obscurity from one of the greatest, and most difficult, of English poets. In these lines by John Donne, a man preparing to travel overseas comforts his wife by assuring her that the two of them will still be united in spirit:

> Our two souls, therefore, which are one,
>   Though I must go, endure not yet
> A breach, but an expansion,
>   Like gold to airy thinness beat.
>
> "A Valediction: Forbidding Mourning"

The two lovers are compared to two segments of a chunk of gold that is beaten until it is flat and thin, a standard process in the making of jewelry. The two segments, though separated, will not be broken apart—will "endure not yet a breach." The husband and wife, then, while separated physically, will still be joined emotionally and spiritually. By comparing their love to gold, the husband implies the value of that love. And a rough nugget of gold becomes even more valuable once it is beaten into a fine sheet—a suggestion that their love will become more valuable

26

after their separation. The love, by suffering this "beating," will achieve an "expansion."

Much of the power of these lines comes from the very complexity and compression that make them difficult. But the purpose of those lines, and of most poetry, is far different from that of expository and argumentative prose. Poetry calls for slow contemplation. Our paraphrase of those four lines is too brief to be adequate. The lines require long, leisurely reflection on sounds and implications. They require the patience and perseverance with which an Oriental reader might ponder, for hours or days, a three-line Zen haiku or a stanza from a Confucian ode. The purpose of expository and argumentative prose, however, is to convey ideas and information with as little exertion on the reader's part as possible. Exposition tries to explain. Obviously, then, it must try to be clear. Argumentation tries to persuade. Obviously it can't achieve that end by being hard to understand.

These points seem obvious, and yet some writers of this kind of prose insist on being unintelligible. They advance several arguments to defend their perverse preference—four arguments in particular. One goes something like this: "Clarity is too easy. It's only for beginners. It doesn't let me test my intellectual abilities to the fullest." On the contrary, clarity is anything but easy. "Easy writing," as Sheridan said, makes "curst hard reading." The easiest way to write is to set down your thoughts in whatever order, and whatever words, first come to mind, no matter how imprecise the words or illogical the order. To achieve clarity, however, a writer may have to wrestle at length with problems of wording and arrangement. In the end, it's true, his prose may be so clear and fluent that it will seem spontaneous, as if he had written without the slightest difficulty or doubt. We find this semblance of spontaneity in many accomplished writers—Mark Twain, Matthew Arnold, and George Orwell, for instance. But it is almost always an illusion. The appearance of spontaneity is usually the result of hard work. Somerset Maugham confessed that though he always sought to convey "the effect of ease" in his writings, he could achieve that effect "only by strenuous effort." He found the same to be true of Colette, who achieved her lucidity and naturalness, her semblance of spontaneity, only by writing every page over and over again.[1]

A second argument often used against clarity is that it can't be achieved when the ideas to be expressed are truly complicated or profound. This is partly true. Subjects inherently complex or perplexing cannot be expounded with perfect clarity—economic theory, for instance, or religious mysticism or Jungian psychology or Einsteinian physics. But

---

[1] *The Summing Up* (New York: Doubleday, 1938), p. 43.

even such matters as these can be explained with surprising clarity if the writer (1) truly understands the subject and (2) adheres to Joubert's aphorism, "It is better to be profound in clear terms than in obscure terms." Economics has had such lucid expositors as Adam Smith, George Bernard Shaw, Robert Heilbroner, and Henry Hazlitt. Religious mysticism has had William James, Gershom Scholem, and Walter Stace (though admittedly even these writers have refrained from trying to explain the ultimate mystical vision). Jungian psychology has had Jolande Jacobi, Frieda Fordham, and June Singer. And Einstein's theory of relativity has had Lincoln Barnett, Max Born, and Bertrand Russell. Why then should matters simpler than these seem to resist clear explanation? Sometimes the answer is merely that the writer lacks the necessary skill or industriousness. But other times the writer *prefers* to be obscure. He likes to believe that his thoughts are too deep to be clearly expressed, even if the truth is that his thoughts are merely confused.

A third argument against clarity is that it is not sufficiently impressive. Difficult words and elaborate sentences, we are told, are more impressive than simple clarity. But if this were true, how could we account for the impressiveness of so much clear, straightforward prose? How could we account for the undisputed greatness of Swift, Defoe, Addison, Hazlitt, Newman, and Arnold, not to mention such modern masters as Shaw, Orwell, and E. M. Forster? Which of the following styles, we ask, is more impressive—the difficult circumlocution of the first or the simple straightforwardness of the second?

> Human beings are completely exempt from undesirable behavior patterns only when certain prerequisites, not satisfied except in a small percentage of actual cases, have, through some fortuitous concourse of favorable circumstances, whether congenital or environmental, chanced to combine in producing an individual in whom many factors deviate from the norm in a socially advantageous manner.

> All men are scoundrels, or at any rate almost all. The men who are not must have had unusual luck, both in their birth and in their upbringing.[2]

The first writer, fearing perhaps that his naked thought is too thin to be attractive, clothes it in gaudy words and showy sentences. The second version says the same thing as the first, but says it more directly and, we believe, more impressively, by virtue of what Yvor Winters has termed "the power attainable through simple accuracy."[3]

[2] Both passages are cited by Bertrand Russell, "How I Write," *Portraits from Memory* (New York: Simon and Schuster, 1956), p. 213.

[3] *Edwin Arlington Robinson* (New York: New Directions, 1971), p. 4.

The last major argument against clarity goes like this: "When I write, I'm trying to express my personality, my unique sensibility. The clarity you ask for violates that personality. It just isn't me." Often this is merely a high-sounding rationalization for a writer whose muddled prose comes from muddled thinking. Such a writer should indeed "violate his personality," however demeaning the process might seem. He should train himself to think more precisely. But perhaps there are other writers whose sensibility is truly too complex to be expressed in a clear style. To that kind of writer we can only say that if he wants to write competent expository and argumentative prose, he may have to refrain from expressing the full richness of his personality. Would a television newscaster keep his job if he insisted on speaking in vague words and twisted sentences because his personality was vague and twisted? Would students admire a college instructor who delivered incomprehensible lectures because her personality was subtle and enigmatic? Well, the writer of expository and argumentative prose has a job very much like that of a newscaster or a teacher. His primary function is to communicate ideas and information, not to convey the complexities of his personality.

But must the writer choose? Why not do both—write clearly and yet at the same time express his personality? Most stylists, after the first fumblings of apprenticeship, find that they can accomplish both purposes. Over the years clear styles have succeeded in reflecting the rich sensibilities of a great variety of writers. Consider the stylists mentioned in the last few pages—Swift, Hazlitt, Arnold, Orwell, and the rest. Each one's prose is distinctly and unmistakably his own, the product of a markedly individual and highly complex personality.

Once a writer has seen the defects in the arguments for obscurity, what can he do to achieve clarity? The answers to that question will appear in a great many pages throughout this book. In the present chapter we offer only a few general considerations regarding (1) the chief kinds of obscurity and (2) the best means of avoiding them.

Our survey of the various kinds of obscurity should contain one example of total nonsense:

He enables the observable reality to rage against history, particle by particle. And the dreamy stagnation implies our collective destiny.

This came from a student writer still enthralled by several of the false arguments against clarity. No writer genuinely wishing to communicate would produce such gibberish.

But he (or she) might produce something like this:

Most women are relegated to work that is not really prestigious, and

> they do not make as much money as men. Only 13 percent of working women have risen above low-status jobs, and they earn $2750 less per year than men do.

This is not totally unintelligible. The gist is clear: women have a hard time getting prestigious, well-paid jobs. But when we look at the passage more closely, we see that vital information has been omitted, information essential to the writer's meaning. (1) What does the writer mean by "not really prestigious"? Is the work almost prestigious, definitely not prestigious, or what? To be quite clear, the writer could give examples of the kind of work she means—pumping gas, cleaning teeth, filing triplicate forms, or whatever. (2) What is meant by "they do not make as much money as men"? Are the salaries of women in nonprestigious jobs being compared to the salaries of *all* men or only men in the same jobs? (3) We are told that only 13 percent of women "have risen above low-status jobs." To what have they risen, exactly? Jobs as typists? As executive secretaries? As lawyers and doctors? (4) We are told that women who have risen above low-status jobs "earn $2750 less per year than men do." Again, which men? All men or only those in comparable jobs?

Another kind of prose is almost as bad. The prose contains a definite meaning, but the meaning becomes clear only after labored analysis. We offer two examples:

> Qualities which in the American educational system do not have much attention given to them, such as compassion, sensitivity, cooperativeness, are not by any means treated that way in the Peace Corps, but rather the opposite.

> One of the things satisfied by earlier America was a liking for fleeing away from things, an attitude that some people think ought to be called something different, like the frontier spirit. Up to our time there was still exploring. And this was happening in many places, in the Mid-West, in the West, and in the Northwest Territory. Instead of being restricted to a few, great challenges were open to just about everyone to leave.

This sort of writing sounds like a first draft. Because the writer fails to revise, his meaning lies buried under extraneous and misleading words, rather than standing out sharply and clearly. In short, the writer's laziness makes the reader do extra work. Here we attempt revisions:

> The Peace Corps emphasizes the very qualities that American education ignores—cooperativeness and compassion.

> Earlier America could satisfy the normal human desire to escape from the past, a desire some people like to call "the frontier spirit."

With open land in the Mid-West, the West, and then the Northwest Territory, almost any man who felt confined, frustrated, or troubled could escape from his old life by setting out for the wilderness.

Finally we come to *ambiguity*—the label for any word, phrase, or sentence that carries more than one possible meaning. Sometimes the ambiguity is insoluble; the reader has no way of deciding which of the available meanings was intended. But even if an ambiguity can be resolved, even if the reader can puzzle out the intended meaning, he will lose much of his respect for the writer—will consider him careless or incompetent for having failed to express himself precisely.

Consider a few illustrations—the italicized pronoun in the following sentence, for instance: "James hated his father; *he* was neurotically shy and insecure." Does the *he* refer to James or the father? What about the italicized phrase in this next sentence? "The youngster watched his grandparents arguing *with anger and indignation*." Does the phrase refer to the youngster or the grandparents? And consider the ambiguity in one further sentence: "Janice did not drop the chemistry course because the lab work was so challenging." Did Janice drop the course or not? The sentence could mean that Janice did not drop the course and that her reason for staying in was the valuable challenge afforded by the lab work. Or it could mean that she *did* drop the course but not because the lab work was so difficult. Let's clarify those faulty sentences:

James hated his father, who was neurotically shy and insecure.
Angrily, indignantly, the youngster watched the argument between his grandparents.
Because the lab work was so challenging, Janice didn't drop the chemistry course.

How easily the ambiguities can be removed once they are spotted. The hard part is to spot them. Because we know what we intend to say, we sometimes have trouble seeing that our sentences might lend themselves to several interpretations.

These observations bring us to the question of how the various kinds of obscurity can best be avoided. For the moment we offer only three general recommendations.

The first is that you must think out your ideas—must know exactly what they are. If they are not entirely clear in your own mind, you can't make them clear to anyone else. As Somerset Maugham has said, one cause of obscurity is that "the writer is himself not quite sure of his meaning. He has a vague impression of what he wants to say, but has not, either from lack of mental power or from laziness, exactly formulated it in his mind and it is natural enough that he should not find a precise expression for a confused idea." [4]

Our second piece of advice is that you should not try to sound impressive. Relax. Use wording that sounds easy and natural, not the fancy language of the High Style. We argued earlier that a clear style in itself can be sufficiently impressive, but even if you found our reasoning unassailable, even if you are intellectually committed to a clear style, you are likely to find that once you actually sit down to write, you will undergo a strange transformation. It happens to almost every writer at one time or another. The words that come most easily to mind strike him as being too ordinary, too commonplace, too dull. And he searches for impressive replacements—not merely synonyms of greater pungency and precision (about which we would certainly not complain), but big, far-fetched words he would never use in conversation. And because he fears that short, clear sentences will sound amateurish, he stretches out his sentences to two or three times their normal length to "impress" the reader. The result may be something like this:

> It is my personal observation that those youths who repeatedly have recourse to actions which fall under condemnation of the law of this land tend to display negative rather than positive emotional reactions toward those who instruct them in academic pursuits in our institutions of learning and toward those who have been officially entrusted with the task of enforcing the legal statutes.

Impressive? No—merely a pompous and very confusing way of saying no more than this: "Juvenile delinquents usually dislike teachers and policemen."

Our third piece of advice is the most important. *Be considerate toward your readers.* Keep them in mind at every stage of your writing, constantly asking yourself whether your arrangement of ideas, your sentences, your wording will cause them the smallest difficulty, the slightest misunderstanding. The inexperienced writer assumes that if the prose is clear to the writer it will be clear to everyone else. He forgets that the writer has the special advantage of knowing his intended meaning in advance, so that he can find it in his prose even when the prose does not express it clearly. This kind of egocentrism leads to a great deal of prose that the writer thinks perfectly clear but the reader finds deplorably muddled. For example, the writer of the following passage knew exactly what she meant:

> It should not always be assumed that the slogan "Let people do their own thing" is indicative of a genuine willingness to abide by the

[4] *The Summing Up,* p. 31.

deeds of others because it often is indicative of only a low-level interest rather than what it at first appears to be.

A teacher, conferring with this student about her writing, asked, "What is that passage supposed to mean?" And the student, rather impatiently, explained her meaning as follows:

> Well, I just meant that when someone says "Let people do their own thing," that doesn't always mean that he's really tolerant of other people. And it doesn't necessarily mean that he believes in freedom for everyone. Lots of times it just means that he doesn't care what happens to other people. He just doesn't give a damn. He might see a friend of his about to make a big mistake, but instead of helping him, he'll just say, "Let people do their own thing."

Why was she able to express these thoughts so much more clearly in conversation than in writing? Largely because she now had a flesh-and-blood audience, someone sitting in front of her waiting to be enlightened. While writing, she had forgotten her audience—had forgotten that her words were supposed to convey meaning not only to herself but to other people.

The spoken version of her thoughts, though it could not serve as her final draft, was able to serve as the basis for that draft. She jotted down the words she had spoken, then hacked and pruned and trimmed until she liked the results:

> Not everyone who says "Let people do their own thing" has genuine tolerance or a true love of freedom. Sometimes the slogan merely reflects a lack of concern for other people's welfare. Seeing someone on the verge of trouble, a hypocrite can hide his indifference behind that fashionable slogan.

If you tend to be forgetful of your audience, you can overcome this handicap in a variety of ways. One is to talk over your ideas with a friend. Outline the ideas in advance, then explain them one at a time, staying with each point until your listener fully understands. Then go back to your desk and write, keeping your friend in mind and using essentially the same wording you used when talking. (One student went so far as to record his remarks on tape. Then he did a rough draft by simply playing back the tape and writing down what he had said.) The rough draft you produce will be very rough indeed, but it can probably serve as a good starting point for your final draft.

After revising and polishing the prose, you can again use your friend as a listener. Read the prose aloud and see which phrases strike him as being opaque, which sentences seem hard to follow, which paragraphs wander off the point. Or let your friend read the prose himself.

Your oral interpretation might give him too much help, since you might pause during hard sentences or raise your voice to emphasize important words. A better test is how well he understands the prose on his own. Tell him to be honest and, if necessary, unkind. Let him mark up your writing however harshly it requires, underlining any phrase that makes him pause, any sentence he has to read twice, and so on. And then you can revise accordingly.

After a few such experiments, you can release your friend—if he is still your friend—from his chores. Now when you write you should be able to visualize your reader and summon up his reactions in your imagination.

Occasionally you might try the valuable exercise of writing for a person much younger and much less knowledgeable than yourself. Try arguing the pros and cons of capital punishment or the "open classroom" or the legalization of marijuana so that a freshman in high school would understand every sentence. A similar exercise is to translate difficult literary prose into language understandable to a younger person. You can find suitable passages by leafing through the essays of Emerson or, better yet, by turning to almost any page in the *Rambler* essays of Samuel Johnson.

Clarity is not merely a fetish of English teachers and textbook writers. The person who learns to express his thoughts more clearly will obviously have a better chance of getting along well with other people—friends, lovers, neighbors, co-workers. Equally important, he will be better able to formulate his beliefs and goals and courses of action—better able to decide what he wants out of life and how he can get it. We have all known someone whose life has been damaged, or ruined, by his inability to think clearly. In a time of cruel pressures and confusing problems his words proved inadequate: they strained, cracked, and broke under the burden. Rather than helping him size up his situation, they could express only unexamined platitudes, hand-me-down slogans, and fuzzy phrases from old sermons and graduation speeches. In critical moments he could not attain clarity.

Clarity is valuable not only in individual lives but in the life of a society. As Ezra Pound repeatedly insisted, unclear language is so much loose thread in the social fabric:

> . . . the individual cannot think and communicate his thought, the governor and legislator cannot act effectively or frame his laws, without words. . . . [When] the application of word to thing goes rotten, i.e. becomes slushy and inexact, or excessive and bloated, the whole

machinery of social and of individual thought and order goes to pot. This is a lesson of history, and a lesson not yet half learned.[5]

Perhaps a nation of inarticulate people could fumble along for a while, but suppose a majority of our legislators used language as vague and equivocal as the following. Recently, at a political dinner in California, a candidate for public office was asked for his opinion on a bill to legalize prostitution. This was his reply:

> It goes without saying that this is a matter which deserves careful attention and deep scrutiny. I can definitely promise you that I will seek to establish a just balance between the right to privacy and self-determination, embedded deeply in our American Constitution, and the need to prevent exploitation of women or the cheapening of sex.

Some listeners thought he was endorsing the bill. Others thought he was condemning it. Most were confused. And the quality of our public discourse slipped another notch downward.

Exercises

I. The following passages have all appeared in print. Actual authors have written them; actual editors have consented to publish them; and yet the pasages badly need clarification.

Rewrite *two* of the passages in a clear Middle Style.

1. From a business report:

> We believe that, notwithstanding the many uncertainties in the outlook, an effort of foresight and preparedness will prove helpful in overcoming the problems that will arise and in promoting that expansion of trade and enterprise at home and abroad which is indispensable to the attainment and maintenance of healthy economic conditions.[6]

2. From a sociological study of swindlers and con artists:

> The fraudulent predatory parasites engage in a form of exploitation characterized by simulation or deceit. Their victims are induced to

[5] Ezra Pound, *Literary Essays*. Copyright 1935 by Ezra Pound. All rights reserved. Reprinted by permission of New Directions Publishing Corporation. "How to Read," *Literary Essays* (New York: New Directions, 1968), p. 21.

[6] Quoted by Ivor Brown, *A Word in Your Ear and Just Another Word* (New York: E. P. Dutton, 1963), pp. 8–9.

cooperate voluntarily with them under the mistaken impression that they are receiving a countervalue or counterservice for whatever they have been persuaded to give.

In sharp contrast to the methods of compulsive predators, which hinge upon force, stealth, or intimidation of some sort, the essential element in the parasitism of those who live by fraud is successful persuasion. The art of deception is their stock in trade, and they continually occupy themselves with schemes to gain access to the resources of others by false pretenses. Cunning decides the most effective bait, and the victims are inveigled into accepting semblance for reality.[7]

3. From another sociological study:

The typical, dominant speech-mode of the middle class is one where speech becomes an object of perceptual activity, and a "theoretical attitude" is developed toward the structural possibilities of sentence organization. This speech-mode facilitates the verbal elaboration of subjective intent, sensitivity to the implications of separateness and difference, and points to the possibilities inherent in a complex conceptual hierarchy for the organization of experience. [The lower working classes] are limited to a form of language use which, though allowing for a vast range of possibilities, provides a speech form which discourages the speaker from verbally elaborating subjective intent, and progressively orients the user to descriptive rather than abstract concepts.[8]

II. These next passages exemplify various kinds of obscurity likely to be perpetrated by apprentice writers. The first passage suffers from excessive informality; the second, from excessive formality. The first is guilty of the imprecision and discontinuity likely to appear in casual conversation; the second illustrates the wordiness and the abstruse phraseology likely to appear when a writer cares more about sounding sophisticated than about conveying a message. Rewrite both passages in a clear Middle Style.

1. The lives of two old people who might be called typical should be considered. I'm referring to the lower middle class. The kind of money that would be needed for food to take care of their needs in a nutritional way is not available. Lesser items have to be depended on for survival. Baked beans, macaroni, and potatoes tell just about the whole story. A lot of money might be spent on heat, too. So the low

[7] James Wyatt Marrs, *The Man on Your Back* (Norman: University of Oklahoma Press, 1958).

[8] Quoted by H. W. Fowler, *A Dictionary of Modern English Usage*, 2nd edition, revised by Sir Ernest Gowers (New York: Oxford University Press, 1965), p. 570.

fifties would not be a surprising temperature during the winter months. The cold condition in their apartment doesn't do much for their infirmities. The man has had arthritis and rheumatism. And imagine the shame. Seedy clothing as well as cheap furniture are two ways in which poverty is likely to affect people. They don't see their old friends any more, and new friends would be something else they wouldn't want because of their shame. Spending all the time in three rooms isn't my idea of a good time, but they hardly ever see a movie or the inside of a church. Television isn't exactly my idea of entertainment, either. But it's the only thing available. There are plenty of old movies, and Sunday mornings have some church services with hardly any personal emotion in them for the viewers.

2. There is a perplexity involved in the task of concocting a treatise on the art of pedagogical endeavors, in view of the fact that the subject is perpetually in a state of flux. The art of pedagogy may be found to be transmuted into diverse forms in diverse nations of the planet, at any single instant in the onward movement of the chronometer. Pedagogical procedures peculiar to any particular geographical location undergo a certain amount of transformation during the course of a lapse of years equivalent to a generation, as a corollary of the transformations inherent in the shifting patterns and paradigms of the community as a societal entity. One representative member will conceive of educational pursuits as a privilege, will labor zealously and husband sufficient pecuniary emolument to achieve entrance into a post-secondary center of academic accomplishments, and will place an elevated value on whatever erudition becomes his possession. Thirty years further into the future, his male offspring may harbor a detestation toward intellectual cultivation, may generate a resistance to all academic activity, may expend his collegiate incumbency in a profligate fashion, and may inculcate in his own progeny an animosity toward literary productions. . . . Each of these generations necessitates a variant form of pedagogy.

III. Dig out an essay you wrote at some time in the past—at least two or three weeks ago. Try to reread it with as much objectivity as you would have if it had been written by someone else. Mark any passages, or single sentences, which, as you now see, might have been written more clearly. Write clarified revisions of those passages. If you find that the essay contains a great many unclear passages, rewrite the entire essay.

4

Specificity

Abstract and *general* words enable us to express ideas. *Specific* words enable us to refer to definite entities—definite people, things, actions, or whatever. Obviously both kinds of language are indispensable, and the accomplished writer can take advantage of both—can move back and forth between the language of ideas and the language of hard realities. Inexperienced writers, however, tend to rely so heavily on abstract, general words that their prose becomes vague and imprecise. Such prose needs large doses of specificity.

Let us define these terms more exactly.

Abstract language refers to intangibles, things that can't be seen or touched: freedom, fulfillment, love, intelligence, greatness, socialism, courage, hypocrisy, and so on. You can see specific instances of these abstractions, but not the abstractions themselves. You can see a courageous act or a loving person or a socialist politician, but not courage, love, or socialism.

General language refers to things that can be seen and touched, but it refers to them only in groups. It lumps them into categories. Specific language can refer directly to "the Baxters' gas-guzzling 1973 Roadhog," while general langauge would refer to it as "an automobile" or, more general still, "a four-wheeled vehicle," "a vehicle," "a moving thing," or simply "a thing." Here are two more series that move from specific to general:

38

my Norwegian Elkhound	Maria Montessori
an elkhound	an innovative educator
a hunting dog	an educator
a dog	a woman
a canine	a human being
a mammal	a mammal
an animal	an animal
a living thing	a living thing

Notice that as the words become more general, they become less precise, less able to express fine distinctions. At a certain level of generality a Norwegian Elkhound seems no different from Maria Montessori: both are subsumed by the word *mammal*.

The examples given thus far have been nouns. But other parts of speech can also be regarded as leaning toward either the specific or the abstract and general. The adjective *brightly colored* is not as specific as *red* or *scarlet*. The adverb *slowly* is not as specific as *five miles an hour*. And the verb *move* is not as specific as *run* or *walk*. *Run*, in turn, is not as specific as any of these synonyms for *run: sprint, dash, gallop, bolt, race, dart, trot, scurry, scamper, lope*. And *walk* suggests an even greater variety of more specific synonyms:

amble	trudge
saunter	clump
stroll	tramp
waddle	shuffle
mince	stride
toddle	march
stagger	strut
stumble	swagger

And we could continue.

Both kinds of language, as we have said, are indispensable—both the specific and the abstract and general. Specific language allows us to say things like this:

> When the Baxters added up the cost of insurance, depreciation, and upkeep, they realized that they laid out $1500 a year for that second car of theirs, a gas-guzzling 1973 Roadhog that did nothing but carry Mrs. Baxter to Sak's or Stop-n-Shop twice a week.

Abstract and general language allows us to say things like the following (which is half quoted, half paraphrased from Philip Slater [1]):

---

[1] *The Pursuit of Loneliness* (Boston: Beacon Press, 1970), pp. 44–45.

Americans did not ask themselves if the trivial conveniences offered by the automobile could really offset the calamitous disruption and depersonalization of our lives that it was destined to bring about.

Without specific language we could not talk about such definite things as Sak's or Stop-n-Shop or the Baxters' Roadhog or the $1500 they spend on it every year. Without abstract and general language we could not formulate comprehensive propositions about society or human nature—could not discuss such notions as "the calamitous disruption and depersonalization of our lives."

But prose in which abstract and general language predominates is likely to leave the reader dissatisfied. One reason is that such language often becomes unclear.

Suppose you were working in an office building in which the following petition was circulated:

A sandwich-vending machine would cost a large sum, but we can afford to buy one if everyone on this floor sets aside a small part of his paycheck from time to time. If you'd like to support this project, please sign below.

Would you sign? Would anyone sign? Only a fool. For only a fool would sign a petition whose most important points were hidden behind cloudy abstractions—"a large sum," "a small part of his paycheck," and "from time to time."

During World War II a government agency circulated a classic example of the obscurity that comes from the misuse of abstract, general language. Some well-meaning but inarticulate bureaucrat was trying to tell federal workers what to do in the event of a nighttime air raid.

Such preparations shall be made as will completely obscure all Federal Buildings and non-Federal buildings occupied by the Federal Government during an air raid for any period of time from visibility by reason of internal or external illumination. Such obscuration may be obtained either by blackout construction or by termination of the illumination.

Beset by requests for clarification, President Roosevelt translated the order into more specific terms:

Tell them in buildings where they have to keep the work going, to put something across the window; and in buildings where they can afford to let the work stop for a while, to turn out the lights.

The moral of all this is obvious. When you present abstractions and generalities, check them for clarity. And if they are not sufficiently clear, restate them in more specific language. The following adaptation of an illustration from Herbert Spencer's *Philosophy of Style* shows how easily a proposition stated in abstract, general language can be clarified by restatement in more specific terms:

> When the customs and amusements of a nation are cruel and barbarous, its penal code will be severe. When men delight in battles, bullfights, and the combats of gladiators, they will punish by hanging, burning, and the rack.

The first sentence might puzzle some readers, but the second sentence—with its more specific language—would clear away any misunderstandings. The same strategy is at work in the next two passages. The first sentence in each passage states an idea in abstract, general terms. Then the following sentences clarify the idea with language of greater specificity.

> Earlier Americans could hardly be called fastidious. As recently as 80 years ago most men were oblivious to many rules of cleanliness and decorum that are now taken for granted. The typical middle-class male didn't bother to wash his hands before eating, didn't bathe more than once a week, didn't brush his teeth until the debris lodged there became uncomfortable, didn't mind slurping his coffee or soup from a saucer, and didn't much care if he missed the living-room spittoon when he spat out tobacco juice.

> His excessive eating and drinking have contributed to his deterioration. He gorges on doughnuts and coffee, pasta and potatoes, cheap hot dogs and vending-machine cherry pies, and, every day, a pint of gin. Then he wonders why his weight is high, his energy low, and his thinking slow and muddled. Two or three years ago he spent his evenings with lively friends or a thoughtful book, but now he settles into an armchair and drifts into suspended animation, watching cowboys or cops on the boob-tube until the black-and-white images yield to solid gray at sign-off.

The following passage by George Orwell is another good example of the way in which specific language can clarify an abstract, general statement. In his essay "Politics and the English Language," Orwell offered this proposition: "Political language [consists] largely of euphemism, question-begging and sheer cloudy vagueness." The specifics with which he then clarified that idea occupy the better part of a paragraph:

> . . . Defenseless villages are bombarded from the air, the inhabitants driven out into the countryside, the cattle machine-gunned, the huts set on fire with incendiary bullets: this is called *pacification*. Millions of peasants are robbed of their farms and sent trudging along the roads with no more than they can carry: this is called

transfer of population or *rectification of frontiers.* People are imprisoned for years without trial, or shot in the back of the neck or sent to die of scurvy in Arctic lumber camps: this is called *elimination of unreliable elements.* Such phraseology is needed if one wants to name things without calling up mental pictures of them. Consider for instance some comfortable English professor defending Russian totalitarianism. He cannot say outright, "I believe in killing off your opponents when you can get good results by doing so." Probably, therefore, he will say something like this:

> While freely conceding that the Soviet régime exhibits certain features which the humanitarian may be inclined to deplore, we must, I think, agree that a certain curtailment of the right to political opposition is an unavoidable concomitant of transitional periods, and that the rigors which the Russian people have been called upon to undergo have been amply justified in the sphere of concrete achievement.[2]

Most of Orwell's examples of vague political language were meant to typify the speeches with which some British politicians and intellectuals sought to justify the purges and deportations of Stalinist Russia. But if Orwell were alive today he could easily update his examples by citing a few cloudy phrases from speeches on the Vietnam War, the "war on inflation," and the Watergate scandals.

One advantage of specific language, then, is that it can serve as clarification. A second advantage is that it can serve as evidence.

Not only does abstract, general language tend to be unclear, it tends to be unconvincing. It often leaves a skeptic skeptical. It tends to confirm the disbelief of the nonbeliever. Consider three assertions whose abstract, general language gets no help from specific language—no clarification and no supporting evidence. Would you accept these assertions as they now stand? (The first and second come from essays by students; the third, which was quoted earlier, comes from Philip Slater, a sociologist.)

Young people of today are more mature than those of earlier times.

The members of our encounter group learned the value of love.

Americans did not ask themselves if the trivial conveniences offered

[2] Excerpted from "Politics and the English Language" in *Shooting An Elephant and Other Essays* by George Orwell; copyright, 1945, 1946, 1949, 1950, by Sonia Brownell Orwell; copyright 1973, 1974 by Sonia Orwell. Reprinted by permission of Harcourt Brace Jovanovich, Inc. and A. M. Heath & Co. Ltd., London. George Orwell, "Politics and the English Language," *Collected Essays, Journalism, and Letters* (New York: Harcourt, Brace and World, 1968), IV, 136.

by the automobile could really offset the calamitous disruption and depersonalization of our lives that it was destined to bring about.

None of these statements, we believe, is acceptable on its own. The first is so extravagantly abstract and general that its defense would require a book as fat as an unabridged dictionary—a study of patterns of growth and maturation throughout human history. The third idea, to be solidly defended, would also require a book, with an abundance of specifics to support such dubious abstract and general phrases as "trivial conveniences" and "calamitous disruption and depersonalization." Probably the second assertion, the one about the marvelously successful encounter group, could be defended in a shorter piece of writing, an essay of fifteen or twenty pages. First the writer would have to use specific language for clarification. What does he mean by "the members"? (How many were there? Did they *all* "learn the value of love"?) What does he mean by the much-abused abstraction "love"? (Sexuality? Tolerance? Kindness? Active altruism?) And what does he mean by "learned the value"? (Did the members merely nod their heads when the group leader declared that love is valuable? Did they voice the belief themselves? Did they act on the belief? Did they continue to act on it after the meetings had come to an end?) The answers to these questions would occupy several pages. Then, once the writer had clarified his meaning, he would come to the larger part of his job. He would have to defend his assertion with specifics—specific evidence regarding each group member who had "learned the value of love." Perhaps a page or two of specifics would be devoted to each member—to the words and deeds that would convince us of the radical change in that member's life.

Consider another idea presented in abstract and general terms:

A good memory can be a great misfortune.

This notion from Mark Twain's *Life on the Mississippi* does not seem very promising. Most people would regard a good memory as an asset rather than a liability. But Twain added specifics, for both clarification and evidence. Here is the clarification:

[Mr. Brown] could *not* forget anything. It was simply impossible. The most trivial details remained as distinct and luminous in his head, after they had lain there for years, as the most memorable events. . . . Such a memory as that is a great misfortune. To it, all occurrences are of the same size. Its possessor cannot distinguish an interesting circumstance from an uninteresting one. As a talker, he is bound to clog his narrative with tiresome details and make himself an insufferable bore. Moreover, he cannot stick to his subject. He picks up every little grain of memory he discerns in his way, and so is led aside.

Twain became even more specific in adding evidence:

> Mr. Brown would start out with the honest intention of telling you a vastly funny anecdote about a dog. He would be "so full of laugh" that he could hardly begin; then his memory would start with the dog's breed and personal appearance; drift into a history of his owner; of his owner's family, with descriptions of weddings and burials that had occurred in it, together with recitals of congratulatory verses and obituary poetry provoked by the same; then this memory would recollect that one of these events occurred during the celebrated "hard winter" of such-and-such a year, and a minute description of that winter would follow, along with the names of people who were frozen to death, and statistics showing the high figures which pork and hay went up to. Pork and hay would suggest corn and fodder; corn and fodder would suggest cows and horses; cow and horses would suggest the circus and certain celebrated bare-back riders; the transition from the circus to the menagerie was easy and natural; from the elephant to equatorial Africa was but a step; then of course the heathen savages would suggest religion; and at the end of three or four hours' tedious jaw, the watch would change, and Brown would go out of the pilot-house muttering extracts from sermons he had heard years before about the efficacy of prayer as a means of grace. And the original first mention would be all you had learned about that dog, after all this waiting and hungering.[3]

Twain's readers would now be ready to concede that a good memory can be a great misfortune.

Let us quote one more passage in which specifics are effectively used as evidence. This time our example is a paragraph written by a student. The central idea, the idea to be supported by specifics, has been italicized.

> In Western Europe, from 1450 to 1700, more than a hundred thousand witches were tortured and executed, the great majority of them women. *To extract confessions from suspected witches, the inquisitors used a variety of brutal tortures.* The rack, as everyone knows, would stretch the woman's body until she either confessed or died. For the *peine forte et dure* she lay upon her back and was pressed with heavy weights until, again, she confessed or died. The thumbscrew slowly twisted her thumb and crushed it. *La fosse* was devilishly ingenious. The victim was buried, up to the neck, in wet cement. As the cement hardened and contracted, it slowly cracked the victim's bones. Other kinds of torture would prevent the woman from

[3] *Life on the Mississippi,* Chapter 13.

sleeping until she confessed her witchcraft or went insane. One form of this torture was to set the suspected witch in the stocks and allow goats to lick salt from her bare feet—for days at a time, without pause for rest or sleep. Perhaps the most vicious torture recorded was one in which a tin box holding a rat was strapped onto the woman's belly. The side of the box pressed against the victim was slid out. Then the box was heated, and the rat, in its agony, tried to escape by eating its way into the woman's body.

This lurid passage is an excellent introduction to our next point. Not only does specific language serve as clarification and evidence, but it has a third function as well. It adds interest. It can spice up a passage that might otherwise be bland. Abstract and general language can be interesting too, especially if it expresses original or controversial ideas. But specific language stays closer to actual experience. It can generate some of the excitement we get from a good story or a vivid description. If you look back at the illustrative passages earlier in the chapter, you will find that typically their rhetorical power comes not from their central ideas but from their specifics. The pasage about witches derives its power chiefly from the descriptions of tortures. Twain's remarks on Mr. Brown's unfortunate memory (pp. 43–44) arouse interest chiefly through the details about Brown's loquacious rambling from one trivial topic to another. Orwell's charge (on pp. 41–42) that politicians disguise reality with vague language would not, we hope, surprise many contemporary readers; but Orwell's specific illustrations remain interesting nonetheless. And we quoted two other passages (on p. 41) whose main ideas were less interesting than the specifics that followed. The main ideas held no special excitement: "Earlier Americans could hardly be called fastidious" and "His excessive eating and drinking have contributed to his deterioration." But the specifics dealt vividly with the sloppiness of earlier Americans and the deterioration of the glutton.

The following passage further illustrates this point. It shows the dullness and feebleness that often result when abstract, general language gets no help from specifics.

Consider the hardships of typical old people in the lower middle class. Lacking adequate pecuniary resources, they are unable to purchase the kinds of foods that are typically recommended for the promotion of health. In winter they are unable to maintain adequate heating. Not surprisingly, they experience an aggravation of any illnesses they might have, particularly those disorders affected most adversely by the absence of adequate warmth. Because their attitude toward their destitution is strongly negative and guilt-inducing, they seek to minimize all social contact. Their offspring maintain only minimal contact with them, except on certain standard festive occasions, at which time they give their parents gifts of relatively inconsequential value.

It may seem unlikely, but the student who wrote this passage knew what she was talking about. As a part-time social worker in a small town in northern California, she had day after day seen the hardships suffered by the elderly. Yet her prose seems to say little about the real problems of real people. We seem to be looking at the old people through a mist that disguises and softens their hardships. This results partly from the author's penchant for fancy-sounding words, her fondness for such terms as "pecuniary resources," "disorders affected most adversely," and "gifts of relatively inconsequential value." But the haziness of her prose results even more from the absence of specifics—from the almost unrelieved abstractness and generality of her language. Undeterred, this young woman revised her prose several times to discard far-fetched words and to replace abstractions and generalities with language of greater specificity. Her final version took this form:

Consider the lives of a typical elderly couple in the lower middle class. Too poor to buy wholesome food, the Arnolds (as I'll call them) survive mostly on baked beans, macaroni, and potatoes. They can't afford to heat their apartment adequately, so the temperature generally stays in the low fifties during the winter months. Not surprisingly, the cold aggravates their infirmities, particularly Mr. Arnold's arthritis and rheumatism. Because they are ashamed of the poverty revealed by their seedy clothing and cheap furniture, the Arnolds avoid their old friends and don't make any new ones. They spend all their time in their three-room apartment, rarely going out to a movie or even to church. Instead they watch television, where they get plenty of old movies and, on Sunday mornings, a few impersonal church services. Their son, and his wife and children, visit the Arnolds only at Thanksgiving or Christmas or on a birthday. The son is all smiles; but the wife's smile is strained and the kids are openly impatient, complaining about the low temperature or the lack of candies and cupcakes, and whining about how tired they are and how much they want to get back home. At the end of each visit, the son, smiling because of his generosity, hands over fifteen or twenty dollars to Mrs. Arnold—his only contribution to the old folks' well-being.

The writer might well have added a great many more specifics and turned this brief account into a full-length essay on "the Arnolds." But the present version is certainly an improvement over the earlier one. Thanks to the added specifics, the revision is not only clearer and more persuasive, but more interesting. The old people are no longer faceless forms interesting only to sociologists, but flesh-and-blood people with painful difficulties.

Exercises

I. For each term that follows, supply three additional terms, each one more specific than the last. For example, for the term *reptile,* you might supply *snake, cobra,* and *King Cobra.* For the term *an art object,* you might supply *a painting, a painting by Rembrandt,* and *Rembrandt's "Slaughtered Ox."*

1. a human being
2. a means of transportation
3. a kind of food
4. a piece of clothing
5. an animal
6. a form of entertainment
7. a body of water
8. a form of physical exercise
9. a dangerous occupation
10. an author

II. For each of the following verbs, give three synonyms of greater specificity. For the verb *walk,* you might give *strut, saunter,* and *waddle.* For *run,* you might give *gallop, sprint,* and *scamper.* Use a thesaurus if your memory needs to be prodded.

1. eat
2. drink
3. look
4. see
5. harm
6. hit
7. laugh
8. produce
9. sleep
10. touch

III. Rewrite five of the following passages by adding specific language. Make the passages interesting by packing them with concrete detail. To illustrate, here are two versions of a single passage. The first uses predominantly abstract and general language. The second adds specifics.

I have lived with the migrant workers. I have personally observed their inadequate living conditions and their unappetizing food. I have seen evidence of their malnutrition. And I have observed their strenuous labor as they pick various kinds of fruits and vegetables.

I have lived with the migrant workers. I have visited their hovels: two-room units separated only by plasterboard, with five such units in a single wood-frame barracks. I have shared their supper of stale beans and sow's ears. I have seen evidence of their malnutrition: the dull eyes, the thinning hair, the lean, twisted limbs, the gaps among their decaying teeth as they smile in hospitality. And I have watched their work: ten hours of bending their backs in 90-degree heat to pick tomatoes and strawberries and (after bending over still further) to cut asparagus spears and lettuce.

Obviously we could add yet more specifics; we could write pages on the housing alone, and more pages on the backbreaking work. But we have restrained ourselves. Exercise the same restraint in your own revisions, lest you spend several days on this one exercise and find that your five revisions have stretched out into five long essays.

One thing more. Don't worry about sticking to the truth. Since you probably won't be familiar with all five of the subjects you write about, you may have to fabricate some of your specifics.

1. You can find a great many kinds of entertainment in this city.

2. Winters are severe in Montana. Though sometimes a thaw warms the air, the temperature usually stays very cold, and occasionally it drops to astonishing lows.

3. In certain ways, grocery shopping can be an interesting experience. The shopper encounters a barrage of colors, shapes, sounds, and personalities.

4. After working in several jobs of excruciating dullness, Bill finally happened upon an interesting line of work.

5. He drove his vehicle very fast over the exceedingly rugged terrain. But halfway through the race his vehicle suffered a mechanical disturbance, began acting in a peculiar way, and then came to a stop.

6. I was not in good shape in those days, so basic training was extremely unpleasant. Shortly after waking up in the morning, I had to perform strenuous exercises for quite some time. And throughout the day there were other kinds of exercise, all of them requiring tremendous exertion.

7. Hugh Hefner, king of the Playboy Empire, has made a great fortune and spread his influence throughout our society. Evidence of his success can be found everywhere.

8. It's easy to understand the new enthusiasm for motorcycles. Motorcycles can do many things that automobiles cannot. And driving a motorcycle satisfies certain important emotional needs.

9. As long as the American people are not suffering any serious hardships or deprivation, they will probably not take much interest in the activities of their government.

10. Most of the new films have little to do with the real lives of modern Americans. The films deal with unreal people set in unreal situations. The goal seems to be sensationalism or crude emotionalism rather than realism.

IV. One way to gain an appreciation of good prose, and to discover exactly what makes it good, is to ruin it. Suppose, for instance, that you spot a passage whose eloquence comes partly from well-chosen specifics. Ruin the passage by converting the specifics into abstract and general language, and in the process you will learn a good many things about the uses of specifics—and also about other aspects of style.

Here is the kind of conversion we have in mind. First we quote the opening paragraph of X. J. Kennedy's fascinating essay, "Who Killed King Kong?" Then we offer a weak imitation in which Kennedy's specific wording has been made overly abstract and general.

> The ordeal and spectacular death of King Kong, the giant ape, undoubtedly have been witnessed by more Americans than have ever seen a performance of *Hamlet, Iphigenia at Aulis,* or even *Tobacco Road.* Since RKO-Radio Pictures first released *King Kong,* a quarter-century has gone by; yet year after year, from prints that grow more rain-beaten, from sound tracks that grow more tinny, ticket-buyers by thousands still pursue Kong's luckless fight against the forces of technology, tabloid journalism, and the DAR. They see him chloroformed to sleep, see him whisked from his jungle isle to New York and placed on show, see him burst his chains to roam the city (lugging a frightened blonde), at last to plunge from the spire of the Empire State Building, machine-gunned by model airplanes.[4]

> The experiences of King Kong have undoubtedly been witnessed by more Americans than have ever seen a performance of any of the greatest dramas or any of the modern plays of a more sensational variety. A great deal of time has gone by since *King Kong* was first released, and yet many people still go to see Kong's unfortunate encounter with the forces of civilization. They see him rendered unconscious and carried from his native habitat to a modern metropolis to be placed on show; they see him escape from captivity to move about the metropolis (carrying a human being), at last to fall from the top of a building after being attacked by make-believe aircraft.

Try the same kind of conversion yourself, and see whether the process doesn't give you some valuable insights into style. To be absolutely sure of getting results, you might add one more step to the process. After putting aside your revision for a day or two, take it up again and try to restore it to its original state. If you happen to remember the original wording, use it. If not, use your own. Then compare your results with the original passage. The test of your success in this venture is not whether you re-create the original passage word for word, but whether you create an effective piece of prose and add to your skill in the art of writing.

[4] "Who Killed King Kong?" *Dissent* (Spring 1960).

Choose one of the following passages to work with:

1. Germaine Greer on the modern ideal of feminine beauty (pp. 19-20)
2. The passage on the dirty habits of earlier Americans (p. 41)
3. The passage on the deterioration of a glutton (p. 41)
4. George Orwell on the language of politics (pp. 41-42)
5. Mark Twain on Mr. Brown's unfortunate memory (pp. 43-44)
6. The passage on the torture of witches (pp. 44-45)
7. Bernard Shaw on "the whole country as a big household" (pp. 191-92)
8. Dwight Macdonald on the men of God who sell peace of mind (pp. 214-15)
9. Joyce Maynard on the goals of young people (pp. 236-37)

V. Take another look at an essay that you wrote at some time in the past. See whether you can improve the essay by inserting language of greater specificity—a few words here, a few sentences there, perhaps even a paragraph or two.

II

Sentences

5

Subjects
and Verbs

Words like *subject* and *verb* probably remind you of your old grammar homework, those tedious hours when you repeatedly drew one line under subjects and two lines under verbs—like this:

The sledgehammer fell from his hands.

By the age of seven, George had become a proficient liar.

This sort of thing may have seemed like a dreadful waste of time and a horrible constraint on the hot blood of youth, but actually that time and energy were not entirely wasted. Your knowledge about subjects and verbs can serve you well. It can lead to immediate improvements in your style.

SUBJECTS

A subject is usually a prominent word. Notice how much more emphasis a word can receive when it acts as a subject than when it occurs in some lesser position:

The dictator was forced to resign by the sudden disintegration of the army.

The sudden *disintegration* of the army forced the dictator to resign.

The *suddenness* of the army's disintegration forced the dictator to resign.

53

Which is the best of these sentences? The answer has to depend on which topic the writer wants to emphasize. He will probably use the first sentence if he is chiefly interested in the dictator, the second if he wants to emphasize the disintegration of the army, and the third if he wants to emphasize the suddenness of that disintegration. But in each case the same general principle holds true: *You can emphasize a word by making it a subject.* In rough drafts an important word will sometimes get buried in the middle of a sentence. One way to remedy that problem—one way to give that word the emphasis it deserves—is to convert it into a subject.

A corollary of this principle is that, generally speaking, *you should avoid using an unimportant word as a subject.* It's true that you can find many exceptions to this rule—exceptions like the sentence you are now reading, in which the subject of the main clause is an unimpressive *it* that refers to nothing. But usually the rule should be obeyed. Usually the subject position—an emphatic position—should not be wasted on a word of little importance. Otherwise you might wind up with a sentence as weak as this one:

The *thing* that forced the dictator to resign was the sudden disintegration of the army.

In some contexts you might justifiably use *thing* in that subject position. If your preceding sentence had been a question such as "What single thing was most important in causing the dictator to resign?" you might then have answered with a sentence beginning "The thing that forced. . . ." But usually you can avoid so dull a beginning. In most contexts the trivial word *thing* should give way to a word of greater importance:

The sudden *disintegration* of the army forced the dictator to resign.

Here are two more sentences in which the subjects should probably not be subjects:

I have found Oldham to be the most vicious gossip I know.

The popular *use* of status symbols is more prominent in the mddle class than among the rich.

We can imagine contexts in which these sentences would serve perfectly well. But in most contexts, *I* and *use*—the two subjects—would be getting more emphasis than they deserved. The first sentence is really about *Oldham,* not about *I;* and the second is more about *status symbols* than *use.* So why not make *Oldham* and *status symbols* the subjects?

Oldham is the most vicious gossip I know.

Status symbols are more popular in the middle class than among the rich.

You can easily apply this principle to your writing. If one of your sentences seems less effective than it ought to be, pick out its subject (and the subject of each clause, for that matter) and then consider: Is this word important enough to be a subject? If you have doubts, try recasting the sentence with some other word as subject, some word that seems to merit special emphasis. And when you find the right subject, you can easily recognize the symptoms of your success. The sentence will probably become clearer and more concise, and it will certainly become more forceful.

VERBS

Verbs can add great vitality to your style—but only if you choose them wisely. Verbs can enliven your sentences but can just as easily deaden them. The right verbs can give a sentence the strength and resilience of a bullwhip; the wrong verbs can render it as lifeless as a piece of string.

A single illustration will show how easily ill-chosen verbs can weaken a piece of prose. By larding the previous paragraph with the wrong sorts of verbs, we quickly make it wordy, roundabout, and generally ineffectual:

Verbs have the capacity to give an added vitality to your style—but only if they are wisely chosen. Verbs are capable of giving life to your sentences but are also capable of having a deadening effect on them. There are some verbs that are able to give a sentence the strength and resilience of a bull-whip; there are other verbs that are likely to bring about the sort of sentence that has no more life than is possessed by a piece of string.

This is 30 words longer than the previous version (54 words have become 84); and the added words have ruined the prose. The earlier version, while not destined for immortality, at least had a healthy conciseness and straightforwardness. The second version, unable to digest all those tasteless verbs, has come down with acute verbosity, otherwise known as logorrhea.

A major symptom of this illness is the overuse of *colorless verbs*: the verb *is* and its relatives (*are, was, were, be,* etc.) and also such verbs as *make, have, give, come,* and *take.* The first version of the passage we have been examining contained a single instance of the verb *give* and used no other colorless verbs—not even the handy *is* verbs. The second version contained fourteen colorless verbs, including eight from the *is* family alone: one *is* and seven *are*'s. The misuse of colorless verbs becomes particularly obvious in the following sentence:

> Verbs are capable of giving life to your sentences but are also capable of having a deadening effect on them.

Here the colorless verbs bring about a slow-moving wordiness. By getting rid of them we can let the sentence flow rather than stagnate. We can reduce the two *are capable of*'s to simple *can*'s. We can replace *giving life to* with *enliven*, and *having a deadening effect on* with *deaden*. The result?

> Verbs can enliven your sentences but can just as easily deaden them.

On the left below are other instances of the wordiness that often results from colorless verbs. On the right we offer revisions.

We are of the opinion that a salary cut would be completely destructive of morale.	We believe that a salary cut would destroy morale.
He is in conflict with . . .	He opposes . . .
They were in doubt as to whether . . .	They doubted whether . . .
The news has made General Craven very angry.	The news has infuriated General Craven.
He made a translation of the message.	He translated the message.
The water has had a weakening effect on . . .	The water has weakened . . .
She finally came to the decision that . . .	She finally decided that . . .
He took a careful look at . . .	He examined (*or* studied *or* scrutinized) . . .
She gave an explanation of . . .	She explained . . .

Now obviously our language couldn't function without colorless verbs. They are marvelously useful, and most of the time they do their work effectively. But you should handle them with care. They are like fire or water—common and useful but sometimes dangerous. Each time you spot a colorless verb in your prose, consider whether you really need it—whether it helps your sentence or hurts it.

The *is* verbs are particularly dangerous. Not only do they figure in constructions of the sort we have just looked at but they appear in two other verb forms that can easily weaken your sentences. One is the *expletive;* the other is the *passive voice.*

The expletive is some variety of *it is* or *there is.* Of course, in conversation you often use an inappropriate *it is* or *there is* and yet your listeners forgive you. In talking about the public schools you might say, "There can be little doubt that there is a far longer school day than is truly necessary" or "There are too many administrators in the typical school system, but there are not enough teachers"; and yet even if your listeners sense the wordiness and indirectness of those sentences, they pardon such venial sins. In conversation you are permitted all sorts of stylistic misdemeanors: verbosity, discontinuity, inaccurate wording, aborted or fractured sentences, and so on. But readers are more finicky than listeners. Your readers know that you are not hurried along by the exigencies of conversational give-and-take. As a writer, you can dawdle and reflect. You need not settle for the first words that occur to you. You have time to review and revise until your prose achieves eloquence. And when you spot an *it is/there is* construction you can stop to ask yourself whether you should revise it out of existence.

Often the answer will be yes. Notice how markedly we can improve the sentences cited earlier by banishing the *it is/there is* constructions:

The school day is far longer than necessary.

The typical school system has too many administrators but not enough teachers.

The sentences are now more concise, more direct, more forceful. Here are additional examples of the improvement that often follows the removal of an *it is/there is* construction:

Weak	Stronger
There is no doubt that there are some teachers in this school who should have gone into a different line of work.	Some teachers in this school should have gone into a different line of work.
It was Mencken's belief that there is no decent person who is not ashamed of the government he lives under.	Mencken believed that every decent person is ashamed of the government he lives under.

None of this implies that you should never use the *it is/there is* construction. If it had no legitimate functions, it would long ago have disappeared from our language. Sometimes the construction is indispensable; no other would serve quite as well. For example:

There is no freedom for the weak. (George Meredith)

> There is a demand today for men who can make wrong appear right. (Terence)

> There are three faithful friends—an old wife, an old dog, and ready money. (Benjamin Franklin)

True, we could revise each of these sentences so as to remove the *it is/ there is* construction. But the revision would be no improvement; the original sentence would be as good as, or better than, the revision. Or so it seems to us. Try the experiment for yourself. Get rid of the *it is/ there is* constructions and then compare your revisions with the originals.

And you should do the same thing each time you spot an *it is/ there is* construction in your own prose. Don't worry about such matters as you write your first draft. But when you review the draft and come upon an *it is/there is* construction, see whether you can remove it and thus improve the sentence. Distrust all such verbs and let them survive revision only when they are truly the most effective verbs for their sentences.

You should also distrust another kind of *is* verb: the verb in the *passive voice*. But before we proclaim the advantages of the active voice over the passive, we had better explain the differences between the two.

Active voice is easily understood. Here is a simple illustration:

> Jack *hits* the ball.

The subject (*Jack*) performs an action (he *hits*). And thus we have active voice. *A verb is in the active voice when the subject of the verb performs an action.* Here is another illustration:

> The cook *prepared* the soup.

The subject (*cook*) performs an action (he or she *prepared*). So again we have active voice.

Passive voice is harder to spot. *The chief mark is that the subject does not act. Instead it is acted upon.*

> The ball *is hit* by Jack.

> The soup *was prepared* by the cook.

The subject of the first sentence is *ball*. But the ball doesn't do anything. Instead something is done to the ball. It *is hit*. In the other sentence, too, the subject (*soup*) does not act. It is acted upon: it *was prepared*.

Another sign of the passive voice is that it always uses some kind of *is* verb plus a past participle: *is hit, was prepared, has been shocked, will be destroyed, were saved, will have been warned,* and so on.

Now for the rhetorical applications of these grammatical distinctions. We should make it clear right at the start that although active voice is generally preferable, the passive voice does have certain necessary functions. It is useful when the doer of an action is unknown and thus cannot appear as the subject of the sentence. It is useful when the doer is not important enough to appear as the subject. And it is sometimes useful simply because the active voice would produce an awkward sentence. The following sentences use passive voice for one or another of these reasons:

Her new Plymouth *was stolen* right out of the garage.

During the accident his right leg *was broken* in two places and his left elbow *was crushed.*

Ron Hunt *was hit* by a pitched ball 50 times in a single season.

The strength of a man's virtue *should* not *be measured* by his special exertions but by his habitual acts. (Pascal)

Passive voice has other legitimate uses beyond those we have mentioned. Unfortunately, it has still other uses that are not so legitimate. Two of these show up repeatedly in the prose of bureaucrats. (1) Passive voice can convey a certain formality and impersonality that bureaucrats find comforting. Somehow "Your letter has been received" strikes them as more dignified than "I have received your letter." Perhaps they recall the old, and badly mistaken, schoolmarm adage, "If you want your writing to sound respectable, never say 'I.'" (2) Passive voice lets the bureaucrat evade responsibility. Rather than saying "I have decided to reject your proposal," he can say "It has been decided that your proposal must be rejected" and thus disappear from the sentence as completely as if he had had nothing to do with rejecting the proposal.

But we find overuse of passive voice not only among bureaucrats. The disease has been spreading. A sociologist is likely to write, "It *was hypothesized* by the observer that the data *could be categorized* in any of several different ways." A psychologist is likely to write, "Intensified anxiety and emotional confusion *were experienced* when puberty *was entered.*" An actual literary critic has written, "Philosophers have frequently expressed the expectation that philosophic disagreements *would be resolved* by applying scientific principles to a subject matter for the first time." And an actual journalist begins a chapter with the following ungainly sentence: "His first afternoon in Miami Beach *was spent* by the reporter in Convention Hall."

It's no wonder, then, that apprentice writers catch the disease and start turning out sentences made awkward and roundabout by the inappropriate use of passive voice. If you find this happening in your own prose, the remedy, again, is a careful review of your early drafts. Each time you find a verb in the passive voice, consider whether active voice would be preferable—whether it would make your sentence clearer, more concise, more vigorous. Most of the time it will do just that.

Exercises

I. Revise the following sentences by putting important words in the subject positions. Your revisions will probably be several words shorter than the originals.

For example:

Original: A measure that will help a person lose weight is inhaling large doses of helium.

Revision: Inhaling large doses of helium will help a person lose weight.`

Several of the following sentences might be perfectly appropriate in certain contexts. But here we give them no context.

1. One thing that can be said to have greatly improved the orchestra's violin section was the extra week of rehearsal.

2. A feature of her game that has given her one victory after another in this season's tennis tournaments has been her cannonball serve.

3. One thing that can be observed regarding the new massage parlors is that they offer such strange-sounding delights as "Cherry Jubilee" and "Banana-Cream Ecstasy."

4. A factor that has damaged the ability of developing countries to purchase food and fertilizers has been the high price of oil.

5. I have arrived at the belief that Oldham is a bigot disguised as a liberal.

6. One thing that formed a part of her beliefs was that she soon came to believe that sex should be as pleasurable for women as for men.

7. If you use too much lipstick, it will make you look cheap.

8. The thing that lost him 27 percent of the vote was his desire to preserve the Internal Revenue Service.

9. Anyone who considers the writings of Shakespeare will find that they are superior to those of Ebenezer Cook.

10. Two things that can be said to have greatly decreased the number of salmon have been the water pollution and the new hydroelectric dams.

11. By getting the advice of a good accountant, a person may save himself from going hopelessly in debt.

12. If you read this catalogue, you will find that it offers all the information you need.

13. Because he has used such complicated sentences, he has made this paragraph difficult to read.

14. If it is to be hoped that any chance of feeding the world's hungry will come into existence, then two things that must be recognized are that we will have to improve agricultural production and establish an effective birth control program.

15. As a result of the relentless poaching on the East African plains, extinction seems to be the condition toward which the rhinoceros and the elephant are being driven.

II. The following sentences make inappropriate use of colorless verbs and *it is/there is* constructions. Revise the sentences to remove the inappropriate verbs. Don't be surprised if your revisions are much shorter than the originals.

For example:

Original: She suddenly engaged in the process of embarking upon an attempt to make a leap from the car.

Revision: She suddenly tried to leap from the car.

1. He had always had the desire to have an encounter with knights, dragons, and wicked sorcerers.

2. There are many scholars who have not made any progress in learning about the art of writing.

3. That afternoon the temperature made a sudden change in a downward direction.

4. The hen came up with a frantic clucking kind of noise whenever her chicks made a movement toward an area that was too far away.

5. It is now the belief of the family that their Doberman has need of a psychiatrist.

6. The hawk made a swooping motion in flying down to get a hold on the gopher, which had shown the first signs of making an effort at scampering away.

7. Betty is of the opinion that her friends do not have an understanding of her feelings toward her pet alligator.

8. Aunt Helen pushed the repairman to such a state of fury that he came to the conclusion that he would not take a look at her television tubes.

9. There is one general who is of the opinion that this strategy will prove destructive to the morale of the soldiers.

10. In this state there is no requirement for a license if you have a desire to engage in the occupation of being a psychological therapist.

11. He made an attempt to make use of meditation as a way of bringing about an increase in his energy, but he always had a way of falling asleep.

12. Ambrose came to the decision that he would not pay any attention to his father's advice and would enter into marriage with Ambrosia immediately.

III. The following sentences all use the passive voice. Revise them by converting the passive voice into active. Several of your revisions will probably show definite improvement over the originals. Put "X's" in front of those revisions.

For example:

Original: The youngsters were awakened by the cawing of crows.
Revision: The cawing of crows awakened the youngsters.

Original: A mystical revelation was experienced by Ronald while a massage was being undergone by him.
X **Revision:** Ronald experienced a mystical revelation while undergoing a massage.

We didn't put an "X" in front of the first revision, because it strikes us as being no better than the original. The revision would sound appropriate in some contexts, but the original would sound appropriate in others. Our second revision gets an "X," however. The original was awkward and wordy; the revision is direct and concise. We can imagine no context in which the original would be more effective than the revision.

1. The entire group was startled by his honesty.

2. As soon as a dam has been built by the beaver, mating is begun by it.

3. For years brutal indignities have been suffered by the mentally ill.

4. The basic social skills necessary for survival in American society are often lost by the inmates of mental institutions.

5. To finish knitting all 87 sweaters by Christmas, much boredom will have to be endured by Sally.

6. I wonder when the mail will be delivered today. by the postman.

7. An interesting book entitled *The Atheist's Handbook* was bought by Gerald the last time a visit to the bookstore was made by him.

8. In Tibet corpses were not buried but cut up and strewn on the ground to be devoured by wolves and vultures.

9. The ancient Egyptians were greatly impressed by the serpent's ability to shed its skin, and thus they viewed the serpent as a symbol of rebirth.

10. It was never admitted by Susan that an act of thievery had been committed by her.

IV. Again, re-examine one of your old essays, perhaps one you have already worked over for a previous exercise in this book. Rewrite any sentence in which you find an ill-chosen subject or a weak verb—that is, an inappropriate colorless verb, *it is*/*there is* construction, or passive voice.

6

Conciseness

Conciseness promotes both clarity and forcefulness. When useless words are omitted, the remaining words—the essential words—stand out more sharply:

Wordy: During the period in which Jack was learning the process of flying the new jets, he also learned something in regard to treating his fellow workers with what is generally called consideration.

Concise: While learning to fly the new jets, Jack also learned to be more considerate toward his fellow workers.

Wordy: It is quite obvious that the person who was flying this airplane and not the woman who was taking care of the passengers is the one who was responsible for the fact that this airplane made a crash landing.

Concise: Obviously, the pilot, not the stewardess, was responsible for this crash landing.

Of course, if the prose becomes *too* brief, if it is filled with such sawed-off sentences as "Jack, learning jets, learned consideration for co-workers," then it will be just as unclear as if it were filled with verbiage. But so long as the prose doesn't omit any words necessary for the reader's understanding, then conciseness will foster clarity as well as vigor.

One kind of superfluous wording is known as *deadwood*. The term is appropriate. Dead wood, in a tree or a sentence, not only looks ugly but weakens the life of the organism. Pruning restores vitality. "Life," said Wallace Stevens, "is the elimination of what is dead."

In writing, the term *deadwood* refers to words that can be deleted without any loss of meaning. Sometimes the words serve no function whatever; other times they repeat ideas that don't need to be repeated. To get rid of such unnecessary words, you don't have to do any rewriting but simply a great deal of crossing out. Your equipment? A dull pencil is helpful; a sharp eye is indispensable.

Wordy: He took the course, not because he wanted to learn about chemistry, but because he wanted to be near the woman who was the instructor.

Concise: He took the course, not ~~because he wanted~~ to learn ~~about~~ chemistry, but ~~because he wanted~~ to be near the woman ~~who was the~~ instructor.

Wordy: As a young man, Walt Whitman was intelligent, perceptive, energetic, and hard-working.

Concise: As a young man, Walt Whitman was intelligent/~~perceptive/energetic/~~ and hard-working.

Wordy: His contemptuous sneer obviously contradicted his extravagant but insincere compliments.

Concise: His ~~contemptuous~~ sneer ~~obviously~~ contradicted his ~~extravagant but insincere~~ compliments.

Have we deleted too many words from that last sentence? Let's see. A sneer is by definition contemptuous, so we don't need the word *contemptuous.* The contradiction between the sneer and the compliments is obvious, so we don't need the word *obviously.* Compliments delivered with a sneer are certainly insincere, so we don't need the word *insincere.* But what about the word *extravagant?* Our shortened revision doesn't contain any word indicating the exuberance of those hypocritical compliments; so if the writer insisted on preserving that idea, he'd have to keep the word *extravagant,* even at the cost of losing some conciseness and forcefulness.

The sentence about Walt Whitman and the one about the sneering hypocrite both illustrate the need for caution in the use of adjectives. "The adjective is the enemy of the noun," said Voltaire, meaning that each time you add an adjective you draw some attention away from the noun it modifies. His point is exemplified in the sentence about the hypocrite, in which, by deleting the adjectives *contemptuous, insincere,* and possibly *extravagant,* we allow the nouns *sneer* and *compliments* to stand out more sharply. Voltaire might also have pointed out that the adjective can be the enemy of other adjectives—as we can see in the first version of the sentence about Whitman. The series of four adjectives in that sentence is woefully repetitive. *Intelligent* is almost the same as *perceptive; hard-working* is almost the same as *energetic.* If we use only two adjectives—*intelligent* and *hard-working,* let's say— we express ourselves clearly and firmly. When we add two more adjectives without adding any new ideas, we blur the meaning and muffle the impact. Needless adjectives are always the enemy of clarity and forcefulness.

Adverbs can be enemies too, particularly qualifiers and intensifiers —words like *very, exceedingly, extremely, actually, definitely, slightly, quite, rather,* and *somewhat.* Notice their effect in the following sentence:

It is actually quite true that people in the very early stages of therapy will definitely tend to become rather egocentric.

The student who wrote this sentence intended to sound precise but wound up sounding fussy. Do we lose any precision if we leave out all those qualifiers and intensifiers?

People in the first stages of therapy tend to become egocentric.

Use an adverb, or an adjective, only if its inclusion can be justified by an added vigor, vividness, or precision. Otherwise regard it as so much dead wood to be hacked away so that the rest of the tree, the remaining words, can thrive. Writers who use too many modifiers are following the dangerous American slogan, "You can't have too much of a good thing." But modifiers, and a great many other things, are like medicine. The proper dose helps; an overdose hurts—and sometimes kills.

Deadwood requires only deletion. Other kinds of wordiness require active revision: the rechoosing of words and reshaping of sentences. But this sort of revising, rather than being a chore, is likely to be a pleasure. You can derive aesthetic satisfaction from changing flabby, slow-moving prose into lean, hard sentences which (in the words of William Carlos Williams) are "quick" and "sharp to strike."

Of the kinds of wordiness that require revision, two were considered in the previous chapter: (1) failure to choose the right subject; (2) failure to choose the right verb. A few illustrations can serve as reminders:

Wordy	Concise
The thing that prevented the plane from landing was the thick fog.	The thick fog prevented the plane from landing.
If the writer deletes these three useless words, he will make the sentence more vigorous.	Deleting these three useless words will make the sentence more vigorous.
A visit to the Riviera was made by Queen Hortense.	Queen Hortense visited the Riviera.
Mrs. Calisher and the Reverend Pontifex were extremely surprised to hear what sounded like a rattlesnake; they suddenly brought an end to their chortling and guffawing noises.	Mrs. Calisher and the Reverend Pontifex were startled to hear what sounded like a rattlesnake; they suddenly stopped their chortling and guffawing.
It is unfortunate that there are many teachers who use their old lecture notes until both teachers and notes have faded with age.	Unfortunately, many teachers use their old lecture notes until both teachers and notes have faded with age.

As the final example suggests, *it is, there is,* and their relatives frequently cause sluggish sentences. Beware, in particular, such roundabout phrases as those on the left below.

Wordy	Concise
It is obvious that . . .	Obviously . . .
It is certain that . . .	Certainly . . .
There is no doubt that . . .	Undoubtedly . . .
It is probably true that . . .	Probably . . .
It is possible that . . .	Perhaps . . .
There is a slight possibility that . . .	Possibly . . .

Another cause of wordiness is *inadequate subordination.* This will be considered at length in later chapters, but it is so dangerous an enemy of conciseness that it deserves to be mentioned here as well. Simply put, it consists of using a clause where a phrase would do, or a phrase where a single word would do.

The following sentence contains an obvious instance of inadequate subordination:

He decided that each week he would eliminate one of his *habits which he considered objectionable.*

The italicized wording—a noun plus a clause—can easily be reduced to a phrase:

He decided that each week he would eliminate one of his *objectionable habits.*   )

And a second look shows that by using a more precise word than *habits,* we can reduce the italicized phrase to a single word:

He decided that each week he would eliminate one of his *vices.*

Here are further examples of inadequate subordination:

Wordy: Most of the animals which have been introduced into this country have become creatures of the kind that is commonly known as pests.

Concise: Most of the animals introduced into this country have become pests.

Wordy: After he had renovated the old house that was in the country, he asked all the people who were his friends at the time to come to a party which would be sumptuous.

Concise: After renovating the old country house, he invited all his friends to a sumptuous party.

Wordy: I admire several of his virtues. The ones I admire are his modesty, his good judgment, and his readiness to lend me money.

Concise: I admire several of his virtues: his modesty, his good judgment, and his readiness to lend me money.

Wordy: Rebecca abhorred the eroticism of contemporary literature and enjoyed nothing but the classics. In particular, she enjoyed the *Satyricon,* the *Decameron,* and Balzac's *Droll Stories.*

Concise: Rebecca abhorred the eroticism of contemporary literature and enjoyed nothing but the classics—particularly the *Satyricon,* the *Decameron,* and Balzac's *Droll Stories.*

The last two examples, the sentence about virtues and the one about eroticism, reveal some unexpected friends of conciseness—namely, colons and dashes: punctuation marks that will often help you to reduce clauses to phrases. But the first and second examples reveal some enemies of conciseness: clauses beginning with *that, which,* or *who,* and then some variety of the verb *to be.* Clauses starting with a *that is,* a *which is,* a *who is,* or the like can often be reduced to phrases or single words.

Finally, we should mention *wordy connectives*—a special pet of writers who yearn to sound impressive. Such writers can stretch out a simple *how to* until it becomes *the way in which to,* or change *so that* into *to such an extent that* or *to the point where.* For example:

Wordy: She showed him *the way in which to* conduct a reliable survey.

Concise: She showed him *how to* conduct a reliable survey.

Wordy: The president became indiscriminate in his cruelty *to such an extent that* even his toadies and spies doubted their safety.

Concise: The president became *so* indiscriminate in his cruelty *that* even his toadies and spies doubted their safety.

Here are some other wordy connectives and their simpler equivalents:

Wordy	*Concise*
in order to	to
with regard to	about
in the event that	if
during the time in which	while
because of the fact that	because
as a result of the fact that	because

For a while you may have to be quite deliberate in applying the principles introduced in this chapter. But gradually you will develop an automatic distrust for clauses beginning *which is,* sentences beginning *there are,* and so on. You will come to share Samuel Johnson's disdain for prose containing so many superfluous words that its thoughts are "lost like water in a mist." You will become impatient with every fat sentence that waddles slowly across the page. Your respect for conciseness will become second nature.

And perhaps you will go too far—will devote yourself so single-mindedly to this one virtue that you neglect all others. If you become obsessed with conciseness your writing may sound curt and impersonal. It will have too little variation in rhythm, too little explanation and qualification, and too few of the narrative and descriptive details that might give it color and drama. For example:

Teaching is hard to discuss because it constantly changes. Different countries have different ways of teaching, and each way alters with time. One man prizes education; his son despises it; the grandchildren hunger for it. Each generation needs a different kind of teaching.

This writer has been fanatical in his quest for conciseness. Here is a more leisurely rendition of the same ideas:

It is difficult to write a book on the art of teaching, because the subject is constantly changing. There are different ways of teaching in different countries of the world, at any one time. Methods in any one country alter every generation or so, as the structure and ideals of society alter. One man will think of education as a privilege, work hard and save money to go to the university, and treasure all the knowledge he can get. Thirty years later his son may despise education, resist schooling, waste his time at college, and teach his children to hate books. Thirty years more, and the children will be eagerly educating themselves, perhaps in an unorthodox or wrong-headed way, perhaps late in life or without entering any educational institution, but still with a genuine hunger for learning. Each of these generations needs a different kind of teaching.

Gilbert Highet [1]

Since it comes at the very outset of Gilbert Highet's book, that paragraph has to guide his readers easily and amiably into his thoughts on the art of teaching. It accomplishes the task far more successfully than would the truncated version we looked at a moment earlier. Perhaps that briefer version had a certain vigor and muscularity, but it was lacking in warmth, clarity, specificity, and rhythmic variety. The hypothetical writer of that version confused conciseness with mere brevity. He deleted all the words he possibly could, regardless of the qualities he thereby sacrificed. The principle of conciseness does not require the terseness of a telegram. It does not proscribe details or images or qualifications, or even words that do nothing but impart a friendly informality or add some extra beats for the sake of a graceful and vigorous rhythm. Instead, conciseness requires the omission of *useless* words. It requires the deletion of words that contribute nothing, either logically or stylistically, to the prose in which they appear, and have no effect but to slow the pace and hide the meaning.

If we criticize Highet's paragraph according to this rectified notion of conciseness, we might decide that he should have deleted a few words. We might wish that he had canceled either the "it is" in the first sentence or the "there is" in the second, and that he had omitted the unnecessary phrases "of the world" and "at any one time" in the second sentence. Possibly his opening sentences should have taken the following form:

It is difficult to write a book on the art of teaching, because the subject is constantly changing. Different countries have different kinds of teaching, and the methods in any one country alter every generation or so, as the structure and ideals of society alter. . . .

Is this an improvement? Perhaps we ourselves are becoming too finicky

[1] *The Art of Teaching* (New York: Knopf Vintage Books, 1950), p. 3.

in the name of conciseness. In any case, we would certainly leave the rest of the paragraph as it stands. Do you agree?

Exercises

I. Rewrite the following sentences and passages to make them more concise. Try not to change the basic meaning of the passages, though perhaps you will have to sacrifice a few nuances.

1. The medicine did not have a soothing effect on the patient.

2. My father was annoyed by the fact that I arrived late instead of being on time.

3. I spotted a butterfly which was green in color; I would have caught it in my net if it had not been for a log which caused me to trip.

4. He did a good job of delivering his speech in terms of persuasive delivery.

5. I admired his writing not only for its terse conciseness but also for the fact that its ideas were expressed in a clear, lucid, straightforward manner.

6. The thing that caused the failure of the army to avoid defeat was the nature of its leadership, which was not competent.

7. As a result of the fact that he had never learned the basic fundamentals of algebra, he found calculus difficult to such an extent that he had to withdraw from the course.

8. The smoke was moving in such a way as to cover up the level prairie, until soon nothing was visible to our eyes except for a thick blanket of dense smoke.

9. The audience was unable to find enjoyment in the final conclusion of the play, the part in which Ralph Barnes, a hero with admirable qualities which were quite respectable, suddenly turned abruptly into an evil villain with truly objectionable qualities.

10. Since Jarvis's allowance had already been spent by him, he found that buying a ticket so that he could attend the dog races was something he simply could not afford to do.

11. Sociologists have tried to make a determination as to why so many people who grow up in the upper classes have a tendency to become the sort of people who consistently ignore and break the law.

12. The reason the people of Somaliland do not achieve an understanding of the problems arising in the American economy is that they have never had the experience of living through a period in which prices have risen rapidly.

13. The most opportune period of time to go out to hunt mountain

quail if you wish to do your hunting in New Mexico is during the month of December. By that time of the year the birds have made their descent down in a drifting manner to the desert valleys in order to make their escape from the deep snow of the high country in the mountains which are in close proximity to the desert valleys.

14. Primitive people are very often highly timorous about exchanging words in conversation with people whom they have never met before, for they are afraid that intercourse of a verbal nature with people who do not belong to their tribe will constitute an offense to the departed souls of their deceased ancestors, all of whom are potentially nasty, evil, malevolent, and quite prepared to harm the living.

15. The Carthaginians of the ancient world made a sacrifice of a great number of their children to the cruel and brutal god whose name was Moloch. The children who were to be sacrificed to the god Moloch were placed on the hands of an idol constructed of bronze. The hands of the idol were stretched out, and they sloped downward toward the ground. The children slid down the sloping hands of the idol into an oven below, which was fiery hot with the burning of fires. Meanwhile the people who worshiped Moloch danced to the considerably loud musical sounds made by flutes, timbrels, and drums in order to drown out the screams of the children who were being sacrificed by being made to slide down the sloping hands of the idol into the flaming furnace.

II. The following wordy passages are derived from two well-written pieces of prose by X. J. Kennedy and Germaine Greer. Rewrite the passages to make them more concise. The first one adds roughly 110 useless words to Kennedy's original 129. The second is even more bloated; it adds 130 words to Greer's 60.

1. The difficult ordeal and the highly sensational, spectacular death of King Kong, who was an ape of gigantic proportions, undoubtedly have been witnessed by a greater number of Americans than have ever laid their eyes upon a performance of *Hamlet, Iphigenia at Aulis,* or even *Tobacco Road.* Since the time when the film was first released by RKO-Radio Pictures, a quarter-century has made its way past us; yet year after year, from prints that have been growing increasingly more rain-beaten, from sound-tracks that have been growing increasingly more tinny, ticket-buyers who number in the thousands still are found to be in pursuit of the luckless fight that is carried on by Kong in opposition to the forces of technology, journalism of the tabloid variety, and the DAR. They see him as he is chloroformed to sleep, see him as he is whisked from his isle which is covered with jungle, see him as he is whisked from that isle to the city of New York and there is placed on show, see him when he is able to burst his chains so that he is able to roam around the metropolitan city (at the same time as he is lugging a blonde who

is extremely fearful), at the very last to make a plunge from the spire of the Empire State Building, having been shot by the machine guns of airplanes which are, in actuality, make-believe model airplanes.

2. I am not able to make the claim that I have achieved a full and complete emancipation with respect to the dream that some man of enormous size, say six foot six, heavily shouldered and so forth to match, will hold me close to his tweedy clothing apparel, so close that he might be said to crush me. He will look down so as to look into my eyes. And he will do no less than leave what might be called the taste of heaven on my lips, which will be waiting in expectation. Or it is possible that on my waiting lips he will leave the extremely intense heat which will be the concomitant of his intensely passionate emotion. As a matter of fact, the truth is that for a period of time extending over three weeks, I was involved with this very man in a state of matrimony.

III. In the previous exercises you've been aiming for conciseness. Now aim for verboseness. Ruin one (or more) of the passages listed below by adding every conceivable kind of redundancy and prolixity —so many useless words, phrases, and sentences that the passage swells to at least twice its initial length. Next, after putting aside your mutilated version for a few days, revise it again to restore its original conciseness. Then compare your results with the original passage. (This procedure, and the rationale behind it, is explained more fully in Exercise IV on pages 48–50.)

1. The passage on the dirty habits of earlier Americans (p. 41)
2. The passage on the deterioration of a glutton (p. 41)
3. The passage on the torture of witches (pp. 44-45)
4. The passage on the plight of a typical elderly couple (p. 46)
5. Henry Miller on our lack of spiritual progress (p. 79)
6. Katherine Anne Porter on the true nature of babies (p. 115)
7. The passage on Jason's attempt to engage in socially useful work (p. 129)
8. Mark Harris on the hippie scene in San Francisco (p. 154)
9. The passage on "gentle strength" in men (p. 177)
10. Caroline Bird on the modern liberated woman (p. 217)

IV. Return to one of the writings you produced at some earlier time and make it more concise. Especially watch out for deadwood, weak verbs, and inadequate subordination (particularly in clauses beginning with *that is, which is, who is,* or the like); but be alert for verbosity in whatever form it occurs.

7

Coordination

This chapter and several of the following ones will be concerned with one of the chief skills of the prose stylist—the ability to connect ideas so that they form graceful, expressive sentences. The writer not skillful in combining ideas has to make do with short sentences and a staccato style:

> A great task remains before us. We must be dedicated to that task. We must take increased devotion from these honored dead. They gave their lives to a great cause. They gave the last full measure of devotion. Therefore we must increase our devotion to that cause. . . .

Short sentences can be valuable, of course—particularly for emphasis and variety—but the writer who uses only short sentences is destined to be an ineffectual stylist. If Lincoln had used only short sentences in dedicating the national cemetery at Gettysburg, his sentences would soon have been forgotten. He did not so limit himself.

> It is rather for us to be here dedicated to the great task remaining before us—that from these honored dead we take increased devotion to that cause for which they gave the last full measure of devotion; that we here highly resolve that these dead shall not have died in vain; that this nation, under God, shall have a new birth of freedom; and that government of the people, by the people, for the people, shall not perish from the earth.

This, said H. L. Mencken, "is eloquence brought to a pellucid and almost gem-like perfection." Perhaps it's only fair to add that Mencken went on to accuse Lincoln's "poetry" of being an elaborate disguise for bad logic:

> The Union soldiers in that battle actually fought *against* self-determination; it was the Confederates who fought for the right of their people to govern themselves. . . . The Confederates went into battle free; they came out with their freedom subject to the supervision and veto of the rest of the country—and for nearly twenty years that veto was so effective that they enjoyed scarcely more liberty, in the political sense, than so many convicts in the penitentiary.[1]

Well, maybe so. But we are concerned here with style, not logic. And the Lincoln passage (the Mencken too, for that matter) clearly displays the advantages of being able to combine phrases and clauses into sophisticated sentences.

One way of tying ideas together is *coordination*. This technique can connect sentence elements that have the same grammatical function. For instance, in the sentence "I walked slowly away from her, and then I felt for my wallet," we have two coordinate elements—two independent clauses ("I walked slowly away from her"/"then I felt for my wallet").

The words most often used to coordinate sentence elements are the seven coordinating conjunctions *and, but, or, nor, for, yet,* and *so.* Here are some examples of the work they can do:

> Miss Smidgin was *courteous* **but** *cool.* (coordinate adjectives)

> The next five minutes will determine whether we *win* **or** *lose.* (coordinate verbs)

> This chimp is crazy *about peanuts,* of course, **but** also *about strawberries.* (coordinate prepositional phrases)

> Major Sabo spoke so *quickly,* so *softly,* **and** so *tremulously* that I thought he had lost his mind. (coordinate adverbs)

> *He once lived in mansions,* **yet** *now he is living in an empty packing case.* (coordinate independent clauses)

> *You probably won't have any trouble spotting him,* **for** *he weighs almost three hundred pounds.* (coordinate independent clauses)

---

[1] Copyright 1922 by Alfred A. Knopf, Inc., and renewed 1950 by H. L. Mencken. Reprinted from *A Mencken Chrestomathy,* by H. L. Mencken, by permission of Alfred A. Knopf, Inc. "Abraham Lincoln," *A Mencken Chrestomathy* (New York: Alfred A. Knopf, 1949), p. 223.

She didn't offer to help, **nor** *did she offer any excuse for her laziness.* (coordinate independent clauses)

I wanted to live closer to Nature, **so** *I built myself a cabin in the swamps of Louisiana.* (coordinate independent clauses)

These versatile conjunctions are the most frequent means for achieving coordination, but they are not the only means. Punctuation can sometimes do the job all by itself—as in these sentences by Henry Miller:

The aim of life is to live, and to live means to be aware, *joyously, drunkenly, serenely, divinely* aware.[2]

What seems *nasty, painful, evil,* can become a source of beauty, joy and strength, if faced with open mind.[3]

And occasionally coordination is brought about by means of *correlative conjunctions*. These always occur in teams of two: *either . . . or; neither . . . nor; not only . . . but (also); both . . . and.* For example: "An honest man will receive **neither** *money* **nor** *praise* that is not his due" (Ben Franklin, of course).

We should add a word of caution. Coordinate elements should be *parallel*—should be similar in grammatical function. A noun should be linked to a noun, a verb to a verb, a dependent clause to a dependent clause, and so on. Here is a flagrant violation:

While confined to bed, he *read* the complete works of Plato, *listened* to Stravinsky on the phonograph, and *he would* also *watch* the soap operas on television.

The writer begins this coordinate structure well enough with the two verbs *read* and *listened,* but then switches to the noun-verb combination *he would . . . watch.* How can we restore parallelism? Probably the neatest way is this:

While confined to bed, he *read* the complete works of Plato, *listened* to Stravinsky on the phonograph, and *watched* the soap operas on television.

Here are some other instances of nonparallel construction:

Priscilla decided not to befriend anyone who was *poor* or *without an education.* (An adjective is linked to a prepositional phrase.)
Revision: . . . *poor* or *uneducated.*
Jon *loved* to peer through the window of the "adult" book store, but

[2] *The Henry Miller Reader,* ed. Lawrence Durrell (New York: New Directions, 1959), p. 359.
[3] *The Henry Miller Reader,* p. 356.

never *being* bold enough to go in. (The verb *loved* is yoked to the participle *being*.)

Revision: Jon *loved* to peer through the window of the "adult" book store but *was* never bold enough to go in.

Dorothy Parker's book reviews were *cutting, cruel,* but always *displayed* intelligence. (Two adjectives—*cutting* and *cruel*—are mistakenly coordinated with the verb *displayed*.)

Revision: Dorothy Parker's book reviews *were cutting* and *cruel*, but always *displayed* intelligence. (*Cutting* and *cruel* form one coordinate structure. The two verbs *were* and *displayed* form another.)

The problem of parallelism becomes a bit more problematic when it involves correlative conjunctions: *either . . . or; neither . . . nor;* and so on. The rule to keep in mind is that the correlatives should occur immediately to the left of the coordinate elements—as in "He was **neither** a *borrower* **nor** a *lender*." The following sentences violate this rule:

Joan **not only** *made* three interceptions **but** several ferocious *tackles.* (The verb *made* is linked to the noun *tackles.*)

Revision: Joan **not only** *intercepted* three passes **but** *made* several ferocious tackles. (Verb is linked to verb.)

Transcendental Meditation was becoming a fad **both** *among students* **and** older *searchers* for tranquility. (A prepositional phrase is linked to a noun.)

Revision: . . . a fad **both** *among students* **and** *among older searchers* for tranquility. (Phrase is linked to phrase.)

Revision: . . . a fad among **both** *students* **and** older *searchers* for tranquility. (Noun is linked to noun.)

The senator was **either** an honest *man* **or** *he was* an extremely skillful liar. (A noun is linked to a subject-verb combination.)

Revision: The senator was **either** an honest *man* **or** an extremely skillful *liar.* (Noun is linked to noun.)

Revision: Either *the senator was* an honest man **or** *he was* an extremely skillful liar. (Subject and verb are linked to subject and verb. It makes no difference that the second subject is a pronoun. In coordinate structures a pronoun is equivalent to a noun.)

You can find exceptions to the rules of parallelism—as you can to most rules of usage. Benjamin Jowett, the great translator of Plato, chose to write the nonparallel sentence "they not only tell lies but bad lies" rather than the proper but less graceful "they not only tell lies but tell bad lies." [4] Still, this example *is* an exception. Usually nonparallelism will

---

[4] Bergen and Cornelia Evans, *A Dictionary of Contemporary American Usage* (New York: Random House, 1957), p. 350.

sound off-key—will grate on the ear of the sensitive reader. (And of course you should write for the sensitive reader, not turn out shoddy prose and hope the reader won't know any better.) When skilled writers use coordination as a means of strengthening their prose, they almost always take pains to keep the coordinate elements parallel.

The writer who has mastered the techniques of coordination will find them an invaluable asset. One of their advantages, as we have suggested, is their proficiency in combining short sentences into longer ones. If a passage is deadened by a monotonous sequence of short sentences, the writer might well be able to relieve the monotony through the judicious use of coordination. To illustrate this point, we present two versions of a single passage. The earlier one sounds like a first draft. Apparently the writer has labored to express his ideas with precision but has not yet had time to worry about the finer points of style. His sentences all have the same length, like so many boards measured and cut by a bench saw. In the second version, however, he has varied the length and structure of his sentences by a skillful use of coordination.

> These rationalists attempted to study man "scientifically." They regarded man as a soul-less object not much different from any other animal. Man belonged to nature in the same way as a plant. He could even be viewed as a machine. The interactions among men could be studied like those among fish. The interactions could be studied like the relations among trees. They could be studied like the relationships between the parts of a steam engine. The needs of men could be investigated with rigor. The investigations would lead to precise results. Man was merely a bundle of automatic responses. What previous philosophers had called the "mind" was merely a function of a machine-like brain.

> These rationalists attempted to study man "scientifically." They regarded man as a soul-less object not much different from any other animal *and* not much different from a plant *or* a machine. The interactions among men could be studied like those among fish *or* trees *or* the parts of a steam engine. The needs of men could be investigated with rigor *and* precision. Man was merely a bundle of automatic responses, *and* what previous philosophers had called the "mind" was merely a function of a machine-like brain.

The second version of the passage has gained in both economy and variety merely through the use of two coordinate conjunctions—*and* and *or*.

Another advantage of coordination is that it can achieve great forcefulness. Chapter 12 will discuss this point at length, but here we should offer at least one passage in which the point is exemplified. Once again we quote Henry Miller:

> Morally, spiritually, we are fettered. What have we achieved in mowing down mountain ranges, harnessing the energy of mighty rivers, or moving whole populations about like chess pieces, if we ourselves remain the same restless, miserable, frustrated creatures we were before. To call such activity progress is utter delusion.[5]

The first sentence begins its accusation with the two strong beats of the coordinate adverbs *morally, spiritually*. The second sentence names some of our dubious activities with the stronger three beats of *mowing down mountain ranges, harnessing the energy of mighty rivers,* and *moving whole populations about like chess pieces,* and then finishes us off with three cruel adjectives: *restless, miserable, frustrated*. The message is an urgent one, and the harsh regularity of its rhythm intensifies the sense of urgency.

Exercises

I. The following sentences illustrate several kinds of nonparallel construction. Rewrite the sentences to achieve parallelism.

1. We survived the torrid summer only by turning on the air conditioner to its full strength and when possible stayed out of the sun.
2. Most critics agree that *Citizen Kane* was well acted, skillfully directed, and it had a powerful screenplay.
3. In interviewing job-seekers, the personnel manager looks for intelligence, sound education, and, above all, to see whether they have perseverance.
4. Getting ready for his walk across the park, James decided to take along a bottle of sulfa tablets, a box of salt, and he included his well-thumbed copy of *Lolita*.
5. The hunter wearing a green jacket and with a red cap turned out to be a game warden looking for poachers.
6. The defeated players left the field looking exhausted, despondent, and as if they were angry.
7. Jacobus peered through his binoculars with shrewd alertness but sometimes hiccupping.
8. If you insist on reading the Old Testament all the way through and to do the same with the New Testament, you are in for some big surprises.
9. Richard was intelligent, well-read, but a failure.

[5] *The Henry Miller Reader,* p. 358.

10. To survive this inflation, the company must reduce expenses either by firing some people or it will have to slash everyone's salary.

11. The plate umpire warned the pitcher that either he must abide by the rules or suffer the consequences.

12. In South Africa the baboons not only annoy farmers by raiding corn fields but also chicken coops.

13. Jonathan was either a true lover of poetry or he was reading Shelley just to impress Gwendolyn.

14. She owed her shrewdness both to her years of reading Aristotle and her years of commuting on the New York subways.

15. When Mr. Oldham gave his wife a copy of *The Ecstasy of Sex,* she knew that he intended the gift either as a joke or he was trying to tell her something.

II. Turn each of the following passages into a single sentence through the techniques of coordination. For easy reference, here is a list of the conjunctions you can use (though you will not have need for all of them).

Coordinating conjunctions: *and, but, for, or, nor, yet, so*
Correlative conjunctions: *either . . . or; neither . . . nor; not only . . . but (also); both . . . and*

1. Acupuncture can dispel migraine headaches. It can relieve many other illnesses as well.

2. Baker is short and stubby. He can play a powerful game of tennis.

3. Ex-convicts often return to crime soon after their release. They find it difficult to get a legitimate job.

4. Yogis can voluntarily change the rate of their heartbeat. They can also voluntarily control the rate of their blood pressure. They can even raise their body temperature. They can lower it too.

5. Stanley fancies himself a great song writer. So far he has received nothing but rejection notices saying that his melodies are imitative. They also say that his lyrics are lifeless.

6. The depression of the thirties was not only unexpected. It was also unnecessary.

7. The British historian Froude was pitied by his colleagues rather than admired. He suffered from a chronic inability to remember important dates.

8. When Francis Bacon died, the scientific revolution had not yet arrived. He had laid the foundations for it, though. He had also bestowed upon it the prestige of his name.

9. The new bookstore manager discovered that she would have to curtail expenses by 25 percent. Otherwise the store would go out of business.

10. At one point in Mahler's *Song of the Earth* three bassoons reach and hold their lowest note. At the same time two flutes warble their high woodwind tones. Meanwhile a lone trumpet blares in the middle register.

11. During his lunch hour, one of the things Barney would do was to look out the windows. Thus he could watch the girls go by. The other thing he would do was to study his favorite book, *The Imitation of Christ.*

12. The tendency toward romantic love is stronger in some generations than in others. Furthermore, it is stronger in some people than in others. Since the end of the Middle Ages, however, it has remained a constant element in Western civilization.

13. The true fire-arm enthusiast gets excited not only by shooting a gun. Touching or cleaning a gun will also excite him.

14. Anger is a common result of low self-esteem. Violence is another. The most common result, however, is withdrawal from reality through drugs. Sometimes this withdrawal is achieved through alcohol.

15. Harold thinks he might devote his spare time to reading the complete works of Plato and John Dewey. He thinks that the only other possibility would be to devote his spare time to perfecting his skill in poker.

III. The following sentences use too much coordination and thus become painfully repetitive in their rhythm. Improve the sentences by whatever means you like. Here is a sample revision:

Original: A poltergeist seems to be at work in this house, for yesterday the refrigerator lifted itself two feet off the floor, and then it stayed aloft until midnight, and meanwhile a chair leaped onto the kitchen table, and then the chair danced a polka.

Revision: A poltergeist seems to be at work in this house. Yesterday the refrigerator lifted itself two feet off the floor and stayed there until midnight. Meanwhile a chair leaped onto the kitchen table and danced a polka.

1. We packed our belongings carefully, but we forgot to include toothpaste, so the next morning we had to rush out to buy some before we could brush our teeth, and so we were late in meeting the tour group, but fortunately they were too considerate to leave without us.

2. Billionaire Paul Getty was the richest man in the world, and he had been married five times, but all of his wives died; but he didn't want a sixth marriage, for a card reader had warned him that he would die shortly after his sixth marriage.

3. I began reading Carl Jung's book on "modern man in search of a soul," but it was hard to understand, so I put it down, and I began

playing solitaire instead, but the game soon bored me, and so I lay back and went to sleep.

4. A number of animal species have been disappearing, but fortunately many of those vanishing species reproduce themselves in captivity, and recently such a reproduction took place at the zoo in Buffalo, New York, and a baby orangutan named Rusty was born.

5. Victims of skin cancer run a high risk of developing other forms of cancer, and those other forms are likely to be more serious, so all people with skin cancer should visit their doctor at least once a year, and this practice should continue even after the skin cancer has been cured.

8

Subordination

Coordination can be forceful by virtue of its repetitiveness—as in Henry Miller's phrase "restless, miserable, frustrated creatures." But if this sort of thing were to appear in paragraph after paragraph, the forceful repetition would soon become tiresome regularity. Sometimes coordination becomes tiresome within just a sentence or two:

> I studied hard for the next exam, and I got Bill to help me, but I still did poorly, but I did much better than on the previous exam. The teacher was obviously displeased with me, but his frowns did not shatter my self-confidence.

The overuse of coordination actually causes several problems. One is the dull regularity. Another is a lack of emphasis. The most important ideas don't get the emphasis they deserve. Coordination makes all ideas seem equally important, or equally unimportant. The problem becomes clear in the sentence "I studied hard for the next exam, and I got Bill to help me." Although the writer probably meant to emphasize how hard he studied, the coordinate structure makes it sound as if the hard studying was no more important than the help from Bill.

The remedy for these problems is *subordination*. For one thing, this device can prevent monotony. The techniques of subordination are so diverse that they enable you to give your sentences a rich and varied rhythm. Second, subordination can help you emphasize important ideas. You can *subordinate* the lesser ideas and thus allow the important ones to stand out more sharply.

83

Here is an example of subordination at work—a revision of the passage about the hardworking student:

> With some help from Bill, I studied hard for the next exam; and even though I still did poorly, I did much better than on the previous exam. The teacher's frowns could not shatter my self-confidence.

This is not immortal prose, but it is considerably better than the version that used too much coordination.

The chief devices of subordination are (1) the dependent clause, (2) the phrase, and (3) the single word. Generally speaking, an independent clause is more emphatic than a dependent clause, a dependent clause is more emphatic than a phrase, and a phrase is more emphatic than a single word:

Independent clause: Ruth Jackson told us about the sordid aspects of the medical profession; *we chose her to be our family doctor.*

Dependent clause: Ruth Jackson, *whom we chose to be our family doctor,* told us about the sordid aspects of the medical profession.

Phrase: Ruth Jackson, *our family doctor,* told us about . . .

Single word: *Dr.* Ruth Jackson told us about . . .

This chapter will focus on the dependent clause and the phrase. Please bear in mind that we don't plan to present the kind of exhaustive and exhausting analysis that sets forth every rule and every exception. Instead, we will offer the kind of information most likely to be useful to apprentice writers.

THE DEPENDENT CLAUSE

A *clause* is a group of words containing a subject and a verb. An *independent clause* can stand alone as a sentence. A *dependent clause,* in most instances, cannot.

> Little Emily grabbed the dollar bill.
> As little Emily grabbed the dollar bill . . .

These are both clauses because each one contains a subject and a verb (*Emily* and *grabbed*). The first clause is independent. The second is dependent: in most contexts it could not serve as a sentence.

A dependent clause ordinarily uses one or another of the following words near the beginning.

after	unless
although	until
as	what (*and* whatever)

because	when (*and* whenever)
before	where (*and* wherever)
how	whereas
if	whether
since	which (*and* whichever)
than	while
that	who(m) (*and* who(m)ever)
though	whose

Sometimes this sort of word is omitted—as in "I knew [*that*] *he was heading in the wrong direction*" and "There's the woman [*whom*] *I met at the dog races last week.*"

We have listed only the most common words by which you can link a dependent clause to the rest of its sentence, but even this partial list can give you some idea of the flexibility and versatility of which the dependent clause is capable. Certainly it is more versatile than the co-ordinate clause. Suppose you were trying to link the two independent clauses we looked at earlier: "Ruth Jackson told us about the sordid aspects of the medical profession" and "we chose her to be our family doctor." If you coordinated these clauses, you would probably have to use *and* or *but* as your connective, although neither of these would do a good job of indicating the logical or chronological relations between the clauses. But if you subordinated one clause to the other, you would have a much greater variety of connectives to choose from. We have already seen that you could use *who(m)*: "Ruth Jackson, *whom* we chose to be our family doctor, told us about the sordid aspects of the medical profession." But you could also consider other possibilities:

After we chose Ruth Jackson to be our family doctor, she told us . . .
Although we chose . . .
As soon as we chose .'. .
Because we chose . . .
Before we chose . . .
Even though we chose . . .
When we chose . . .

And you would have still other possibilities—other ways of linking the two clauses. You could reverse the emphasis—that is, you could subordinate the clause about Dr. Jackson's thoughts on the medical profession and make the other clause independent. For example:

After Ruth Jackson told us about the sordid aspects of the medical profession, we chose her to be our family doctor.

And in place of the *after* you could use any of the other connectives that appeared in the last batch of illustrative sentences: *although, as soon as, because,* and so on.

So far, then, the dependent clause has enabled us to derive roughly fifteen different sentences from those two ideas about Dr. Ruth Jackson. But the possibilities are not yet exhausted. The dependent clause has yet another source of flexibility: it can come *before* the independent clause, *after* it, or *in the middle.*

Before: *As soon as we chose Ruth Jackson to be our family doctor,* she told us about the sordid aspects of the medical profession.

After: Ruth Jackson told us about the sordid aspects of the medical profession *because we had chosen her to be our family doctor.*

In the middle: Ruth Jackson, *whom we chose to be our family doctor,* told us about . . .

Before leaving dependent clauses, we must re-examine a few of the words that introduce such clauses. Some of these words can be troublesome.

To begin with, consider *while,* a word that can generate confusion because it has several meanings. It can mean *during the time that:* "He studied *while* I stared out the window." It can mean *but:* "My sister likes Stravinsky *while* I prefer country music." And it can mean *although:* "*While* I sympathize with your motives, I deeply disapprove of your actions." The versatility of this word can lead to ambiguity—as in the following sentence, in which *while* can mean either *although* or *during the time that:*

> *While* Milhouse was under doctor's orders, he downed two jiggers of 100-proof bourbon every night before going to bed.

Did the doctor insist that Milhouse drink bourbon, or did Milhouse do his drinking in violation of doctor's orders? The second interpretation is almost certainly the right one, but the *while* leaves us in doubt. The writer could have avoided the problem simply by replacing *while* with *although.*

Another marker inclined to be ambiguous is *since. Since* not only signifies the passage of time; it can also mean *because.* Here it can be taken either way:

> *Since* Sabo left town three weeks ago, most people have concluded that he is guilty as charged.

At first the reader would probably interpret the *since* to mean *after,* but a moment later he might well decide it means *because.* You can prevent such lapses in clarity by using *since* only when there can be no doubt about whether it means *because* or *after.* In the sentence about Sabo, a *because* should replace the *since.*

As can be another source of confusion. It can mean either *while* or *when* or *because.* What does it mean here?

Tina started out for home *as* daylight was turning to darkness.

Mark sneaked out the side door *as* the party began to get larger and more boisterous.

The first *as* can mean either *while* or *because;* the second, either *when* or *because.* Whenever *as* threatens to be ambiguous, replace it with a word that will leave no doubt as to your meaning:

Tina started out for home *because* daylight was turning to darkness.

Mark sneaked out the side door *when* the party began to get larger and more boisterous.

One final caution—with regard to the word *because. Because* is likely to be ambiguous when it follows *not:*

She did not read the works of Albert Jay Nock because he ridiculed the public schools.

This sentence could mean either of two things. (1) She did not read Nock; she refused to read him because she disliked his attitude toward public education. (2) She *did* read Nock, but not because he ridiculed the schools; she read him for other reasons. How can the sentence be clarified? If we wish to express the first meaning, we can simply insert a comma before *because.* To express the second meaning, we must revise more extensively—for example, "She read the works of Albert Jay Nock, but not because he ridiculed the public schools," or, "Her interest in the works of Albert Jay Nock had nothing to do with his scorn toward public education."

THE APPOSITIVE PHRASE

The appositive, though neglected by amateur writers, is a great favorite among professionals. It is remarkably useful—a handy means of subordination, a help in achieving conciseness, and a sure way of attaining diversity in sentence structure. One reason for its usefulness is that, like the dependent clause, it can occupy a variety of positions with respect to an independent clause; it can come *before, during,* or *after* the clause. Since the *during* position is the most common, we'll start with that one.

Here is a simple illustration:

Macaulay Jones, a local *businessman,* was found to be the organizer of a state-wide ring of bicycle thieves.

An appositive is usually a noun that refers to, and helps to explain, another noun. Here the *appositive noun* is *businessman.* The word it refers to (the *antecedent*) is *Macaulay Jones.*

In this simple form, perhaps, the appositive doesn't seem very promising as a rhetorical device, but a second look shows that even this brief appositive serves valuable functions. A writer unskilled in the use of appositives might have needed two sentences to convey the information about Jones:

Macaulay Jones was a local businessman. He was found to be the organizer of a state-wide ring of bicycle thieves.

By converting the first sentence into an appositive phrase, the writer can save words, can do away with an unnecessary sentence, and, most important, can de-emphasize the fact of Jones's being a local businessman and thus put the chief emphasis where it belongs—on the fact that Jones has been convicted of thievery.

Appositives need not be as brief as the one just cited. Using the noun *businessman* as the base of the appositive, we could easily add modifiers to fill out the portrait of our white-collar bicycle thief:

Macaulay Jones, a widely respected businessman who had twice won the city's Man-of-the-Year award, was found to be the organizer of a state-wide ring of bicycle thieves.

Similarly, the following sentence makes use of an expanded appositive whose central word is the noun *sin:*

Forgive Us Our Sins, a literary *sin* that should have led to everlasting damnation for the author, has just won the Robbins Prize for being the longest pornographic novel of the year.

Another possibility is the appositive phrase that contains two, three, or four nouns in a row:

Without apposition: Several of the *New Yorker* humorists have excelled in the art of nonsense. The humorists I have in mind are Robert Benchley, S. J. Perelman, and Woody Allen.

With apposition: Several of the *New Yorker* humorists—Robert Benchley, S. J. Perelman, and Woody Allen—have excelled in the art of nonsense.

Without apposition: Charles Lamb's personality made him the most popular member of that little circle of Romantics. His most endearing traits were his warm friendliness, his lively wit, and his dependable common sense.

With apposition: Charles Lamb's personality—his warm friendliness, his lively wit, and his dependable common sense—made him the most popular member of that little circle of Romantics.

Notice that when an appositive phrase contains commas, you may have to use dashes to set it off from the rest of the sentence. Otherwise the sentence is likely to be a puzzle: "Three plays about love, *Twelfth Night, Romeo and Juliet,* and *Antony and Cleopatra,* formed the entire curriculum of Professor Nelson's course in Shakespeare." The reader would probably make sense out of this after a moment or two, but why should he be forced to pause at all? The writer could easily have prevented puzzlement by the simple expedient of inserting dashes (instead of commas) before *Twelfth* and after *Cleopatra*.

Occasionally you may wish to use appositive *adjectives* rather than nouns:

Those children—*selfish, deceitful, and sadistic*—were evidence of their parents' muddled sense of values.

And as you experiment with appositive phrases you will discover still other possibilities—permutations and combinations more elaborate than any we have mentioned. Beware one danger, however. When a long and complicated appositive phrase intrudes between a subject and its verb, the resulting sentence is likely to be clumsy and unclear:

His cruelty—the snarling tone, the cutting words, the savage eagerness to scold and insult and condemn anyone who disagreed with him on the smallest point—remains in my memory.

This sort of sentence can easily be repaired. As we mentioned earlier, an appositive phrase does not have to come in the middle of an independent clause; it can also come at the end. And when the phrase is a long one, the end of the clause may be a good place to put it:

I can still remember his cruelty—the snarling tone, the cutting words, the savage eagerness to scold and insult and condemn anyone who disagreed with him on the smallest point.

The reward for his hard work seemed more like a punishment— ruined eyesight, headaches, insomnia, loneliness.

The end of the sentence is often the best place for the sort of phrase that begins with its appositive noun and then adds a good deal of modification:

Without apposition: She asked her friends if they knew a reliable mechanic.

She wanted the kind of mechanic who would do simple repairs without charging as if he had a Ph.D. in automotive engineering.

With apposition: She asked her friends if they knew a reliable mechanic, a mechanic who would do simple repairs . . .

Without apposition: He learned how to fix cars from Miss Alice McMahon. She was an elderly spinster who used to spend all her spare time at the Ford garage.

With apposition: He learned how to fix cars from Miss Alice McMahon, an elderly spinster who used to spend . . .

As you may have noticed, an appositive at the end of a sentence is likely to be especially emphatic. This is true not only of long appositive phrases (like those in the last four illustrative sentences) but also of short ones:

She has a new goal in life—the presidency of the P.T.A.

He values only one thing—his new color television set.

Consider the second sentence. It might have taken other forms ("His new color television set is the only thing he values" or "He values only his new color television set"), but no other form would emphasize the television set quite as strongly. The same principle applies to adjectives as well as nouns. If you wish to focus special attention on an adjective, try turning it into a sentence-ending appositive:

The children finally came home, exhausted and hungry.

The guru sat before them for the entire morning—silent, serene, oblivious to all their questions.

We come now to the least customary position for the appositive—the beginning of the sentence. For example:

Silent and serene, the guru sat before them for the entire morning.

A caustic and demanding critic, John Simon delights in tearing apart mediocre films.

Plato, Nietzsche, Henry James, Henry Miller, and Robert Benchley—works by this strange collection of authors dominated his bookshelves.

The noose, the knife, the shotgun, the telescopic sight, the magnum revolver, the gushing blood, the face contorted with pain, the body writhing in agony—these have become standard fare in the movies of violence.

Be careful not to use this structure too often. Frequent use of the introductory appositive would make it stand out as a mannerism—a clever strategy allowed to become a fetish. How often is "too often"? How many uses would be too many? There is no fixed rule. In one passage you might well use three introductory appositives in three consecutive sentences to achieve a special rhetorical effect, while in another piece of writing three introductory appositives spread out over three pages might call too much attention to themselves, or just *one* introductory appositive, if it is awkward or ostentatious, would be one too many.

In any case, these cautions are not meant as an absolute prohibition. You should certainly add the introductory appositive to your stock of rhetorical techniques. It can serve two purposes. (1) It can serve as yet another means of varying the shape of your sentences. (2) It can emphasize the appositive words. As you can see from the examples given above, an appositive at the beginning of a sentence is almost as emphatic as one at the end.

THE VERBAL PHRASE

Verbals, not surprisingly, are derived from verbs. For example:

Singing the blues makes him happy.

Singing, though derived from the verb *sing,* is not itself a verb. Instead it is a *gerund,* a verb form used as a noun. Here is another kind of verbal —an *infinitive:*

To live in the manner to which he is accustomed, he will need at least $50,000 a year.

Both the gerund and the infinitive are valuable subordinators. They can often reduce an imposing clause to a not-so-imposing phrase. Note the italicized clauses on the left below. On the right they have been reduced to phrases.

Ron used to read Walt Whitman. Whitman was Ron's infallible cure for insomnia.	*Reading Walt Whitman* used to be Ron's infallible cure for insomnia.
He sprayed the bushes with garlic juice. Thus he got rid of all those hungry insects.	He got rid of all those hungry insects *by spraying the bushes with garlic juice.*
The film did not contain a great deal of sex or violence. *Therefore it did not attract big crowds of paying customers.*	The film did not contain enough sex or violence *to attract big crowds of paying customers.*

During the lunch hour Arnold reads Gibbon's *Decline and Fall of the Roman Empire*. He does this so that he can show the other clerks that he's more intelligent than he looks.	During the lunch hour Arnold reads Gibbon's *Decline and Fall of the Roman Empire to show the other clerks that he's more intelligent than he looks.*

You will have plenty of chances, then, to use both the gerund and the infinitive. You will have even more chances to use the *participle*. A participle, roughly speaking, is a verb form that functions as an adjective:

> The man *scolding* that child is not the child's father.

Present participles—such as *scolding*—always end in *ing. Past participles* usually, though not always, end in *ed:*

> *Exhausted,* he stared at the words without forming the slightest conception of their meaning.

> *Caught* in the sudden hailstorm, the girls took refuge in a nearby farmhouse.

What are the chief advantages of the participial phrase? One, of course, is that, like the other kinds of phrases we have looked at, it makes an excellent replacement for a clause that should not be a clause —a clause whose ideas use up more words than they require and are likely to get more of the reader's attention than they deserve. Take another look at the sentences just cited. Without help from participles, each of those sentences might have stretched out into two separate sentences:

> *A man is scolding that child,* but the man is not the child's father.

> *He was exhausted.* Therefore he stared at the words without forming the slightest conception of their meaning.

> *The girls were caught in the sudden hailstorm.* They took refuge in a nearby farmhouse.

Possibly the idea expressed in each of the italicized independent clauses truly deserves the emphasis it gets by being expressed in an independent clause. If not, then maybe the independent clause should be converted into a dependent clause—as in this sentence:

> The man *who is scolding that child* is not the child's father.

But if the idea still occupies too many words and gets too much emphasis, we can simply cut out the *who is* (often a sign of wordiness) and wind up with the tidy participial phrase with which we started:

> The man *scolding that child* is not the child's father.

The participial phrase shares yet another advantage with some of the other kinds of phrases we have examined. It is remarkably flexible. It can function at several positions within a sentence: (1) It can come before the subject of a clause; (2) it can intrude between the subject and its verb; (3) it can wait until the end of the clause.

The following sentences exemplify both these advantages of the participial phrase—both its mobility and its talent for cutting overweight clauses down to size. The italicized clauses on the left are reduced to phrases on the right.

Johnson was terrified by the possibility of failing the exam. Therefore he became so nervous that he did indeed manage to fail.	*Terrified by the possibility of failing the exam,* Johnson became so nervous that he did indeed manage to fail.
She threw her calculating machine out the window, and she vowed never again to look at a column of figures.	*Throwing her calculating machine out the window,* she vowed never again to look at a column of figures.
Reginald was convinced of his greatness as a poet. As a result he stored all his sonnets in a safety deposit box.	Reginald, *convinced of his greatness as a poet,* stored all his sonnets in a safety deposit box.
Reverend Cooper had failed to win the argument by appealing to faith, so he decided he had better appeal to reason.	Reverend Cooper, *having failed to win the argument by appealing to faith,* decided he had better appeal to reason.
The little boy hid way in the back of the closet. *He was trembling at the thought of being detected.*	The little boy hid way in the back of the closet, *trembling at the thought of being detected.*
The job troubled him deeply. *It forced him to meet people he didn't like* and *it was steering him toward a future he detested.*	The job troubled him deeply, *forcing him to meet people he didn't like* and *steering him toward a future he detested.*

The *absolute phrase* is equally versatile. Like the participial phrase, and like other subordinate elements we have examined, the absolute phrase can come before, during, or after the clause it depends on.

Usually an absolute phrase contains both a noun and a participle:

His confidence broken, he doubted whether he could ever again appear before an audience.

Sometimes the participle is omitted:

Martini [held] *in hand,* he sauntered over to the girls by the fireplace.

Here are further examples. On the left appear italicized clauses. On the right these have been converted into absolute phrases.

After Fairfax had completed his novel, he decided to go back to writing limericks.	*His novel completed,* Fairfax decided to go back to writing limericks.
The robot found that his strength was failing. Therefore he reached for a can of spinach.	The robot, *his strength failing,* reached for a can of spinach.
He waited impatiently. *His courage was sinking fast. The old anxieties were returning. The twitch on his brow was becoming just as violent as it used to be.*	He waited impatiently, *his courage sinking fast, the old anxieties returning, the twitch on his brow becoming just as violent as it used to be.*

The absolute phrase has something distinctive about it. And the same is true of several of the other devices mentioned in this chapter. The writer who uses them sets himself apart from the raw beginner who plods along from one pedestrian sentence to another, ignorant of the means by which he might add some variety and vitality. Yet the very distinctiveness of these devices makes them dangerous. Used too often, any one of them calls too much attention to itself. It becomes a tiresome mannerism. The reader guesses, perhaps correctly, that the writer, having just gained command of the technique, is so proud of his acquisition that he can't keep from showing it off.

A kindred danger is that the writer may overuse not merely one technique of subordination but all of them. He becomes so absorbed in the pleasure of joining phrase to phrase and clause to clause that he forgets that the reader, however much he enjoys complexity, must also have clarity. Something of this sort may have led to the tortuous sentence quoted below. Edmund Wilson, a master of prose architecture, apparently got carried away by his own mastery—by the aesthetic thrill of putting together a labyrinthine sentence. Wilson is discussing the fantastic *Ingoldsby Legends* by Richard Harris Barham, particularly the "malignant mischief" that continually appears in the *Legends* in the form of minor devils and the Devil Himself. We quote two sentences. The first is clear enough; the second, we believe, is not.

The Devil is always erupting, and though the saints usually succeed in curbing him, it is sometimes a near thing. In the case of those devils who, in "The Lay of Saint Cuthbert," have, in a moment of profane fury, been invited to dinner by Sir Guy Le Scroope, the victim himself of a malicious hoax on the part of one of his friends, who has contrived that the guests shall not come, St. Cuthbert, in rescuing Sir Guy's little son, with whom the devils are playing catch, is nevertheless so little confident as to how far his authority extends that he is forced to make a kind of deal with them by allowing them to remain and gobble up the dinner.[1]

A few minutes devoted to pondering that passage will convince just about anyone that excessive subordination is a terrible vice and that the virtues of the short sentence should never be forgotten.

Exercises

I. In each passage that follows, connect the two sentences by converting one of them into a dependent (or subordinate) clause. Change the wording if necessary. Here are some subordinate conjunctions you'll find useful:

after	since
although	unless
as	when
because	where
before	whereas
provided that	while

1. After eating, you should wait two hours before meditating. The digestive process prevents the full use of the mind.
2. The American actor Bobby Bixby is now relaxing at Nantucket. There he will soon play the part of Ahab in the new filming of *Moby Dick*.
3. George has worked as a ticket-taker in a movie house for the last twenty years. Nevertheless, he has managed to save enough money to buy a Rolls-Royce.
4. In the nineteenth century gasoline cost nothing. It was considered a useless byproduct of kerosene.
5. Most teachers oppose extending the school year beyond the customary nine months. Most parents favor the plan.
6. Koplin was working as head butcher in the Kansas City stockyards. At this time Oldham offered him a partnership in a company that sold organic foods.

[1] Edmund Wilson, *The Devils and Canon Barham* (New York: Farrar, Straus and Giroux, 1973), pp. 12–13.

7. Faith's mother told her she could marry any man she chose. The only condition was that he had to be a nobleman.

8. The audience stood and cheered. The new tenor, making his debut in *Daughter of the Regiment,* hit seven splendid high C's in a row.

9. The Kodiak bear never attacks human beings. This generalization does not hold true, however, if the bear is starving or believes her cubs to be in danger.

10. The new Dutch army has dispensed with short hair, saluting, and most barrack-room spit-and-polish regulations. The Dutch army seems just as efficient as ever.

II. Each of the following exercises contains two sentences. Link the two sentences by turning the second one into a dependent clause introduced by *who(m), whose, which,* or *that.* For example:

Original: There are three species of gnat in California. All of them now appear on the list of endangered species.

Revision: There are three species of gnat in California, all of which now appear on the list of endangered species.

Original: The desk had been thoroughly searched. It was the desk in which I sometimes kept my intimate diaries.

Revision: The desk in which I sometimes kept my intimate diaries had been thoroughly searched.

1. Alfonso Smith introduced me to four newcomers. They were all interested in joining the Young Socialists.

2. Simone de Beauvoir has written a brilliant book on old age. The book exposes and condemns our society's cruelty toward old people.

3. Buffalo Bill was a buffalo hunter and an Indian fighter. Unfortunately he became the symbol of the American West.

4. Buddhism comes closest to what the Western world calls "worship" in *bhatki yoga.* This consists of dedicating one's life to a beloved person, activity, or cause.

5. In ancient mythology, the argument about which sex gets more pleasure from love-making was settled by old Tiresias. He had been both a man and a woman.

6. Napoleon's expedition to Egypt in 1798 failed in its primary aim, but it produced the first accurate map of Egypt and the first detailed study of the pyramids. The primary goal of the expedition was to block England's routes to the Far East.

7. According to the Hellenic Greeks, there had been five periods in human history. All but the last of these had been matriarchal.

8. The ancient Egyptians were sufficiently skilled in mathematics to predict the exact date of the summer solstice. The Greeks learned the rudiments of geometry from the Egyptians.

III. Each of the following sentences contains two or more sentences. Change every sentence but the first into an appositive phrase. For example:

Original: Debbie Bone has become one of the foremost karate experts in the country. She is a black-belt expert from Florida.

Revision: Debbie Bone, a black-belt karate expert from Florida, has become one of the foremost experts in the country.

Original: Rollo was deeply disturbed by the cruelty and treachery in *Measure for Measure.* This play is one of Shakespeare's "dark comedies."

Revision: Rollo was deeply disturbed by the cruelty and treachery in *Measure for Measure,* one of Shakespeare's "dark comedies."

1. The appositive is a great favorite among professionals. However, it is a device neglected by beginners.

2. Isis grants special favors to all who perform the ritual we are about to enact. Isis is the Egyptian goddess of the moon.

3. George Smithers charges $25 an hour for tiddley-winks lessons. Smithers is the best tiddley-winks player in the valley.

4. Dr. Holmquist has been invited to speak to the Linguistics Club. Dr. Holmquist is our new specialist on morphemes.

5. In 1840 the *Rosalie* was discovered drifting off the coast of the Bahamas, with its cargo intact but without the slightest trace of its crew. The *Rosalie* was a French merchant ship bound from Hamburg to Havana.

6. The audience grew impatient with the bumbling amateurs. The audience was tired and hot.

7. *A Vindication of the Rights of Women* was written by Mary Wollstonecraft. She was an eighteenth-century feminist who boldly challenged male supremacy.

8. The safari sponsored by the Merchantville Chamber of Commerce somehow wandered into the territory of the Urubu Indians. The Urubu are bloodthirsty headhunters who hate all white people.

9. The witch doctors of central Sumatra initiate their disciples through a ritual called the King Cobra Dance. This ritual has been kept so secret that no anthropologist has learned any details about it.

10. Oedipus succeeded in solving the riddle posed by the Sphinx. The Sphinx was a monster with the head of a woman, the body of a lion, the wings of an eagle, and the tail of a serpent.

11. One fascinating character from medieval England was John Master. He was a renowned alchemist. He was an astrologer who predicted hailstorms with perfect accuracy. He was a Satanist who molded wax figures of his enemies. He was a murderer who plotted to kill Edward II with black magic.

12. I remember Uncle David well. He was a quiet man with a hunched back and a shuffling walk. He was a misanthrope whose only pleasures were drinking bourbon and wielding a flyswatter.

13. The young Americans dipped their hands into the water of the River Ganges and then lifted them solemnly toward the sun. This is an ancient ritual practiced by Hindu holy men. It is a rite of purification for both body and soul.

IV. In each of the following exercises you are to combine two sentences into one. The resulting sentence will contain a series of appositive nouns at the beginning of the sentence, the middle, or the end—whichever position you choose. The foregoing chapter offers the following examples of the kinds of sentences you'll wind up with:

> The noose, the knife, the shotgun, the telescopic sight, the magnum revolver, the gushing blood, the face contorted with pain, the body writhing in agony—these have become standard fare in the movies of violence. (The appositive series comes at the beginning.)

> Several of the *New Yorker* humorists—Robert Benchley, S. J. Perelman, and Woody Allen—have excelled in the art of nonsense. (The appositive series comes in the middle.)

> The reward for his hard work seemed more like a punishment—ruined eyesight, headaches, insomnia, loneliness. (The appositive series comes at the end.)

1. Several women's magazines are now featuring male nudes. These magazines are *Viva, Playgirl,* and *Cosmopolitan.*

2. Several Asian animals seem headed for extinction. These are the panda, the orangutan, the gibbon ape, and the Bengal tiger.

3. Fortune-tellers say that certain cards represent joy and fulfillment in the near future. These cards are the nine of hearts, the ten of hearts, and the ace of clubs.

4. Some men thrive on duplicity. Among them are card sharks, poolroom hustlers, and gigolos.

5. Several kinds of writers have contributed to the myth of the cowboy. These writers have been novelists, historians, journalists, and, above all, film writers.

6. He wanted food, a place to sleep, a worthwhile job, and a few close friends. That was all he wanted out of life.

7. Bow-hunters enjoy several privileges denied to gun-hunters. These privileges are a longer season, freedom to hunt on lands closed to gun-hunters, and permission to kill deer of either sex and any age.

8. Certain masters of American prose didn't receive a single mention in the third edition of the *Literary History of the United States.* These

writers are Frederick Douglass, John Jay Chapman, and Albert Jay Nock.

9. Several concepts in modern physics are in conflict with traditional logic. These concepts are anti-matter, black holes in space, the fourth dimension, and the relativity of time.

10. Almost every person imposes symbolic meaning on some common object. Perhaps the object is a book, a ring, a watch, or an automobile.

V. Each of the following exercises contains two or more sentences. Combine the sentences by converting every italicized sentence into a participial phrase. Change wording if necessary, but don't change the arrangement of ideas. For example:

Original: *I was standing by his grave.* I suddenly realized what a heel he had been.

Revision: Standing by his grave, I suddenly realized what a heel he had been.

Original: More than 40 percent of American blue-collar wives now work outside the home. *They are trying to supplement the family income.*

Revision: More than 40 percent of American blue-collar wives now work outside the home trying to supplement the family income.

1. *Professor Bumble was trying to follow democratic principles.* He asked his class to vote on whether they should receive A's or F's.

2. *Arnold suspected he had done something wrong.* He begged Frieda to explain why she had kicked him so hard.

3. *Price hoped to win the professor's approval.* He started waving his hand wildly and exclaiming, "I know the answer, sir. I know, sir. Sir! Sir!!"

4. *Lester listened to the sermon more intently than he had ever listened to anything else.* He decided that his way of life—including the peeps into *Playboy*—was entirely free from sin.

5. *Moore had knocked Marciano down with a splendid punch.* So Moore was astonished to see Marciano get up at the count of two —fresh, strong, and ready to charge in again.

6. *Gordon was reading his* Mad *magazine. And he was popping chocolates into his mouth.* He ignored his mother's coaxing and pleading and sobbing.

7. *Marcia was delighted by his words. She was enchanted by the very sound of his voice.* She still felt that this man was not to be trusted.

8. *Archibald was abandoned by his family. He was cold-shouldered by his friends. He was hounded by his creditors.* He took a slow boat to New Zealand.

9. Arthur kept his ear pinned to the keyhole. *He was straining to hear what Lancelot and Guinevere were saying.*

10. Marshall swore eternal devotion. *He promised that he would never leave his beloved Gwendolyn for more than a year at a time.*

11. He typed away at his manuscript right through the night. *He was prodded on by his high ideals and his need for money.*

12. Maxwell was on the verge of hysteria. *He knew that if he had stayed in the game for one more bet, his three kings would have won $65.*

13. Mabel slammed down the receiver. *She was infuriated by Roger's indifference. And she hoped she could damage his eardrum.*

14. *Marmaduke was terrified by the approaching daylight.* He knelt and uttered his favorite curses. *He desperately hoped that Satan and Beelzebub would protect him.*

15. *The mongoose was brought into the West Indies to destroy poisonous snakes.* Instead it has almost wiped out the poultry industry. *The mongoose has found chickens easier to kill than snakes.*

VI. Each of the following exercises contains two or more sentences. Combine the sentences by converting every italicized sentence into an absolute phrase. Change wording if necessary, but don't change the order of ideas. For example:

Original: *His confidence was broken.* He doubted whether he could ever again appear before an audience.

Revision: His confidence broken, he doubted whether he could ever again appear before an audience.

Original: He waited impatiently. *His courage was sinking fast. The old anxieties were returning. The twitch on his brow was becoming just as violent as it used to be.*

Revision: He waited impatiently, his courage sinking fast, the old anxieties returning, the twitch on his brow becoming just as violent as it used to be.

1. *His imagination was running wild.* He went out to investigate the strange noise in the back yard.

2. *Her beliefs were shattered.* She decided she might just as well eat, drink, and be merry.

3. *Her interviews were done. Her library research was completed.* She was ready to write the whole truth about General Douglas MacArthur.

4. *His eyes were cold. His face was impassive. His arms were crossed.* He would not extend the slightest courtesy to the ill-bred interloper.

5. The doe stood motionless. *Her nose was lifted to catch the strange and terrifying scent.*

6. A skid-row bum tottered in the wind. *Both hands were clutching a half-empty bottle of wine.*

7. Harmon ran for the thicket. *The bullets were zinging through the air. The hounds were yapping eagerly only twenty yards behind him.*

8. The professor abruptly fell silent. *His eyes were wide. His hands were grasping the lectern. His chest was heaving in a desperate effort to get more air.*

VII. Convert each of the following passages into a single sentence, using any devices of coordination or subordination that seem appropriate. These chopped-up passages are derived from skillful sentences by accomplished authors: James Baldwin (passages 1–7), Caroline Bird (8–13), and X. J. Kennedy (14–16).

1. My father could be chilling in the pulpit. He could be cruel in his personal life. This cruelty was indescribable. He was certainly the most bitter man I have ever met.

2. He claimed to be proud of his blackness. This blackness, however, had also been the cause of much humiliation. It had fixed boundaries to his life. These boundaries were bleak.

3. We were growing up. He was not a young man at the time. He had already suffered many kinds of ruin.

4. He loved his children. He loved them in an outrageously demanding way. He loved them in an outrageously protective way. His children were black. They were black just as he was black. They were also menaced. They were menaced just as he was menaced.

5. All these things sometimes showed in his face. They sometimes showed when he tried to establish contact with any of us. He never to my knowledge had any success in establishing contact.

6. He would take one of his children on his knee. He would do so in order to play. The child always became fretful. The child always began to cry.

7. He would try to help one of us. The help would concern our homework. A tension emanated from him. It was absolutely unabating. It caused our minds to become paralyzed. It caused our tongues to become paralyzed. As a result, he flew into a rage. He scarcely knew why. The child was punished. The child did not know why.

8. The modern liberated woman is liberating herself not so much from sex. She is liberating herself from what goes with being a girl. She is liberating herself from all that sugar and spice and everything nice. All that sometimes seems especially attractive to frigid women.

9. She sees exploitation associated with those things. As a result,

she has discarded some other things. They are things that invite a man to look her over. They are cues and clues. They are also buttons and bows. They are also smiles and wiles.

10. She wants one thing above all. She wants freedom from tyranny. The tyranny is that of being a girl.

11. She is like the heroine of a recent Women's Lib play. She is likely to whack off her hair. She is likely to wear it scraggling around her face. That would be wearing it witch-style. Or she may conceal her hair. She may conceal it under a tight bandana. That would be wearing it nun-style.

12. She wears no makeup. She wears no frippery.

13. There is a growing number of young women of a certain kind. They are otherwise conventional. They refuse to squeeze themselves into brassieres. As the spirit moves, they may do other things. They may dispense also with shoes. They may dispense with stockings. They may dispense with underwear of any kind.

14. King Kong was a giant ape. He underwent an ordeal and a spectacular death. These have undoubtedly been witnessed by more Americans than have ever seen a performance of *Hamlet* or *Iphigenia at Aulis.* They have even been witnessed by more Americans than have ever seen *Tobacco Road.*

15. RKO-Radio Pictures released *King Kong.* Since then a quarter-century has gone by. The prints are growing more rain-beaten. The sound tracks are growing more tinny. Yet year after year the ticket-buyers number in the thousands. They still pursue Kong's luckless fight. They see him fight against the forces of technology. They also see him fight against the forces of tabloid journalism and the DAR.

16. They see him chloroformed to sleep. They see him whisked from his jungle isle to New York. They see him placed on show. They see him burst his chains to roam the city. While he roams the city he is lugging a frightened blonde. At last he plunges from the spire of the Empire State Building. He is machine-gunned by model airplanes.

VIII. Review one of your old essays to see whether you can improve its style by applying the principles of subordination.

1. See whether you used subordination to emphasize the ideas that truly deserved to be emphasized. Did you make the mistake of over-subordinating important ideas, giving them only a single word or a phrase when they actually deserved a dependent or even an independent clause? On the other hand, did you give too much prominence to minor ideas, expressing them in clauses when they deserved no more than phrases or single words? Revise any sentences in which you committed such mistakes.

2. See whether you used subordination to achieve sentence variety. Are any passages guilty of the "choppy style" that results from the overuse of short sentences? Revise such passages by using both coordination and subordination to join some of those skimpy sentences.

Are any passages guilty of *excessive* coordination? Did you connect too many independent clauses with *and's, but's, or's,* etc. rather than consigning the less important ideas to dependent clauses or to phrases or single words? Revise such passages.

What about the passages that avoid both choppiness and overcoordination? Did they achieve sentence variety by means of the subordinate patterns mentioned in this chapter? Surely you used plenty of dependent clauses, but did you use them in a variety of positions within their sentences—*before* the main clause, *during* the clause, and *after* the clause? Did you make appropriate use of appositive and verbal phrases? And, again, did you use them in various positions within their sentences? Revise any passages in which the sentence patterns are not sufficiently varied.

9

Precision

As a style matures, it inevitably suffers growing pains. The writer runs into troubles he could have avoided if he had stayed with the safe mediocrity of the infantile style—if he had continued to write nothing but short, simple sentences. As soon as he begins to combine short sentences into longer ones, as soon as he begins to capitalize on the possibilities offered by coordination and subordination, he encounters a danger that threatens to keep his style just as amateurish as ever. Briefly, the danger is this. As the sentences become longer, their parts are more likely to become disconnected. The relationships between the parts are likely to become imprecise, illogical, or downright unclear.

SUBJECTS AND VERBS

Here is one kind of discontinuity:

In hard times people vote their pocketbooks, / but in good times prejudices determine voting patterns.

This sentence is not impossibly obscure. It does not defy comprehension. But neither does it achieve lucidity. It fails to convey its ideas as clearly as it might have, because its two clauses (the clauses separated by a slash) are not as clearly related as they might have been. Read the sentence again, and then compare it with the following revision:

In hard times people vote their pocketbooks, but in good times they vote their prejudices. (Gore Vidal)

Why is this version so much clearer? The reason is simple. The earlier version changed from one subject to another as it moved from the first clause to the second. The first clause presented *people* as its subject; the second shifted to *prejudices*. In reading the sentence, then, you were forced to refocus your attention, were forced to shift your attention from *people* to *prejudices*. Admittedly, that effort kept you busy for only a fraction of a fraction of an instant; but it was more effort than you should have been asked to expend—enough effort to make that first version slightly more difficult than the second. In the second version the two clauses share the same subject, the only change being that the noun *people* is replaced by the pronoun *they.*

The principle illustrated here can be simply stated: Whenever possible, stick to the same subject as you move from one clause to another. But immediately we must add major qualifications. Often you won't be able to stick to the same subject. Often you will have splendid reasons for changing from one subject to another. Often you will express your meaning more precisely, more economically, perhaps even more clearly, by violating the very rule we have just taken such pains to expound. So it is with rules of style—and with books that expound such rules. Borrowing from Samuel Johnson, we might say that such books are like watches. "The worst is better than none, and the be t cannot be expected to go quite true."

Another kind of discontinuity can occur within a single clause. This happens when a subject becomes disconnected from its verb—that is, when the meaning of the subject doesn't quite fit the meaning of the verb. For example:

The main source of the readings in this book *has been taken* from the Old Testament.

The flaw here is obvious. The writer didn't really mean that the source *has been taken* from the Old Testament. He meant

The main source of the readings in this book *is* the Old Testament.

Now the sentence expresses its meaning precisely (though the sentence would be more vigorous, we might add, if it were more concise and used a stronger verb: "Most of the readings in this book come from the Old Testament").

Here are two more sentences in which subject and verb are not quite suited to one another:

According to many psychologists, the stereotyped masculine and feminine *roles* displayed in elementary school textbooks *should* not *be read* by children.

Before a major fight, a boxer's *strength* sometimes weakens from too much training and *needs to rest* for a day or two.

These sentences don't make sense. The first one says that *roles* should not be read, whereas the writer actually intended to say that certain *books* should not be read. The next sentence says that *strength* needs to rest, whereas the intended meaning was that a *boxer* needs to rest. These imprecisions are corrected in the following revisions:

According to many psychologists, children should not read elementary school textbooks that display stereotyped masculine and feminine roles.

Before a major fight, a boxer sometimes finds that because he has lost his strength by training too hard, he has to rest for a day or two.

The verb *is* requires extreme caution. When a predicate fails to match its subject, the predicate usually involves an *is* or one of its relatives—*are, was, were,* and so on. *Is,* you should remember, implies that one thing equals another:

Two plus two is four.

Life to the great majority is only a constant struggle for existence. (Schopenhauer)

Life is one long process of getting tired. (Samuel Butler)

Life is a festival only to the wise. (Emerson)

Here the *is*'s are used with precision. The writers truly intended to equate the things coming before the *is*'s with the things coming after. But in the following sentences, the equations are incorrect. (In each sentence we have italicized the *is* verb and the two things falsely equated.)

The students' *anger* over the rejection of the plan *is* chiefly the president's *refusal* to explain why she rejected it.

Revised: The students are angry about the rejection of their plan chiefly because the president has refused to explain why she rejected it.

Casal's *dislike* for modern music *was,* as he said, its *lack of "soul"*— its inability to elevate the spirit.

Revised: Casals explained that his dislike for modern music arose from its lack of "soul"—its inability to elevate the spirit.

The *horror* he felt while watching *The Exorcist was* the little girl's hideous *obscenities,* not the idea of her being possessed by the devil.

Revised: The horror he felt while watching *The Exorcist* resulted from the little girl's hideous obscenities, not from the idea of her being possessed by the devil.

Perhaps we should mention one other point regarding *is*: Avoid writing *is when* or *is where*. The rationale behind this dictum is so complicated that only professional grammarians get excited about it, but even to writers who know little grammar the *is-when* and *is-where* constructions usually (though not always) sound awkward and imprecise. Consider these examples:

The official cause of America's declaration of war against Japan *was when* the Japanese bombed Pearl Harbor.

Better: The official cause of America's declaration of war against Japan was the bombing of Pearl Harbor.

A quiet, book-lined corner of the attic *was where* he did his best thinking.

Better: A quiet, book-lined corner of the attic was the place where he did his best thinking.

A similar point of usage is the distinction between *the reason is because* and *the reason is that*. The best writers and editors generally prefer *the reason is that*, although the other phrasing continues its slow, steady campaign to be accepted into standard written English. For the time being, we advise that you follow the practice of the accomplished writers and editors who would be pleased to see that the following sentence says *the reason is that* rather than *the reason is because*:

The reason Ernest has become a Zen Buddhist *is that* his Aunt Edith has converted him.

COMPARISONS

Comparisons are indispensable. Almost every essay will contain several sentences in which two things are compared—sentences like these:

Dr. Harvey's *newest kind of therapy* is much more exciting than his *previous one.*

Unlike *other psychologists, Dr. Harvey* changes his style of therapy at least once every six weeks.

He has now decided that *Yoga* does more for his patients than the *steam baths* he was prescribing last week.

In each sentence we have italicized the two things being compared; but even if we had not done so, you would have had no trouble understanding the comparisons. They are eminently clear and logical.

But some comparisons depart from logic and wander off toward obscurity. Here is a blatant example:

> Our cat chases worms as eagerly as birds.

This can mean either of two things—that the cat chases worms as eagerly as birds do or that the cat is eager to chase both worms and birds. But rarely is a comparison put together as badly as this one was. The following sentence comes closer to being typical:

> The *prose* of Theodore Dreiser was slower and heavier than *H. L. Mencken.*

We can see what the writer was trying to say, but we also see that he doesn't quite say it. Though he intended to compare two styles of writing, he actually compared a style with a man—compared *prose* with *H. L. Mencken.*

Faulty comparisons can be repaired in a variety of ways—as we can show by offering three revisions of the sentence about Dreiser and Mencken:

> The *prose* of Theodore Dreiser is slower and heavier than the *prose* of H. L. Mencken.

> The *prose* of Theodore Dreiser is slower and heavier than *that* of H. L. Mencken. (The pronoun *that* replaces the second reference to prose for the sake of variety.)

> The *prose* of Theodore Dreiser is slower and heavier than *H. L. Mencken's.* (The second reference to prose is understood. The fact that *Mencken's* is in the possessive form shows that the man's prose, and not the man himself, is being compared with the prose of Dreiser.)

Here are a few more instances of false comparison. We offer only one revision of each sentence, but you can readily imagine other possibilities.

> Henrietta finds the *words* of the Bible much more satisfying than *Billy Graham.*
>
> **Revision:** Henrietta finds the *words* of the Bible much more satisfying than *those* of Billy Graham.

> According to Alan, the *symbolism* of Charles Schultz, the author of *Peanuts,* is more profound and more comforting than *Melville.*
>
> **Revision:** . . . more profound and more comforting than the *symbolism* of Melville.

After the demonstrations and confrontations had subsided, the students issued a *manifesto* that showed more good sense than the *faculty.*

Revision: . . . showed more good sense than *any of the statements* circulated by the faculty.

Another kind of comparison that sometimes causes trouble starts off with *like* or *unlike.* Here the comparison is perfectly clear and precise:

Unlike the *typical physical education teacher, Betty* gets up at five o'clock every morning not to do calisthenics but to read a few pages ·from Plato, Aristotle, and Aquinas.

Notice that the way to ensure precision in this kind of comparison is to juxtapose the two terms being compared—in this case, the *typical physical education teacher* and *Betty.* The first term should be followed immediately by the second. Otherwise we get sentences in which the meaning expressed deviates from the meaning intended. We get sloppy comparisons like these:

Like *Karl Marx, very few people* get around to reading the works of the great English economist Adam Smith.

Unlike *his sister, a terribly poor education* was all that Lionel received.

Like *California, all the favorite American virtues and vices* can be found in Hawaii.

These sentences seem to imply that the italicized words are being compared. We know better, of course. We know that in the first sentence, for example, the writer actually intended to compare *Karl Marx* with *Adam Smith,* not with *very few people.* But if the sentence is to express its meaning precisely, it must juxtapose the two things being compared. The same principle applies to the other sentences as well—and to any sentence that starts off with a comparison introduced by *like* or *unlike.* We revise accordingly:

Like *Karl Marx,* the *great English economist Adam Smith* is read by very few people.

Unlike *his sister, Lionel* received a terribly poor education.

Like *California, Hawaii* has all the favorite American virtues and vices.

Finally, we should mention one other kind of imprecise comparison. It shows up in the following sentences:

Edwards was less skillful at throwing passes than anyone on his team.

The 200-pound wrestler knew more about Christian mysticism than anyone in his discussion group.

Edwards cannot possibly be less skillful than anyone on his team, because he himself is on the team. The wrestler cannot know more about Christian mysticism than anyone in the discussion group, because he himself is in the group. Once you have spotted this kind of illogic, you can easily correct it:

> Edwards was the worst passer on his team.

> The 200-pound wrestler knew more about Christian mysticism than anyone else in his discussion group. (Note the addition of *else.*)

PRONOUNS

Every pronoun should be entirely clear in referring to its antecedent. Here are several gross violations of this principle:

> Bannerman spoke with Lang only a few weeks after *he* had read *his* novel about the student rebels of the 1960s.

> When Susan got into that fierce argument with Brenda, *she* insulted *her* so often and so ruthlessly that *she* thought their friendship must come to an end.

> *Crime and Punishment* is a great novel even though *his* final chapter leaves many readers dissatisfied.

> Lumpkin was thought to be an authority on Greek philosophy, but actually he had never read *them*—had never so much as peeked into *their* writings.

In the first sentence we can't tell who read whose novel. In the second sentence confusion is piled on top of confusion. Who did the insulting? Who got insulted? Who thought the friendship must end? The reader can only guess. The faults of the third and fourth sentences are somewhat different. There the reader can infer that the *his* in the third sentence refers to Dostoevsky, the author of *Crime and Punishment,* and that the *them* and *their* in the fourth sentence refer to the Greek philosophers. But the reader should not have to do such inferring. On the contrary, the writer should be so precise in his handling of pronouns that each one will refer clearly, explicitly, unmistakably, to its antecedent. The reader should not have to pause to decide between several possible antecedents or, as in the third and fourth sentences, to supply antecedents not even mentioned by the writer. The reader may succeed in bringing clarity out of confusion—may succeed in identifying the intended antecedents of those puzzling pronouns—but in the process he will lose much of his respect for the writer.

Sometimes a pronoun refers not merely to a noun or a group of nouns but to an entire idea. As recently as twenty years ago, many arbiters of style condemned any pronoun used in this way, but now that common sense and widespread usage have prevailed over that arbitrary prohibition, the writer is free to use such pronouns whenever they pass the test of clarity:

> Harkness believes that all public schools are mediocre. *This* has led him to educate his children at home.

> Webster arrived late, *which* surprised no one.

But pronouns of this kind must be handled with care. They often lead to trouble:

> Webster appeared briefly at the party, *which* surprised no one.

> She enlivened the conversation with anecdotes from her lion-hunting sojourn in Africa. *This* irritates her dull, stay-at-home husband every time he thinks about *it*.

In the first sentence, what was it that surprised no one? The party? Webster's appearance there? The briefness of his appearance? We can't be sure. And in the second sentence the possible antecedents of *this* and *it* are even more numerous. Those pronouns may refer to (1) the wife's ability to enliven conversation, (2) her anecdotes, (3) her lion hunting, (4) her trip to Africa, or (5) all of the above.

The simplest way to repair a defective pronoun is to replace it with its antecedent:

> She enlivened the conversation with anecdotes from her lion-hunting sojourn in Africa. *Her ability to enliven a conversation* irritates her dull, stay-at-home husband every time he thinks about it.

Sometimes, however, this cure is almost as bad as the illness. The repaired sentence, though free from problematic pronouns, may sound awkward because of too much repetition of nouns:

> Bannerman spoke with Lang only a few weeks after Bannerman had read Lang's novel about the student rebels of the 1960s.

We would have to revise further to eliminate the excessive repetition:

> Bannerman spoke with Lang only a few weeks after reading Lang's novel about the student rebels of the 1960s.

We have no objection to mentioning Lang twice, but if you would prefer to eliminate even that trace of repetition, you would have to revise still further. You might write:

> Only a few weeks after reading Lang's novel about the student rebels of the 1960s, Bannerman spoke with the author.

MODIFIERS

Modifiers must refer clearly to the words they modify. The modifiers italicized in the following sentences are guilty of unclear reference.

Madame Eva saw the nation enter an economic crisis and tumble into a depression *while looking into a crystal ball.*

Mrs. Gildersleeve looked at the students as they whispered, passed notes, and played blackjack *with only faint signs of disapproval.*

Semantics is the study of words *that Humpeldorf considers supremely important.*

His psychologist advised him *repeatedly* to say to himself, "Every day, in every way, I am growing better and better."

As a result of faulty modification, the first three sentences suggest that (1) the nation was tumbling into a depression while looking into a crystal ball, (2) the students, not the teacher, showed signs of disapproval, and (3) semantics studies only those words that Humpeldorf considers important. The fourth sentence is unclear as to whether the psychologist or his patient does the repeating. This sentence is the most seriously flawed of them all, since the meaning of *repeatedly* remains a mystery. But even though we can deduce the intended meanings of the other three sentences, those sentences, too, are unsatisfactory. They show a disparity between intention and expression. They don't quite say what they were intended to say.

Fortunately, unclear modification can usually be repaired with no great difficulty:

While looking into her crystal ball, Madame Eva saw the nation enter an economic crisis and tumble into a depression.

With only faint signs of disapproval, Mrs. Gildersleeve watched the students as they whispered, passed notes, and played blackjack.

Humpeldorf regards semantics as the supremely important approach to the study of words.

His psychologist advised him to say to himself repeatedly, "Every day, in every way, I am growing better and better."

With three of these sentences we have used the customary means for repairing an unclear modifier: we have simply moved it closer to the word it modifies. Only the third sentence required more extensive revision.

Introductory verbal modifiers need special attention. They are notoriously liable to be unclear or illogical or both. For example:

Leaking badly, Silas kicked over the pail in disgust.

Driving on the highway last night, two deer came into view as Matthew passed through the fields just outside town.

An introductory verbal phrase usually refers to the first noun (or pronoun) that follows it. Hence these sentences seem to imply that Silas was leaking badly and two deer were driving along the highway. In repairing such sentences, you have to make sure that each introductory phrase is followed by the noun to which it refers:

Seeing that the pail was leaking badly, Silas kicked it in disgust.

Driving on the highway last night, Matthew saw two deer in the fields just outside town.

The introductory modifiers in these sentences are participial phrases. Their basic words—*seeing* and *driving*—are participles. But several other kinds of introductory verbal phrases must also be handled with care— particularly gerund phrases, infinitives, and elliptical clauses. Strictly speaking, these are not modifiers in the same way as a participle is; but the distinction makes no difference for our present purposes. The same principle applies: Each introductory verbal phrase should be followed immediately by the noun it refers to.

In applying this principle you don't have to keep in mind the various grammatical labels we have just mentioned. You can spot the instances of unclear reference in the following sentences, and in your own sentences, without being a master grammarian.

Rereading *Ulysses* after ten years, it greatly disappointed him.
Revision. Rereading *Ulysses* after ten years, he was greatly disappointed with it.

After hearing the full story behind his nastiness, he seemed to her to be pitiable rather than hateful.
Revision: After hearing the full story behind his nastiness, she regarded him as pitiable rather than hateful.

While looking at the other clerks, they suddenly appeared to him to be deeply, desperately unhappy.
Revision: While looking at the other clerks, he suddenly thought them to be deeply, desperately unhappy.

To get a high-paying job these days, an enormous amount of good luck must be one of your assets.

Revision: To get a high-paying job these days, you need an enormous amount of good luck.

Hurt by her insults, saddened by her decision to leave him, nevertheless the prospect of life without her was faced with his usual stolid fortitude and superficial cheerfulness.

Revision: Hurt by her insults, saddened by her decision to leave him, he nevertheless faced the prospect of life without her with his usual stolid fortitude and superficial cheerfulness.

The principle illustrated here deserves to be stated again: Each introductory verbal phrase should be followed immediately by the noun to which it refers. This commandment, if adhered to faithfully, will ward off most of the evils of unclear modification.

But not all. Although troublesome modifiers usually occur at the beginnings of sentences, they can occur elsewhere as well, particularly at the *ends* of sentences. Sentence-ending modifiers have a way of getting out of control. Again the modifiers most likely to cause trouble are the verbal phrases, especially the participles:

Lucinda darted a glance at her double-crossing friend Penelope, anxiously *chewing* her fingernails.

The jet zoomed across the sky, leaving only a thin trail of vapor, quickly *disappearing* in the gathering darkness.

The locked car had been stolen right from in front of the house and right in the middle of the day, *infuriating* both the owner of the car and the Citizens Protection Patrol.

Today's young people have many problems to solve and no firm beliefs with which to solve them, *reflected* among teenagers not only in the widespread use of drugs but in a steadily increasing rate of suicide.

In the first sentence and the second the italicized participle could refer to either of two nouns. Who was chewing her nails—Lucinda or Penelope? What disappeared quickly in the darkness—the jet or the trail of vapor? Usually you can clear up such ambiguities easily enough, perhaps simply by moving the offending participle closer to the noun it modifies. The third and fourth sentences, however, present a problem requiring further revision. Each italicized participle, rather than modifying a noun, attempts to modify the entire idea expressed in the main clause. Occasionally this sort of modification is successful, but more often it results in an awkwardness and imprecision not tolerated by experienced writers.

Now we can revise the four sentences we have been examining:

Anxiously chewing her fingernails, Lucinda darted a glance at her double-crossing friend Penelope.

The jet zoomed across the sky, quickly disappearing in the gathering darkness and leaving behind only a thin trail of vapor.

The locked car had been stolen right from in front of the house and right in the middle of the day. This daring theft infuriated both the owner and the Citizens Protection Patrol.

Today's young people have many problems to solve and no firm beliefs with which to solve them. This plight is reflected among teen-agers not only in the widespread use of drugs but in a steadily increasing rate of suicide.

Please don't leave this chapter with the impression that sentence-ending modifiers are too dangerous to be tried. Yes, they demand a watchful eye, but their rhetorical effectiveness can make them well worth the special attention they require. Consider, for instance, two sentences by Katherine Anne Porter:

> *[Babies] lie flat on their noses at first in what appears to be a drunken slumber,* then flat on their backs kicking and screaming, demanding impossibilities in a foreign language. *They are human nature in essence,* without conscience, without pity, without love, without a trace of consideration for others, just one seething cauldron of primitive appetites and needs. . . .[1]

Each sentence begins with its main idea (the italicized independent clause), elaborates upon that idea with a variety of subordinate elements, and yet never lapses into obscurity. And the sentences are much more than clear: they are forceful and compelling—partly because they contradict some orthodox notions about babyhood, but also because their structure is at once graceful and vigorous.

Exercises

I. Each of the following sentences is less clear and less graceful than it ought to be. As the sentence moves from one clause to the next, it switches awkwardly and unnecessarily from one grammatical subject to another. Revise each sentence by giving every clause the same subject (or a pronoun referring to that subject). For example:

Original: Yeast has a sharp, disageeable taste, but the B vitamins are supplied in plentiful amounts in it. (The first clause has *yeast* as its subject; the second needlessly switches to *B vitamins.*)

[1] "Marriage is Belonging" excerpted from *The Collected Essays And Occasional Writings of Katherine Anne Porter.* © 1951 by Katherine Anne Porter. Originally appeared in *Mademoiselle.* Reprinted by permission of Delacorte Press/Seymour Lawrence. Katherine Anne Porter, " 'Marriage Is Belonging,' " *Collected Essays and Occasional Writings* (New York: Delacorte Press, 1970), p. 190.

Revision: Yeast has a sharp, disagreeable taste, but it contains a plentiful supply of the B vitamins. (The subject of the first clause is still *yeast;* the subject of the second is now *it,* a pronoun referring to yeast.)

1. Mass education has helped a great many people to get better jobs, but academic standards have been lowered because of it.

2. After the board members investigated the facts about good and bad driving, the decision was arrived at by them to discontinue all those useless courses in driver education.

3. Defoe wrote excellent prose, but poetry of an inferior quality was the kind that was produced by him. (You may find a way to reduce this sentence to a single clause containing only seven words.)

4. During damp autumns the sea gulls often fly hundreds of miles inland, as if there were an instinctive awareness that hordes of grasshoppers and earthworms were available. (You can use *sea gulls,* or a substitute pronoun, as the subject of all three clauses.)

5. Salmon and trout have once again become plentiful in Lake Michigan, but the disappearance of them will take place again if exposure to waste materials from sewers and factories occurs. (Again you can use the same subject in all three clauses.)

II. Each of the following sentences contains a subject and a predicate that don't add up to a logical statement. Revise the sentences to make them clear and sensible. For example:

Original: The main source of the readings in this book has been taken from the Old Testament.

Revision: The main source of the readings in this book is the Old Testament.

1. The chief reason for his resignation was when the boss tried to force him to cut off his beard.

2. The refusal of government agencies to speak out on UFOs is not so much a lack of knowledge as a fear of public panic.

3. The plot of that Western was where the typical kindly gunslinger meets a pretty schoolteacher from the East and reforms by becoming a lawman.

4. My dislike for Ambrose was his tendency to be an intellectual leech who got all his ideas from books.

5. His first acquaintance with tennis was when he used to hang around the tennis club where his father was a groundskeeper.

6. His favorite method of writing is with red ink on yellow paper.

7. Because major athletes lead a life of glamorous affluence is one reason why many boys from poor families aspire to be professional football players.

8. His experience as a writer was doing feature stories for the *Brooklyn Bugle*.

9. The fact that one out of every seven children is growing up with a single parent is sure to increase in the near future.

10. The idea that meditation strengthens a person's powers of concentration seems quite likely.

III. Revise the following sentences to repair the faulty comparisons.

1. Beef purchased in Hawaii is much more expensive than the mainland.

2. The motor on Sammy's speedboat is more powerful than the average automobile.

3. Even in his own day Shakespeare was esteemed more highly than any playwright.

4. Unlike hockey fans of earlier times, bloody brawls are eagerly anticipated by hockey fans of the new breed.

5. The taboos in our own society strike us as being much more rational than other societies.

6. Our starting quarterback knew more about Frank Lloyd Wright than anyone on the team.

7. The rock star spent $100,000 to protect himself, purchasing security measures that equaled the FBI.

8. Some people believe that Henry George did a better job of analyzing economic issues than anyone in the long history of economic theory.

9. Like my lecherous friend Garry, every woman seems sexually attractive in the eyes of Gus Bell, who runs a school for beauticians.

10. By reading great literature for an hour each day, this high school dropout has acquired an education far superior to the typical college graduate.

IV. Revise the following sentences to repair any pronoun whose antecedent is not entirely clear.

1. The hippie couple insisted on composing their own wedding vows, which shocked the minister.

2. Melissa and Florence said their good-byes, their final good-byes, while she was writing her recollections of life with Picasso.

3. Jake went to college right after leaving the Marine Corps, which changed his life radically.

4. Lynch informed Smith of his belief that the only way he could survive in these turbulent times was to invest in gold, silver, and gasoline.

5. The bighorn sheep of the Rockies are becoming plentiful again,

despite having come close to extinction through disease and hunting, which is heartening.

6. When Rimmer and Higgins got together in those dull days before graduation, he told him that his plan of becoming a prominent journalist was nothing but a pipe dream.

7. Sammy began to spend three hours every night listening to the music of Ravi Shankar and reading aloud from the writings of Alan Watts and Baba Ram Dass, which disturbed and perplexed his psychiatrist.

8. Benjamin did not like his English professor in the slightest; he was a shy, retiring person who detested all class discussion.

9. The rocking chair they discovered in that used-furniture store, which was stained and scarred and battered, was found to be a priceless antique.

10. Every day Samantha celebrated the rising of the sun by running out to the front yard stark naked, bowing to the east twelve times, and shouting out her composition, "Samantha's Prayer to the Sun." This greatly annoyed her husband Herman.

V. Each of the following sentences contains a troublesome modifier —one that "dangles," or is misplaced, or is imprecise for some other reason. Revise each sentence to eliminate unclear modification.

1. Although yelping and squirming and lunging to escape, Siegfried managed to bathe his Doberman pinscher without getting drenched.

2. Ambrose had asked the pet shop to wash down his boa constrictor at least four times.

3. The bold hunter prepared to shoot the skunk that was heading in his direction with a twelve-gauge shotgun.

4. Reclining half asleep in his hammock one summer afternoon, a strange, disembodied voice advised Smithers to invest all his savings in the Esalen Institute.

5. The wounded grizzly crashed into the brush, leaving a faint trail of blood, vanishing within a hundred yards.

6. The piano teacher directed Ludwig to repeat the first twelve bars of the sonata with great impatience.

7. The automobile that was towed away belonged to a young woman —a cheap German model, or perhaps it was Swedish.

8. Lying naked in the back yard, the sun burned him so badly that later he couldn't put his clothes back on.

9. The winters in northern California seem delightfully mild, having spent 30 winters in the sub-zero weather of Minnesota.

10. The guard watched the convicts as they improvised clubs, knives, and zip-guns with no sense of alarm.

11. Charlie predicted that Western civilization would soon come to its terrible demise while slurping down another martini.

12. Seeing *Desire Under the Elms* again after fifteen years, it caused her to wonder why she had ever admired it.

13. The second annual Nectarine Bowl game got started two hours late, disappointing an enormous crowd of spectators.

14. Satan gave Count Dracula the ability to change himself into a bat to demonstrate the power of evil.

15. Martha's long-distance running was deteriorating while training under the regimen set up by the new coach.

16. Indoctrinated by television during every evening of her adolescence, the image of the typical female model—beautiful and narcissistic—became the chief idol in her religion.

17. Mrs. Cain ignored the road signs about the danger of throwing a lighted cigarette out the window, explaining the forest fire that swept across half the county.

18. Dr. Bramble prepared a talk for the national symposium on public education, which asserted the need for much better pay for the best teachers and no increase whatever for the worst.

19. After negotiating for two months, the new contract between the miners and their employers seemed just as far away as ever.

20. In 1955 almost 36 percent of American families subsisted on diets lacking in essential nutrients, leading to the food stamp program enacted in the early 1960s.

21. Mr. Hogan sat there in bewilderment as his wife walked out of the house, and out of his life, without knowing what could be done to resolve their differences.

22. To read and understand Milton's *Paradise Lost,* a thoroughly annotated text is almost indispensable for the modern student.

VI. Review an essay that you wrote at some time in the past. Do you find any infractions of the principles set forth in this chapter? If so, repair them.

10

Transitions

In the prose of skilled writers, sentences are linked so adroitly that, in the words of Winston Churchill, they "fit on to one another like the automatic couplings of railway carriages." [1] Or, to shift the metaphor, the sentences have an easy flow like that of a river whose current has not been impeded by dams or rocks or garbage. Or, to shift again, they have the fluency of music—not the discontinuous discords of electronic music, but the fluency of a Mozart, or of a Stravinsky, whose abrupt rhythmic and melodic changes never violate an essential coherence. Whatever metaphor best implies the fluency of well-written prose, the effect is hard to achieve. We take it for granted in the prose of accomplished stylists; we achieve it ourselves only by hard labor. Eleanor Perényi, speaking of the early essays of Edmund Wilson, remarked that they all had "a clarity and ease that, like Mozart sonatas, seem child's play until you try them." [2]

Transitions are indispensable for achieving continuity. The word comes from the Latin *trans*, meaning *across;* transitions are like bridges across the gaps that often occur between sentences. To use one more metaphor, transitions are like signposts: they guide us from where we have been to where we are going. For example:

---

[1] Quoted by Virginia Tufte, *Grammar as Style* (New York: Holt, Rinehart and Winston, 1971), p. 225.

[2] "Wilson," *Esquire* (July 1963), p. 80.

Helen was an exceptionally generous person. *However,* she was universally despised.

Try reading this passage without the italicized transition and you find that although the sentences still make sense, there seems to be a gap between them. The transition closes the gap by indicating the relationship between the sentences. Another way of saying this is that the transition provides what psychologists call "a mental set." It tells the reader what kind of idea is coming next.

Helen was an exceptionally generous person. *However* . . .

The town council was determined not to levy new taxes. *Therefore* . . .

As soon as you reach the *however* in the first passage, you know what sort of idea to expect; it will contrast with, or maybe contradict, the previous idea. In the second passage, the word *therefore* creates a different mental set; it leads you to expect some sort of *consequence*—some *result* of the council's determination.

Transitions such as *however* and *therefore* are known as *markers* because they explicitly indicate the relationships between sentences. Much of this chapter will be devoted to markers—not *all* markers (that discussion would fill a book) but some of the most common, and most commonly misused. It is not enough to have an abundance of markers in your repertoire; you must know precisely how to use them, precisely what sorts of ideas they can connect. Using the wrong markers can be worse than using none at all. Markers rarely become troublesome in description or narration. Descriptive prose commonly uses markers that express simple spatial relationships: *here, there, higher up, in the refrigerator, under the tree,* and so forth. The narrative markers—*then, later, suddenly, on the third day,* etc.—are no more difficult to use. The markers likely to be troublesome are those that occur in exposition and argumentation—the prose of information, explanation, and ideas.

Consider, for instance, the markers of enumeration: *first, second, third; the first step, the second step; in the first place, in the second place;* and so on. These can be valuable when you are genuinely entitled to enumerate things—reasons, rules, stages in a process, or whatever. Here the writer enumerates stages in a process:

The first step in Ignatian meditation requires the meditator to empty his mind of all secular considerations and put himself in the presence of God. Second, the meditator must ask for God's gracious assistance. The third step is the crucial one. . . .

Precisely because this device is easy to use, it is easy to overuse. Inexperienced writers, once they have discovered the advantages of enumeration, are easily enticed into using it inappropriately. For example:

> First, Martha let loose some jibes and insults. Second, her father-in-law became angry. Third, the two of them had a furious argument on New Year's Eve.

Here the enumerative markers are clumsy and obtrusive; they get more of the reader's attention than they deserve. (To be sure, some writers are even clumsier with enumeration, writing "the second point that I wish to make" when a mere "second" could do the job.) Another disadvantage of using enumeration in the passage about Martha and her father-in-law is that an important cause-and-effect relationship gets lost in the process. The fact that Martha's jibes and insults caused her father-in-law's anger has not been clearly expressed. The following revision drops the obtrusive enumeration and expresses the relationships between the events more accurately:

> Martha's jibes and insults angered her father-in-law and brought about their furious argument on New Year's Eve.

This version uses no markers. To repeat, using the wrong markers can be worse than using none at all.

We can begin our survey of markers by focusing on a group that causes little trouble. These markers introduce the reiteration of an idea just stated.

> The committee has clearly indicated its unwillingness to support this venture. *In other words,* it has refused to grant the necessary funds.

> The metaphysical poets had what T. S. Eliot has called "a unified sensibility." *That is,* they were able to think and feel at the same time.

> This version uses no markers. *To repeat,* using the wrong markers can be worse than using none at all.

Also useful are the markers *briefly* and *in short,* which can introduce a pithy restatement of an idea just presented at greater length. But if you promise briefness, you should keep your promise. Readers are entitled to be impatient if they find that after a *briefly* you fail to be brief.

When the restatement of your idea is more precise than the initial statement, you can use any of several markers: *to be exact, to be specific, to be precise, more specifically,* or *more precisely.* The following passage uses *to be precise* but could have used any of the other markers just as well.

Matthew Hopkins, a seventeenth-century lawyer, attempted to subdue the Satanic forces corrupting his beloved England. *To be precise,* he launched a campaign to exterminate witches.

If you have stated an idea and now wish to illustrate, you can announce the illustration with *for example* or *for instance.*

He tried desperately to appease his landlord. *For example,* he offered to pay all damages, even those for which he was clearly not responsible.

The soldiers carried out a strange kind of pacification. In the first village they pacified, *for instance,* they burned down all the houses and shot all the inhabitants.

Markers of *addition* announce the approach of a new idea, an addition to what has already been said. One such marker is *and:*

The battles of the Napoleonic era continued. *And* through all this period the shopkeepers and merchants quietly heaped up their profits, developing the strong capitalistic structure that would soon support the Industrial Revolution.

Possibly you have hesitated to use *and* (or *but*) at the start of a sentence, fearing that you would thereby violate a basic rule of style. For some reason a number of teachers have insisted on promulgating this superstition. As a cure, they should read some of the great prose in which initial *and*'s and *but*'s appear—for example, the prose of George Bernard Shaw and Jonathan Swift and the King James version of the Bible.

Other "additive" markers are *also, too, besides, furthermore, further, moreover,* and *in addition.* If you suspect you have used one of these markers incorrectly, you can find out by seeing whether *in addition* could be used in its place. *Moreover* and *furthermore* sometimes need to be checked in this way. Here they are used correctly:

Anthony Trollope each day added at least 2000 words to whatever book he was writing. *Furthermore,* he was active in other endeavors —family affairs, post office work, card playing, and horseback riding.

Benjamin Franklin wrote political and scientific tracts and, of course, his great autobiography. *Moreover,* he was an accomplished satirist, an exposer of shams both personal and public.

But in the following instances the markers are used incorrectly:

Queen Elizabeth could not raise enough money for government expenditures. *Moreover,* she sold monopolies to greedy businessmen.

Our nation has achieved unparalleled affluence. *Furthermore,* many of its people are bored, alienated, uncertain about values and purposes and the future.

If we try to replace the italicized markers with *in addition,* we find the markers to be faulty. The *moreover* in the first passage is illogical. The relationship between the two sentences is obviously one of cause and effect, but the marker obscures this relationship. A better marker would be *therefore* or *consequently* or *as a result.* In the second passage, the *furthermore* should be replaced with a marker that can emphasize the sharp contrast between the first sentence and the second. Most of us consider affluence a good thing and uncertainty a bad thing. Rather than disguising the contrast with a *furthermore,* why not point it up with a *but, yet,* or *however?*

Keep in mind that *moreover* and *furthermore* are distinctly formal in tone. In informal prose you may want to replace them with simpler markers such as *but, and,* or *besides.* Look back at the illustrative passages about Anthony Trollope and Benjamin Franklin. Note the slightly different tone you would achieve by substituting *but* for *furthermore* in the Trollope passage and *besides* for *moreover* in the Franklin.

We come now to markers that announce a contrast, a change in direction. *Yet* and *and yet* are two such markers. And one of the most valuable is *but.* The first of the following passages uses no *but;* the second uses *but* to turn two sentences into one; the third uses *but* to close the gap between two sentences.

E. M. Forster was a man of exceeding kindness. It would be a mistake to look upon his kindness as a sign of weakness.

E. M. Forster was a man of exceeding kindness, *but* it would be a mistake to look upon his kindness as a sign of weakness.

E. M. Forster was a man of exceeding kindness. *But* it would be a mistake to look upon his kindness as a sign of weakness.

In the first version we are left unprepared for the contrasting idea in the second sentence. Granted, we catch on anyway, after only the slightest of pauses; but why should we have to pause at all, when a simple *but* could guide us quickly and easily from one idea to the next?

As you may have noticed, a *but* at the beginning of a sentence can give special emphasis to a contrast in ideas. In the second version of the passage about Forster, the two ideas are contrasted clearly enough, but in the third version the contrast is even sharper.

However is another marker commonly used to announce a contrast. A longer and slower word than *but,* it is therefore slightly more formal. Here are three versions of one passage. The first uses an initial *but;* the second uses an initial *however;* the third delays the *however* until later in the sentence.

> Bertrand Russell refused to join any established religion. *But* he did confess that he greatly admired the tenets of Buddhism.

> Bertrand Russell refused to join any established religion. *However,* he did confess that he greatly admired the tenets of Buddhism.

> Bertrand Russell refused to join any established religion. He did confess, *however,* that he greatly admired the tenets of Buddhism.

Notice that when *however* appears as a marker at the beginning of a sentence (as in the second passage), it should be followed by a comma to prevent confusion with this sort of initial *however:* "However he felt about the ceremony, he said nothing." It is sometimes argued that *however,* as a marker, sounds clumsy at the beginning of a sentence and that whenever possible it should be delayed until later. This advice seems arbitrary. Sometimes, though not always, an initial *however* sounds clumsy; but sometimes a delayed *however* sounds even clumsier. Rather than obeying an iron rule, let your ear be your guide. And if *however* seems cumbersome no matter *where* you put it, try switching to *but* or *yet* or *and yet.*

Or you might try one of the other markers that announce a contrast—perhaps *still* or *nevertheless.*

> Francis Bacon, more than any other Englishman of his time, popularized the new science. *Still,* he failed to appreciate the importance of mathematics.

The *still* could be replaced by *nevertheless.* The two words have the same meaning, though *nevertheless* is more formal in tone.

Other markers useful for introducing a contrasting idea are *on the other hand, in contrast, instead,* and *on the contrary.* Perhaps you have been told never to write *on the other hand* unless you have previously written *on the one hand.* This doddering rule has now expired and gone to the same limbo that holds the defunct prohibitions against initial *and's, but's,* and *however's.* The following examples are perfectly acceptable:

> Rocky loves symphonies and chamber music. His brother Wolfgang, *on the other hand,* prefers musical comedies.

> Senator Bromide will certainly win the approval of the Daughters of the American Revolution. *On the other hand,* he will lose the votes of all revolutionaries.

In contrast introduces an idea sharply different from the one preceding it:

The new contract delighted the teachers. *In contrast,* it infuriated the superintendent of schools, the principals, and all the assistant administrators.

Instead sometimes means pretty much the same as *but* or *however,* though perhaps it emphasizes a contrast more strongly:

Ostensibly the new law was intended to rescue the Free Parliament from the London mobs. *Instead,* it resulted in the first parliamentary purge in English history.

At other times *instead* operates in the same way as *on the contrary.* Either term can join (1) the negation of one idea and (2) the presentation of a new and contrasting idea:

Kevin didn't even smile when he saw the new bike. *Instead,* he turned to his father and whined, "Why didn't you get me a red one?"

Phillips did not believe in democracy. *On the contrary,* he yearned for an aristocracy in which he could serve as one of the most intelligent, progressive, and comfortable members of the elite.

The next markers to be examined have the job of tying together cause-and-effect relationships. The most common of these markers is *therefore:*

The ratcatchers wanted to raise their prestige. *Therefore* they renamed themselves "exterminating engineers."

Other markers that work in the same way, and could replace *therefore* in the preceding example, are *hence, consequently, accordingly,* and *as a result.*

When using such a marker, you should double-check its appropriateness. Does it truly join a cause and an effect? One test is to see whether the marker could be replaced by *for this reason.* Failing to test for appropriateness, an intelligent but inexperienced writer produced the following absurdity:

Many people in eastern Kentucky are too poor to buy wool clothing. *Therefore,* they are too poor to buy food.

There is no necessary cause-and-effect relationship between the first sentence and the second. Those people in Kentucky, even if they cannot afford wool clothing, might still be able to buy food. Possibly the writer would have detected his illogic if he had tried the test we just mentioned—had tried replacing *therefore* with *for this reason.*

Here is a different misuse of a cause-and-effect marker:

The editor told Beecher his article was weakened by its monotonous sentence structure. *Hence* Beecher got the article published.

After a moment's reflection we see that the passage took this ludicrous form simply because the writer omitted an important link in a chain of causes and effects. Apparently the editor's criticism led Beecher to revise his article and vary its sentence structure. Once he had done so, he got the article published. But the writer neglected to state the all-important intermediate step—the revision of the article.

Two other markers that deserve comment are *thus* and *so,* both of which may be used as synonyms of *therefore. So,* however, is much less formal than *therefore* and the other cause-and-effect markers we have examined. Use *so* only when you wish to impart an informality to your style.

Thus and *so* sometimes have another meaning: *in this way.*

> His speech led up to his favorite quotation from Samuel Johnson: "A decent provision for the poor is the true test of civilization." And *thus* the speech ended.

Or the writer might have said, "And *so* the speech ended."

Markers are not the only transitions. A less conspicuous transitional device is *the repetition of words or ideas:* the writer can achieve continuity by echoing an important word or idea from previous sentences. For example:

> My opponent argues that this proposal would *cost* the state at least $3 million. Actually, the cost would not exceed $1 million.

> The class stared at the *instructor* with expressions that mutely cried out, "Please *clarify* these points!" But *clarification* was precisely what this *instructor* habitually disdained.

Of course, sometimes the repetition of words would grow tiresome. In that event you can use synonyms:

> *Corporations* have sought to improve their image with college students. But many students still remain cool toward *business* as a vocation.

> He has begun to *question* his family's values and middle-class values in general. This *skepticism* has been both harmful and beneficial.

Or you can use a word that echoes, not simply a single word from the preceding sentences, but an entire idea:

> In the last scene Jake risks his life for his friends. This *heroism* clashes oddly with Jake's earlier cynicism.

> King Charles understood neither the temper nor the strength of the

forces he sought to control. This *faulty assessment* led to his down-fall.

Pronouns offer another means of achieving tight coherence with-out tedious repetition. Note the abundance of transitional pronouns in the following passage from Frances Trollope's *Domestic Manners of the Americans* (1832). (Punctuation and spelling have been slightly revised.)

> The ladies have strange ways of adding to their charms. *They* powder *themselves* immoderately, face, neck, and arms, with pulverized starch. The effect is indescribably disagreeable by daylight, and not very favorable at any time. *They* are also most unhappily partial to false hair, which *they* wear in surprising quantities. *This* is the more to be lamented as *they* generally have very fine hair of *their* own. I suspect this fashion to arise from an indolent mode of making *their* toilet and from accomplished ladies' maids not being very abundant. It is less trouble to append a bunch of waving curls here, there, and everywhere than to keep *their* native tresses in perfect order.

Mrs. Trollope's prose also shows the utility of the so-called de-monstrative adjectives (*this, that, these, those,* etc.). Note the transitional function of the phrase "this fashion" in the sixth sentence. An inexperi-enced writer might have said simply "the fashion" and would thereby have lost the tighter continuity afforded by the demonstrative adjective. Here is one further example of demonstratives at work:

> The new Turtoise four-cylinder engine consumes amazingly little oil. *This* feature is one reason for the popularity of *that* remarkable engine.

We have now surveyed both kinds of transitions—the explicit mark-ers and the repetition of words and ideas. As a way of summarizing, and of adding a few new points, we will take one piece of prose through several different versions, first using too few transitions, then too many, then a mean between the extremes.

Our first version has almost no transitions. It is admittedly a make-believe prose, more fragmentary and discontinuous than any prose a native speaker of the language would be likely to write. But it will serve to emphasize, by contrast, the benefits of using transitions.

> Jason felt a strong urge to engage in socially useful work. The vo-cation chosen was that of teaching in a high school in a poor urban

area. It was discovered that there was much arduous and frustrating activity. The students seemed to be rewarded no more than the teacher. So much exhaustion and demoralization resulted that a breakdown was imminent. A resignation became necessary. Some valuable lessons had been learned. . . .

Now suppose the imaginary writer of this prose happened to read the present chapter and see the need for adding both markers and repetitions. The following passage might be the result. (The markers are underlined twice, the repetitions once.)

Jason felt a strong urge to engage in socially useful work. Therefore he became a high school teacher in a poor urban area. However, he soon discovered that the work was arduous and frustrating. In addition, the work seemed no more rewarding for the students than for the teacher. In short, this labor was so exhausting and demoralizing that he was on the verge of a breakdown. Consequently he resigned after only five months. Nevertheless, this brief experience taught him some valuable lessons. . . .

The writer has gone too far. This prose is littered with transitional words. The repetitions are not at fault; they don't impose themselves unduly on the reader's attention. But the markers do. They are painfully conspicuous. Their frequency seems to tell the reader that he is so imperceptive, so dull-witted, that he must be guided like a child from one sentence to the next.

How can the writer cure this stylistic illness? One means is to combine some short sentences into longer ones. He can let coordination and subordination, rather than markers, tie the ideas together. Once he has done this, he can delete any remaining markers that are not truly necessary for maintaining clarity or continuity. Finally, if it seems advisable, he can shorten the markers that still remain, reducing *furthermore*'s to *and*'s, *however*'s to *but*'s, and so forth. The passage about the frustrated high school teacher, if it were revised in this way, would turn into something like this:

Eager to engage in socially useful work, Jason became a high school teacher in a poor urban area. But he soon discovered that the work was arduous and frustrating, unrewarding for the students as well as the teacher, and in general so exhausting and demoralizing that he was on the verge of a breakdown. He resigned after only five months. Nevertheless, this brief experience taught him some valuable lessons. . . .

Much, much better. Not only can the passage be read from beginning to end with no lapse in continuity, but the means by which continuity is achieved do not call undue attention to themselves. The transitions have served their purpose admirably.

Exercises

I. In each of the following exercises, indicate which transitional marker would do the best job of achieving continuity between the sentences. Occasionally, in the last few exercises, you'll be able to justify either of two choices. Add necessary punctuation.

1. Pamela loves to insult people—to attack their most vulnerable weaknesses with stinging words. _____ she doesn't have a single friend.
(For instance, In short, As a result, That is, On the other hand)

2. American attitudes can shift rapidly. Only twenty years ago divorce led to social disapproval. _____ now it is viewed with sympathy and sometimes with approval.
(Furthermore, For example, Therefore, To be exact, But)

3. The one pornographic movie house in town shows crude, amateurish films and charges an outrageous $7.50 per seat. _____ the place is filled to capacity every night.
(In other words, Nevertheless, Moreover, On the other hand, Furthermore)

4. Igor always did careless work in his college biology courses. _____ he wound up working for the famous Dr. Frankenstein.
(In contrast, Therefore, To summarize, Nevertheless, Moreover)

5. The Blue Mountain Express approached the curve at 60 miles an hour—twice the recommended speed. _____ eight of its cars were derailed, almost three hundred people were injured, and twenty-six were killed.
(Furthermore, Briefly, Nevertheless, Afterwards, Consequently)

6. The growth of the cities, the permissiveness of parents, a widespread disappointment with the democratic process, a hatred for meaningless work, a yearning for religious experience—all these phenomena have been said to explain the current craze for drugs. None of them _____ is nearly as important as another cause that rarely gets mentioned.
(therefore, on the other hand, however, nevertheless, for instance)

7. The spiritual examiners said they had found evidence that justified charging the old woman with witchcraft and putting her to death by hanging. _____ they said they had found the mark of Satan on the old woman's breast.
(Accordingly, Hence, To be specific, Similarly, And yet)

8. A child is likely to repeat an act if the reward is to be kisses and

chocolates. _____ a dog will quickly learn to retrieve if it is re-warded with praise, a petting, and some canine candy.
(However, In contrast, Similarly, Thus, Briefly)

9. Some people said that Priscilla quit school because she hated cutting animals apart in her biology classes. _____ the main reason she quit was to carry out her ambition to tour the country on a motorcycle.
(In contrast, Furthermore, Thus, As a result, But)

10. The editor-in-chief doesn't harbor any favorable feelings toward this article. _____ he thinks it is the worst article ever submitted to the *Hicksville Gazette.*
(However, To be precise, On the contrary, Besides, Moreover)

11. George Bernard Shaw had an amazing capacity for hard work. He wrote a thousand words a day—five pages of small script. _____ he somehow found time to participate in the multifarious political activities of the Fabian Society.
(As a result, In addition, More specifically, Furthermore, On the other hand)

12. Humphrey, whose weight has climbed to 250 pounds, has nothing for breakfast but orange juice and coffee. _____ his wife, who never weighs more than 95 pounds, starts the day with four eggs, four pieces of buttered toast, and a twelve-ounce steak.
(On the contrary, Hence, And yet, On the other hand, Moreover)

13. Brenda's abilities are amazingly diverse. She is a member of the board of education, a free-lance writer whose articles have appeared in leading magazines, and a photographer who has already given three one-woman exhibitions. _____ in her spare time she offers psychological counseling to the old and the indigent.
(And, On the other hand, To be exact, Moreover, For example)

II. Choose five of the following passages to work with. For each of those five passages, compose a sentence (or two) that will carry the thought a bit further. Take the thought in any direction you please, but be sure that your sentence is not discontinuous with the preceding passage. Ensure continuity by echoing important words or ideas. Suppose, for instance, that you were given this passage:

A. J. Liebling, one of the best of the *New Yorker* writers, had no use for Fowler's *Modern English Usage* or any other how-to-do-it books on writing.

You might compose the following sentence:

Liebling reasoned that because *he* was a seasoned and successful professional, *he* was entitled to make *his* own *rules* about *how writing* should or should not *be done,* just as a master chef makes his own rules without bothering to consult Rombauer's *Joy of Cooking.*

We have italicized the words that provide the most obvious echoes of words and ideas in the previous passage.

1. No hard-and-fast line divides sanity from insanity. There are all sorts of intermediate stages.

2. In 1968, 37 percent of college freshmen favored an all-volunteer army. By 1970, 68 percent of college freshmen favored an all-volunteer army.

3. Hating the daily embarrassment of being obese, Milton bought still another book on a sure-fire, easy-does-it way to lose weight.

4. His transistor radio was his closest friend. It woke him up in the morning, kept him company through the day at school and home, and lulled him to sleep at night.

5. Howard died right in the middle of his morning calisthenics. He suffered a massive heart attack just after his seventh push-up.

6. Dr. Marvin Harris, a noted anthropologist, has said that "the death of male supremacy may simply mean that the sexes become equally powerless rather than equally powerful."

7. In stories and essays alike, both Robert Benchley and James Thurber portrayed themselves as ineffectual little men who feared women, children, repairmen, and just about everyone else, but who secretly dreamed of the bold deeds they could perform if they only had the right opportunities.

8. In his seventies Arnold laboriously taught himself to read French, so that he could finally savor the great masters of French prose in the original—Montaigne, Rabelais, Pascal, Madame de Sévigné, Voltaire, Saint-Simon, and all the rest.

9. Certain psychologists believe that their colleagues have spent too much time delving into childhood traumas and probing into unconscious fears and fixations. These therapists say that most people with emotional difficulties don't need all that probing as much as they need practice at thinking clearly and applying common sense.

10. Reading Nietzsche had changed Martha's life. She decided that she had been kind and good and self-effacing long enough. Now she would think of herself first. Her children, her husband, her parents, the PTA, the March of Dimes—they could damn well take care of themselves and leave her alone.

III. Rewrite the following passage. Use pronouns, synonyms, and whatever other devices you please in order to alleviate the excessive repetition of certain words. But don't sacrifice continuity.

Hacker is fond of hockey. In fact, Hacker is fanatically fond of hockey. Hacker has become so fond of hockey that he has neglected his studies. Not only has Hacker neglected his studies but he has neglected his friends. Hacker has actually told his friends not to speak to him during the hockey season.

IV. In the following passage the transitional markers become painfully conspicuous. Revise the passage to achieve continuity through more varied and subtle means.

Melvin is becoming a misanthrope. That is, he has begun to hate and distrust all mankind. To begin with, Melvin had kept a secret regarding himself for over twenty years. Namely, he kept it a secret that he had been jilted by the only woman he ever deemed worthy of becoming his wife. Then, a week ago, Melvin decided to confide in his sister Charlotte. Charlotte, however, revealed his secret the very next day, during a coffee-break at the office. Nevertheless, Melvin still believed that most people are trustworthy. Consequently, he next confided in his Aunt Sophie. However, Sophie held in the secret for only two days. Then she let it out at her weekly bridge game for the local chapter of the Browning Society. Therefore Melvin decided that women in general are not to be trusted. Nevertheless he still hoped to find one person who could appreciate his secret and surround it with reverential silence. Accordingly, he confided in his brother Amos, a deacon in the Baptist church. Amos, however, turned out to be the most treacherous traitor of all. To be specific, at dinner that very evening Amos laughingly divulged the secret to the entire family.

V. Reread an essay that you wrote some time ago. Do you experience any difficulty in following the line of thought—any lapses in continuity between one sentence and the next? Revise accordingly. Rearrange your sentences if necessary. And add transitions.

On the other hand, you might find some passages in which the transitions are too plentiful and too conspicuous. Revise such passages to reduce the number and conspicuousness of the transitions without sacrificing continuity.

III

Advanced Principles of Style

11

The Sound
of the
Sentence

This chapter and the two that follow are all concerned with the sounds made by sentences. Admittedly, the kind of prose discussed in this book—the prose of college essays, business reports, magazine articles, and so forth—is usually not intended to be read aloud. Then why must the writer of such prose worry about sound? The answer is that even if the prose is not to be read aloud, it will be read with "the mind's ear"—an inner sense for the harmony or disharmony of a prose style. The sensitive reader will detect, and resent, the slightest lapses in prose harmony: the silly rhymes, the clumsy repetitions, the awkward collocations of harsh syllables. And even the insensitive reader, the "speed reader" manufactured in a "reading laboratory," will sometimes recognize that defects in prose rhythm can lead to deficiencies in clarity and forcefulness.

Surely the most insensitive reader would notice the deficiencies in the following passage, which, as Fowler would say, has no more rhythm than so much water running from a faucet.[1] The writer of this passage has just confessed his inability to get pleasure or profit from books by systematic philosophers—Schopenhauer, William James, Bergson, and the like. And at that point we turn on the faucet:

> My failure to keep pace with the leaders of thought as they pass into
> oblivion distresses me and makes me wonder whether I am an abso-

---

[1] H. W. Fowler, "Rhythm," *Modern English Usage*, 2nd ed., revised by Sir Ernest Gowers (New York: Oxford University Press, 1965), p. 526.

137

lute fool. My evidence that I am not is that I can listen fairly intelligently and be stirred to not altogether fatuous thoughts if you tell me of some real or fictitious man or woman or place or event in a narrative form that will present some image to me. Anyone who comes to me with a grievous difficulty will discover that I can talk to him like a father or even like a lawyer and exhibit mellow wisdom but the sort of person who wishes to weave theories as to the nature of things in general and try those theories on someone who will luminously confirm them or powerfully rend them must be warned that I am not the man he wants because I suffer from a strong suspicion that things in general cannot be accounted for by any formula or set of formulae and that not even the newest philosophy is any better than another. What I have just said is suspect because it is in itself a sort of philosophy but is acceptable because it has for me the merit of being the only philosophy I can make head or tail of and any other philosophic system expounded to me will get by with all its flaws undetected except the great flaw just suggested and will make no sense to me after a minute or two.

Does anyone actually write such rhythmless prose? We assure you that not only does such stuff get written, it also gets published. And if you doubt our word, we invite you to grapple with the monstrous sentences quoted by Fowler in his entry on "Rhythm." [2]

In the same entry Fowler offers good advice on how you can achieve an effectively rhythmic style. The method has nothing to do with counting vowels, consonants, or accented syllables. Instead, Fowler urges merely that you read large amounts of first-rate prose—and read it aloud, or at least with a lively appreciation of its "internal echo" in the mind. Thus you will gradually enhance your ability to distinguish between rhythmic and rhythmless prose—between the vigor and grace of, say, a Virginia Woolf or an H. L. Mencken, and the droning or babbling indulged in by all too many newspaper writers, business people, bureaucrats, sociologists, literary critics, and textbook writers. And the more sensitive you become to the harmonies and disharmonies in other people's prose, the more sensitive you will become to the same virtues and vices in your own, and the more skillful you will become at multiplying the one and minimizing the other.

This chapter, and the two that follow, are meant to give you a head start in this process by familiarizing you with the most obvious virtues and the most notorious vices, those that have most persistently earned praise or condemnation from writers and rhetoricians. You might eventually discover these do's and don't's for yourself, if you listen closely enough to enough good prose. But you can quicken the process

[2] And his entries on "Hanging-Up," "Officialese," and "Trailers."

by reviewing the advice passed down by lovers of good prose during the last 2500 years.

LONGWINDED SENTENCES

A moment ago you looked at a rhythmless passage about one person's inability to read systematic philosophy. The main failing in that passage is that it doesn't contain enough pauses. Its sentences contain no pauses whatever—no commas or semicolons or dashes—although several of the sentences are unusually long, and one of them, the third, runs on for 107 words.

The result of this longwindedness is that the prose sounds inhuman. No human being talks without pausing for breath; so the passage sounds less like a human being than like some computerized writing machine. By way of contrast, we'll quote a passage by Max Beerbohm, the modern British essayist. Notice that in its meaning and its wording the passage closely resembles the one we have just finished disparaging. But the present passage can hardly be accused of lacking a human voice. Every sentence is infused with Beerbohm's own special blend of irony, urbanity, and common sense.

It distresses me, this failure to keep pace with the leaders of thought as they pass into oblivion. It makes me wonder whether I am, after all, an absolute fool. Yet surely I am not that. Tell me of a man or a woman, a place or an event, real or fictitious; surely you will find me a fairly intelligent listener. Any such narrative will present to me some image, and will stir me to not altogether fatuous thoughts. Come to me in some grievous difficulty; I will talk to you like a father, even like a lawyer. I'll be hanged if I haven't a certain mellow wisdom. But if you are by way of weaving theories as to the nature of things in general, and if you want to try those theories on some one who will luminously confirm them or powerfully rend them, I must, with a hang-dog air, warn you that I am not your man. I suffer from a strong suspicion that things in general cannot be accounted for through any formula or set of formulae, and that any one philosophy, howsoever new, is no better than another. That is in itself a sort of philosophy, and I suspect it accordingly; but it has for me the merit of being the only one I can make head or tail of. If you try to expound any other philosophic system to me, you will find not merely that I can detect no flaw in it (except the great flaw just suggested), but also that I haven't, after a minute or two, the vaguest notion of what you are driving at.[3]

[3] From *And Even Now* by Max Beerbohm. © 1921 by E. P. Dutton; renewal, 1949 by Max Beerbohm. Reprinted by permission of the publishers, E. P. Dutton & Co., Inc., and Heinemann Publishers, London. "Laughter," *And Even Now and A Christmas Garland* (New York: E. P. Dutton, 1960), pp. 166–67.

The monotonous, mechanical voicelessness of the earlier passage has given way to the unmistakable voice of Beerbohm. You may not particularly enjoy or admire that voice, but you can hardly deny that you have heard a voice. And one reason is that although Beerbohm uses long sentences, he uses no *longwinded* sentences such as we found in the earlier passage. His long sentences—the eighth and the concluding ones, for instance—are judiciously broken up by pauses.

LAST WORDS

Pauses are worth your attention for a second reason. They have much to do with emphasis. The opening words of a sentence are emphatic because they follow the pause between sentences: they break the silence. But even more emphatic are the words at the *end* of a sentence, the words immediately *before* the pause. If the words are forceful, and if they express an important idea, then the pause can leave them resounding in the reader's mind.

For this reason you should avoid ending a sentence with trivial words. To end with trivia is to end with an anticlimax. Because the end of a sentence is potentially so emphatic, the reader unconsciously expects the ending to deliver some important words—perhaps not the most important in the sentence, but certainly words of greater interest than the ones italiciized here:

> In reading about Genghis Khan, I was astonished by the magnitude of his power and by the viciousness of the cruelty *that he displayed from time to time.*

> What Mailer means is that a woman's monthly period may in some way disqualify her from piloting a 100,000-ton tanker into harbor, flying a Boeing 747, controlling a subway train, running a computer, *or doing other work of a similar nature.*

> The board of education has postponed its decision on the issue of sex education until late in April, when a citizens' committee set up to investigate the matter will deliver its final report, *Mrs. Edith Ramirez, the board chairperson, has said.*

The ineffectual wording at the end of the first sentence detracts from whatever interest the reader might have built up during those earlier phrases about power and cruelty. The second sentence begins interestingly enough, but then embarks on one long anticlimax, moving from the enormously difficult task of piloting a tanker to such lesser tasks as operating a computer, and then losing all vigor by ending with those feeble words in italics. The third sentence parodies the sort of newspaper reporter who ruins many a good sentence by ending it with an awkward reference to his source of information. Perhaps such reporters are obeying a commandment handed down by their editors. But how much better that sentence would have been if it had mentioned the source at the outset, rather than saving it for a clumsy anticlimax.

If you have ended with trivial words, you can revise by moving them to an earlier point in the sentence or by omitting them entirely:

> In reading about Genghis Khan, I was astonished by the magnitude of his power and the viciousness of his cruelty.

> [What Mailer means is that] a woman's monthly period may in some way disqualify her from running a computer, controlling a subway train, flying a Boeing 747, or piloting a 100,000-ton tanker into harbor.
>
> Michael Korda [4]

> According to chairperson Edith Ramirez, the board of education has postponed its decision on the issue of sex education until late in April, when a citizens' committee set up to investigate the matter will deliver its final report.

The last sentence remains unsatisfactory. "Sex education" is one of its most important phrases, but because that phrase lies buried in the middle of the sentence, it gets too little emphasis. Surely it deserves a more prominent position—the beginning of a sentence or, better yet, the end:

> According to chairperson Edith Ramirez, the board of education has postponed its decision on the issue of sex education. The board will make its decision late in April, when a citizens' committee set up to investigate the matter will deliver its final report.

REPETITION AND VARIETY

You can often gain emphasis through a repetitive rhythm. Listen to the forceful repetition in the following sentence, in which Lord Chesterfield warned his son against lusting after prostitutes:

> The pleasure is momentary, the position ridiculous, and the expense damnable.

The sentence is effective not only because of the repetitive rhythm but also because of the reiterated "p's" in "pleasure," "position," and "expense," and because of the increasingly condemnatory tone in the mild "momentary," the stronger "ridiculous," and the angry "damnable."

[4] *Male Chauvinism* (New York: Random House, 1974), p. 51.

But in talking about Chesterfield's sentence we are talking about controlled artistry, not about such accidental, ineffectual repetition as we find here:

> The *timid* student *reluctantly* knocked at the *massive* door, *suddenly* fearful at the *alarming* prospect of *singlehandedly* facing the *arrogant* professor and his *sneering* disciples.

Writers who produce this kind of sentence have somehow picked up the notion that every noun should be preceded by an adjective and every verb by an adverb. (We have italicized the five adjectives and three adverbs.) The resultant rhythm is as monotonous, as sing-songy, as bad poetry. The only solution is to cut out some modifiers:

> *Timidly* the student knocked at the *massive* door, fearful at the prospect of facing the *arrogant* professor and his *sneering* disciples.

We have kept only four of the original eight modifiers, and, as an added attempt at variety, have changed the adjective "timid" to the adverb "timidly" and separated that adverb from the word it now modifies— that is, "knocked." Have we kept too many modifiers? Are you annoyed by the threefold repetition of the adjective-noun pattern in "massive door," "arrogant professor," and "sneering disciples"?

Another irritating form of repetition comes from the overuse of prepositional phrases. A series of three prepositional phrases is chancy, and four or more such phrases will almost always lead to monotony. Note the tiresome regularity in the following sentence, which contains seven prepositional phrases in close proximity (as we have indicated by italicizing the prepositions).

> Several *of* the younger members *of* the families *of* prominent citizens were placed *under* arrest *for* the possession *of* various kinds *of* illegal drugs.

In these added examples, the prepositional monotony is less obvious but still objectionable:

> Many *of* the surveys *by* American sociologists *in* recent years have made a point *of* an appreciable degree *of* decline *in* our confidence *in* our institutions.

> All branches *of* knowledge have their share *of* fascination and are *of* assistance *in* the maintenance *of* society, but *in* a culture *in* the process *of* rapid evolution, most kinds *of* knowledge quickly fall *into* obsolescence or *into* a state *of* uselessness.

How can you repair such sentences? Obviously, by converting their prepositional phrases into something else. Often the nouns following the prepositions (the so-called "objects" of the prepositions) can become adjectives or verbs.

> Several children of prominent citizens were arrested for possessing illegal drugs.

> Recently many sociological surveys have shown that our confidence in American institutions has been declining.

> All branches of knowledge can be fascinating and can help a society to maintain itself, but in a rapidly evolving culture such as ours, most kinds of knowledge quickly become obsolete.

We should also mention that *any* series of words can become monotonous if the words remain similar in length. If they persist in being polysyllabic, they are likely to become unclear as well as monotonous:

> In audio-visual literature, technical terminology substantially facilitates communication efficiency, ensures sophisticated, professional expression, and achieves comprehension rapidity.

The phrase "comprehension rapidity" exemplifies the problems that sometimes result when you modify a noun with a noun. "Comprehension rapidity" is clumsier and less clear than "rapidity of comprehension"; and yet many writers feel that the noun-noun form sounds more like "sophisticated, professional expression." They favor such cumbersome phrases as (1) "manpower utilization procedures," (2) "teenager peer-group value system," and even (3) "accuracy maintenance strategy"—when it would be clearer and more graceful to write (1) "procedures for making the best use of our employees," (2) "the values of most teenagers," and (3) "a strategy for maintaining accuracy." But of course that passage about "audio-visual literature" has other problems besides the phrase "comprehension rapidity." It needs to be translated into plain English, for the sake of both clarity and sound.

> When writing about audio-visual equipment, you should use a great many technical terms. Thus you will sound like an expert. And at the same time you will make your prose easier to understand.

The second sentence in this version probably indicates the true motive behind the profusion of polysyllabic words in the earlier version. The writer wants to sound like an expert. But will big words, or "technical terminology," really "make your prose easier to understand"?

Small words have been capably defended by Joseph Ecclesine, in an essay written entirely in words of one syllable. But even when used by so sympathetic a writer as Mr. Ecclesine, those tiny words soon become tiresome. Or so they seem to us. Judge for yourself.

> When you come right down to it, there is no law that says you have to use big words when you write or talk.
>   There are lots of small words, and good ones, that can be made to say all the things you want to say, quite as well as the big ones. It may take a bit more time to find them at first. But it can be well worth it, for all of us know what they mean. . . .
>   Small words move with ease where big words stand still—or, worse, bog down and get in the way of what you want to say. There is not much, in all truth, that small words will not say—and say quite well.[5]

As we read this prose, we find ourselves hungering for a little variety —not for esoteric or gargantuan words, but merely for a few words of more than one syllable.

Still, as we have said, Mr. Ecclesine uses his short words adroitly. If he had been less skillful, his words might have become as harshly discordant as these:

> All mud wasps built dirt nests hung from close trees.

Not only are all the words short, but they contain a number of sibilants and hard consonants: all those "s's" and "t's." We can unclog the prose by adding a few softer words:

> All the mud wasps built their nests out of dirt and hung them from nearby trees.

The first version contains ten words; the second, sixteen words. We have sacrificed conciseness for the sake of sound.

Up to this point we have focused on repetition in *rhythm*. Now we will turn to repetition of *words* or *parts of words*.

The repetition of words has several legitimate purposes. For one thing, it can achieve continuity between sentences. For another, it can achieve emphasis—as it did at several points in John F. Kennedy's Inaugural Address:

> . . . man holds in his mortal hands the power to abolish *all forms of human* poverty and *all forms of human* life. [We offer a pledge] to convert our *good* words into *good* deeds, . . . to assist *free* men and *free* governments in casting off the chains of poverty.
>
> . . . the *instruments* of war have far outpaced the *instruments* of peace. . . .

[5] "Words of One Syllable." Quoted by Jerome H. Perlmutter, *A Practical Guide to Effective Writing* (New York: Dell, 1965), pp. 112–13.

. . . only when our arms are sufficient *beyond doubt* can we be certain *beyond doubt* that they will never be employed.

But accidental repetition can be irritating. When a writer repeats his words not because he is aiming for rhetorical effect, but because he is getting careless, the results are likely to sound amateurish:

When they are hunting *antelope,* the Bushmen try to get within 30 feet of the *antelope* before hurling their spears.

At one time the Bushmen *inhabited* all South Africa, but today they *inhabit* only *the Kalahari Desert.* And now there is talk of permitting them to *inhabit* only the northern portion of *the Kalahari Desert.*

You can get rid of such annoying echoes by recasting your sentences or by using synonyms in place of word-for-word reiterations:

When they are hunting antelope, the Bushmen try to get within 30 feet of their *prey* before hurling their spears.

At one time the Bushmen inhabited all South Africa, but today they *are confined* to the Kalahari Desert. And now there is talk of *re- stricting* them to the northern portion of *that* desert.

But Fowler points out that if you work too hard at varying your words, you will commit the stylistic error he has labeled "elegant varia- tion." [6] If you swear never, never to repeat the same words, you will sink to producing such elegant variations as these:

They spend a few weeks longer in their winter home than in their summer *habitat.*

Curiously enough, women played the male parts, while men *were entrusted with the* female *characters.*

Rarely does "Indian summer" linger until November, but at times its stay has been prolonged until quite late in *the year's penultimate month.*

The elegant variation in the first sentence has the sole disadvantage of being too obtrusive—of calling too much attention to itself. "I see," the reader will respond; "the writer thought he would sound too plain if he repeated 'home'; so he tried to sound fancy with 'habitat.'" The writers of the second and third sentences also strain to sound elegant. But those sentences have the added flaw of being unclear—or less clear than if the writers had done less straining for elegance. Would the sentences have sounded impossibly crude if the writers had simply re- peated themselves word for word?

[6] *Modern English Usage,* pp. 148–51. The examples that follow are borrowed from Fowler.

> They spend a few weeks longer in their winter home than in their summer home.

> Curiously enough, women played the male parts, and men played the female parts.

> Rarely does "Indian summer" linger until November, but at times it has lasted well into the second half of November.

The first two sentences seem acceptable as they stand. And if, in the third sentence, the reiterated *November* sounds a bit clumsy, we can change "the second half of November" to "the second half of that month."

So your policy regarding the repetition of words might well boil down to this: Vary your words rather than sound clumsy, but not so much that you seem affected or obscure.

Up to this point we have talked about the repetition of entire words. But we must also mention the dangers of repeating *parts* of words: syllables or even single letters. Here such repetition is subtly effective:

> The mass of men lead lives of quiet desperation.
>
> Henry David Thoreau [7]

> The fear of excessive good fortune is deeply ingrained in man. There is an instinctive sense that the gods envy human success.
>
> Edward Edinger [8]

Alliteration—the repetition of consonants—can emphasize key words: *mass* and *men, lead* and *lives, fear* and *fortune, sense* and *success.* And sometimes alliteration can add a touch of humor—as when Max Beerbohm poked fun at "fashionable philosophers," or when a disaffected student ridiculed "the pomposity of pedagogues."

But the humor in the following passage was unintentional. Indeed, the speaker, Warren Gamaliel Harding, who was later to become president of the United States, regarded himself as an accomplished orator. But here we have Harding's prose at its worst—or at its best, if you enjoy the unintended humor in pretentious speech-making:

> Progression is not proclamation nor palaver. It is not pretense nor play on prejudice. It is not of personal pronouns, nor perennial pronouncement. It is not the pertubation of a people passion-wrought, nor a promise proposed.[9]

[7] *Walden,* Chapter 1 ("Economy").
[8] *Ego and Archetype* (Baltimore: Penguin Books, 1973), p. 32.
[9] Quoted by Harry H. Crosby and George F. Estey, *College Writing* (New York: Harper & Row, 1968), pp. 162–63.

The repetition of sounds need not be that extended to be disconcerting. Although the following samples from student prose are not as tasteless as Harding's runaway alliteration, they certainly need revision.

The American Bar Association has pointed out that prospects for the profession seem unlimited. Prophesying prosperity, the Association has proposed a plan for expansion of the profession.

Although he was a serious student, he disliked courses with a strong stress on stringent requirements.

As you can see, "p's" and "s's" require special caution because they can be especially irritating. Too many "-ly's" or "-ion's" can also be annoying. Two "-ly's" in a row are likely to be one too many—as in "He runs marvelously quickly for a big man." Two "-ion's" are a blemish; more than two, a deformity. "Expansion of the profession" might be tolerable, but "his submission of a proposition for the elimination of costly expenses" is not.

Our favorite piece of sing-songy wording is this one: "the scarlet harlot." This was the brainchild of Noah Webster, the nineteenth-century American lexicographer.[10] Having finished most of his work on dictionaries, spelling books, and the like, Webster devoted himself to an all-important task of expurgation. He set out to clean up the Bible for genteel readers. He sought to rid the King James Version of all its offensive words—"stink" and "belly," for instance, as well as others even more shocking: "bowels," "breasts," "womb," "lust," "fornication," and, of course, "whore" and its many derivatives. And when in the New Testament he came to "the scarlet whore of Babylon," he devised that marvelous phrase, "the scarlet harlot."

Remember that phrase. It will encourage you to review your prose with an attentive ear, lest you, like Webster, commit some terrible sin against the canons of prose harmonics.

Exercises

I. The following passage contains nothing but what we have called "longwinded sentences"—sentences that rush breathlessly ahead from first word to last, with never a pause to slow the pace or vary the rhythm.

[10] We are indebted to Noel Perrin for calling that phrase to our attention. The tale of Webster's attempt to purify the Bible is told in Perrin's thoroughly entertaining book, *Dr. Bowdler's Legacy: A History of Expurgated Books in England and America* (New York: Doubleday Anchor Books, 1971), pp. 98–101; and, at greater length, in his "Noah and the Scarlet Harlot," *A Passport Secretly Green* (New York: St. Martin's Press, 1961), pp. 142–52.

Revise the passage to remedy that shortcoming. Break up the monotony of those lengthy sentences by dividing them into shorter ones or by otherwise inserting some pauses in their midst.

This monotonous prose is derived from a skillfully varied piece of writing by Gore Vidal.

> It is possible to stop most drug addiction in the United States within a very short time simply by making all drugs available and selling them at cost and by labeling each drug with a precise description of what good or bad effect the drug will have on the taker even though this accurate labeling will require heroic honesty. Don't say that marijuana is addictive or dangerous when millions of people know that it is neither although "speed" can kill most unpleasantly and heroin is addictive and difficult to kick. I will go on record as saying that I have tried once almost every drug and liked none and have thereby disproved the popular Fu Manchu theory that a single whiff of opium will enslave the mind but I know that nevertheless many drugs are bad for certain people to take and they should be told why in a sensible way.

II. The following passage loses much of its potential force by ending every sentence with trivial words. Revise the passage so that every sentence will end with an important word or phrase. Delete the trivial words or move them to an earlier point in the sentence.

> To extract confessions from suspected witches, the inquisitors used brutal tortures that took a variety of forms. The rack would stretch the woman's body until she either confessed or died, as probably everyone knows. For the *peine forte et dure* she lay upon her back and was pressed with heavy weights until she confessed or died, just as was the case with the torture mentioned previously. The thumbscrew slowly crushed her thumb by twisting it and thereby causing pain in considerable amounts. *La fosse* was ingenious in a devilish sort of way. The victim was buried in wet cement up to the neck or thereabouts. The cement cracked the victim's bones as it hardened and contracted at a slow pace.

III. The following sentences are marred by a variety of aural offenses—the clumsy reiteration of sounds or whole words, the overly long series of prepositional phrases, the lumping together of discordant short words, and the sing-songy repetition of adverb-verb and adjective-noun locutions. Revise the sentences to remove those disagreeable sound effects.

> 1. The president of Peoria College has persistently rejected all proposals for the promotion of professors without a Ph.D.
> 2. The brave Odysseus finally returned to his patient Penelope, but

he immediately discovered that his faithful Penelope was being cruelly molested by greedy suitors.

3. With tranquil determination and methodical meditation, a dedicated Yogi bravely tries to untie the tangled knots of his troubled thoughts.

4. As soon as he saw the first star shining in the sky's soft darkness, the hermit began the recitation of his meditation on salvation.

5. In 1474, in Basel, Switzerland, one of the most farcical episodes in the ludicrous history of the vile persecution of supposed witches took place when a diabolical rooster was put to death for the unnatural crime of laying an egg.

6. Prairie dogs provide protection for themselves by the practice of establishing sentinels at a distance of a hundred feet from their "town" of burrows. Because of the presence of the sentinels few of the enemies of the prairie dogs succeed in approaching the town without detection.

7. Devout Hindus pray to a great variety of images. The Hindus prostrate themselves before these images and offer the images sacrificial gifts of flowers, rice, and scented oil. And yet the Hindus do not believe that these images are themselves Brahma or Vishnu, but merely the representatives of Brahma or Vishnu. Consequently, the Hindus prostrate themselves not to the images themselves but to Brahma and Vishnu, whom these images represent.

IV. Devise graceful revisions for the cumbersome noun phrases that follow. For example:

Original: manpower utilization procedures
Revision: procedures for making the best use of our employees

Original: teenager peer-group value system
Revision: the values of most teenagers

Original: accuracy maintenance strategy
Revision: a strategy for maintaining accuracy

1. insulation utilization methods
2. efficiency maintenance techniques
3. information transmission procedures
4. suicide prevention therapy
5. profit maximization strategy
6. privacy protection legislation
7. personality disorder evolution
8. reading deficiency correction technique
9. good community relations maintenance procedures
10. childhood indoctrination prevention procedures

V. Take another look at the passage on pages 143–44 in which Joseph Ecclesine limits himself to words of one syllable. Revise that passage in order to vary its rhythm by varying the length of its words. Inject some words with two or more syllables, as a change in pace from the monosyllabic style of Mr. Ecclesine.

While revising, you might want to test out Herbert Spencer's hypothesis that a good way to emphasize important thoughts is to express them in multisyllabic words surrounded by shorter words. See whether you can reserve your lengthier words for thoughts that deserve special emphasis. Then see whether those words do in fact succeed in emphasizing those thoughts.

VI. Reread one of your old essays with your "mind's ear" alert for the sounds of your sentences. Revise the sentences whenever you find them guilty of the various lapses in prose harmony discussed in this chapter. And by all means go beyond the recommendations of this chapter if you feel so inclined. The chapter has been mainly negative in its recommendations; it has pointed out how you can avoid conspicuous blemishes in the sound of your sentences. The following chapters will explain how you can achieve added diversity and forcefulness. Why wait until you have read the following chapters? If you can already find ways to add diversity and forcefulness—and undoubtedly you can—then you should certainly go ahead and do so.

12

Parallelism

Parallelism is one of of the chief means by which you can achieve eloquence. But the kind of parallelism we refer to is not simply *grammatical;* it might better be called *rhetorical parallelism.* An example will clarify this distinction. Here is an instance of mere grammatical parallelism:

> Women are placed on the marketplace with certain fixed values. *Each woman gets so much for long blonde hair; good legs can help raise her value; another asset is good breasts.*

Those three groups of words joined by semicolons are grammatically parallel because they are all clauses, but the clauses differ so much in length and structure that the parallelism is scarcely noticeable. It is too loose to be rhetorically effective—too loose to be called rhetorical parallelism. The following construction, however, would qualify for that term. The parallel elements resemble one another much more closely, and the parallelism is therefore much more effective.

> Women are placed on the marketplace with fixed physical values— so much for long blonde hair, so much for good legs, so much for breasts.

> Michael Korda [1]

Parallel elements with this close a resemblance are said to be *balanced.* Therefore the distinction we have been making can be summarized in

[1] *Male Chauvinism* (New York: Random House, 1974), p. 51.

151

the following formula: Rhetorical parallelism equals grammatical parallelism plus balance.

That sentence about women on the marketplace suggests the eloquence of which parallelism is capable. One reason for this eloquence is the human fondness for symmetry and regularity, the same fondness that lies at the root of our admiration for Greek temples and oriental mandalas. Another reason is the power of repetition, the same power that excites a primitive tribe to anger or ecstasy at the sound of a beating drum.

Unfortunately, apprentice writers generally fail to take advantage of parallelism. It is an easy device to use, and yet, as one scholar has said, "The resourcefulness of student writers in obscuring and avoiding parallels is boundless." [2] This chapter will encourage the opposite kind of resourcefulness—boundless in its zeal to experiment with parallelism. To be sure, this device, like most other rhetorical devices, can be used too often and thus become an irritating mannerism; but the great majority of writers-in-training use it too little rather than too much.

Parallelism can be eloquent even when it contains only two elements—two words, phrases, or clauses. In the last few paragraphs we have aimed for this kind of eloquence with such phrases as "the human fondness for symmetry and regularity," "our admiration for Greek temples and oriental mandalas," and "excites a primitive tribe to anger or ecstasy." Note the effectiveness of the parallel pairs in the following sentences—one by a student and two by professionals:

> *Just when my husband granted that I was a person, just when he granted that I had the right to fulfill myself through a career,* I discovered that I detested him.

> Shakespeare's noblest characters express sentiments of *patriotic or personal* honor which to young modern ears sound *flamboyant or unconvincing.*
>
> Madeleine Doran [3]

> The elders [in the black community] became angry and shouted that this was the way the world was and they [the young] must learn to accept it—how else could they get a job *shining shoes or cleaning toilets?*
>
> Philip Slater [4]

---

[2] W. K. Wimsatt, Jr., *The Prose Style of Samuel Johnson* (New Haven: Yale University Press, 1963), p. viii.

[3] *Something About Swans* (Madison: University of Wisconsin Press, 1973), p. 45.

[4] *The Pursuit of Loneliness* (Boston: Beacon Press, 1970), p. 49.

Perhaps the most forceful kind of two-part parallelism is *antithesis*. This is a balancing of contrasts or opposites. For example:

> To the mighty general war was a glorious enterprise; to the plodding foot soldier it was a grimy hardship.

> Ambition in a man is praised; ambition in a woman is denounced as unfeminine.

> Let both sides explore what problems unite us instead of belaboring those problems which divide us.
>
> John F. Kennedy, Inaugural Address

> We will have to repent in this generation not merely for the vitriolic words and actions of the bad people, but for the appalling silence of the good people.
>
> Martin Luther King, Jr.

Antithesis is a favorite device of experienced writers, but it is certainly not beyond the reach of apprentices. A young black student who moved from Mississippi to northern California wrote the skillful sentence that follows, in which two antitheses are combined in a double-barreled condemnation:

> I soon discovered that the Land of the Redwoods could be as racist as the Land of Cotton, and that the Yankee police could be as bigoted as any good-ol'-boy Southern sheriff.

The student who wrote the following sentences had a similar fascination with double antitheses.

> I was told about good but not about evil; I was shown pictures of saints glowing with ecstasy, but not of the damned souls writhing in the flames of Hell.

> I heard about golden highways but not about dark alleys; I heard about princesses but not about whores.

> I knew about privileges but not about responsibilities; I was eager to partake of all joys, but wished to avoid all pains.

> I learned about the multiple orgasm but not about gonorrhea; I learned about the bites and scratches of lovemaking, but not about the oozing sores of syphillis.

This writer is experimenting, quite skillfully, with one special kind of parallelism. Not only does each sentence contain two antitheses, but those two are closely balanced *with each other*. Consider the final sentence. The first antithesis contrasts a pleasure of sexuality (the multiple orgasm) with a pain (gonorrhea); then the second antithesis does the same thing—contrasts pleasure (the bites and scratches of lovemaking) with pain (the oozing sores of syphillis). We should point to further evidence of this writer's skill: the alliteration that intensifies each antithesis. The hard "g" in "orgasm" is echoed by the "g" in "gonorrhea"; the "s" sounds in "bites and scratches" are echoed in "the sores of syphillis." And let us mention one other sign of the writer's artistry. Note the *onomatopoeia* (the sounds that imitate sense) in her final phrases. "Bites and scratches"—with its sharp "t" and "c" and "tch"—sounds a bit like actual biting and scratching; and "oozing sores" sounds as if it oozes. . . . Does any of this make you wince? If so, you can regard that as evidence of the writer's accomplishment.

If we were to criticize her sentences at all, we would do so only on the grounds that she has put all four of them in a single essay. One sentence with so intricate and emphatic a pattern is certain to be admired. Perhaps two will be admired. But when the reader comes to a third and then a fourth, he is likely to accuse the writer of making too much of a good thing.

Up to this point we have focused on two-part parallelism, but parallels can also be eloquent when they number three or more. Three-part parallelism is so effective that it has earned itself two special labels: *triplet* and *triad*. Mark Harris, in the following passage, goes so far as to use triads within his triads:

> The hippie "scene" on Haight Street in San Francisco was so very visual that photographers came from everywhere to shoot it, reporters came from everywhere to write it up with speed, and opportunists came from everywhere to exploit its drug addiction, its sexual possibility, and its political or social ferment. Prospective hippies came from everywhere for one "summer of love" or maybe longer, some older folk to indulge their latent hippie tendencies, and the police to contain, survey, or arrest.[5]

The first sentence contains three parallel clauses: "photographers came . . . ," "reporters came . . . ," and "opportunists came. . . ." And in the final clause we find a triad of nouns: "its drug *addiction*, its sexual *possibility*, and its political or social *ferment*." Again in the second sentence Harris uses three parallel clauses, though this time the second and third clauses don't make their verbs explicit: "prospective hippies came . . . ," "some older folk [came] . . . ," and "the police

[5] "The Flowering of the Hippies," *Atlantic Monthly*, September 1967, p. 63. Copyright © 1967, by The Atlantic Monthly Company, Boston, Mass. Reprinted with permission of the author and publisher.

[came]. . . ." And again the final clause ends with a shorter triad—this time a series of verbs: "contain, survey, or arrest."

A parallel series of more than three terms can achieve power through the persistent regularity of its rhythm. Philip Slater bangs a steady beat to denounce popular magazines for their love of easy solutions to hard problems. Each month, he says, the magazines announce that

> our transportation crisis will be solved by a bigger plane or a wider road, mental illness with a pill, poverty with a law, slums with a bulldozer, urban conflict with a gas, racism with a goodwill gesture.[6]

And here two student writers experiment with extended parallelism:

> I spent much of my time photographing the living things of the Mohave Desert: cactus flowers in yellow bloom, an indigo bush with dark blue flowers, kangaroo rats hopping frantically over the sand, a vulture circling overhead, a rattlesnake basking in the sun.

> The prose style of William Faulkner has been grossly overrated. The sentences are too long and complex; the parenthetical expressions and interrupting modifiers are annoying; the shifts in tense are often pointless and confusing; the metaphors are usually imprecise and sometimes bizarre.

Occasionally you may wish to extend parallelism beyond the confines of a single sentence. You may wish to use *parallel sentences.* By this device you can achieve special emphasis for important ideas—as Winston Churchill did in one of his radio speeches during World War II:

> We shall fight on the beaches. We shall fight on the landing grounds. We shall fight in the fields and in the streets. We shall fight in the hills. We shall never surrender.

Note the recurrence of the phrase "we shall fight." This is an instance of what the classical rhetoricians labeled *anaphora*—repeated words at the beginning of successive phrases, clauses, or sentences. The device is usually saved for passages of great intensity—Churchill's appeal to the English people, or the following passage by Bernard Shaw, in which Shaw denounces the belief that if a man cannot lift himself out of poverty, we should let him be poor.

> Now what does this Let Him Be Poor mean? It means let him be weak. Let him be ignorant. Let him become a nucleus of disease. Let him be a standing exhibition and example of ugliness and dirt. Let him have rickety children. Let him be cheap and let him drag his

[6] *The Pursuit of Loneliness* (Boston: Beacon Press, 1970), pp. 12–13.

fellows down to his own price by selling himself to do their work. Let his habitations turn our cities into poisonous congeries of slums. Let his daughters infect our young men with the diseases of the streets, and his sons revenge him by turning the nation's manhood into scrofula, cowardice, cruelty, hypocrisy, political imbecility, and all the other fruits of oppression and malnutrition.[7]

The hammering blows of the first half of the passage—the strident short sentences and the insistent "let him's"—soon give way to the longer sentence that ends the passage; but even in that final sentence Shaw hits away at his opponents with the two-part parallelism of "Let his daughters infect . . . and his sons revenge," and then with an angry extended series ("scrofula, cowardice," etc.), and finally with the two-part phrase "oppression and malnutrition." All these parallels combine to convey a tone not much different from that of evangelism or prophecy—the tone of a man who knows he is right and insists that we listen.

The passage by Shaw raises a question we have touched on only in passing: How much parallelism is too much? We can't answer this question precisely—can't set down rigid rules to prevent you from going too far with parallels. The only reliable guide is your own good taste. As you reread your prose, does the parallelism seem too conspicuous? Does it call too much attention to itself? If so, you must revise accordingly.

The Shaw passage on the consequences of poverty is so remarkable a display of parallelism that an essay might not be able to accommodate more than one such passage. If a writer exhibited such pyrotechnics twice or three times, the reader's initial admiration might change into amusement or annoyance. But this has not always been the case. Readers in the eighteenth century admired, and many writers sought to emulate, the sustained and elaborate parallelisms of Samuel Johnson. But today, though we may still admire Johnson's style, not many of us would be tempted to emulate it. Here are two samples of the Johnsonian "balanced style"—both from the *Rambler* essay (number 14) in which Johnson pointed out that an author's writings are likely to be wiser and wittier than his conversation.

[When the author enters public life,] if his temper is soft and timorous, he is diffident and bashful, from the knowledge of his defects; or if he was born with spirit and resolution, he is ferocious and arrogant, from the consciousness of his merits. He is either dissipated by the awe of company, and unable to recollect his reading and arrange his arguments, or he is hot and dogmatical, quick in oppo-

---

[7] Preface to *Major Barbara*. Reprinted by permission of The Society of Authors on behalf of the Bernard Shaw Estate.

sition and tenacious in defence, disabled by his own violence, and confused by his haste to triumph.

A transition from an author's book to his conversation is too often like an entrance into a large city after a distant prospect. Remotely, we see nothing but spires of temples and turrets of palaces, and imagine it the residence of splendor, grandeur, and magnificence; but, when we have passed the gates, we find it perplexed with narrow passages, disgraced with despicable cottages, embarrassed with obstructions, and clouded with smoke.

Each sentence in these passages has at least two instances of parallelism. And in several spots we find extremely close balancing—almost a word-for-word correspondence between the parallel elements. Consider the balanced phrasing in the first sentence:

if his temper is soft and diffident
if he was born with spirit and resolution

he is diffident and bashful
he is ferocious and arrogant

from the knowledge of his defects
from the consciousness of his merits

Remarkably skillful—but probably too symmetrical to be imitated by contemporary writers. Modern prose, as we have said, makes abundant use of parallelism; but the parallelism is more varied—less balanced, less symmetrical—than that which we find in Johnson.

Here, for instance, is a passage from Alan McGlashan's *The Savage and Beautiful Country*, a study in Jungian "depth psychology." The "Dreamer" of which McGlashan speaks is the Unconscious—the mysterious force that lurks beneath the conscious mind.

With the Dreamer you never know where you are. At one moment he chills by an inhuman cruelty, at another uplifts with a sheer grandeur of spiritual vision; he irritates us by trivialities, silences us with an unreasonable wisdom, charms us by his subtlety and wit, and often enough disgusts us with his coarse and bestial fantasies. In fact, he behaves with the strangeness, the power, the fascination and the unpredictability of a being from another world. . . .[8]

The first sentence contains no parallelism. The second contains an extended series of parallels and thereby risks becoming too symmetrical to please the modern reader. But the sentence displays variety as well as regularity. It is neither so symmetrical as to sound rigid or contrived nor so unsymmetrical as to lose its emphatic rhythm.

[8] *The Savage and Beautiful Country* (Boston: Houghton Mifflin, 1967), p. 147.

Take a close look at those parallel constructions.

he	chills	by	an inhuman cruelty
	uplifts	with	a sheer grandeur of spiritual vision
he	irritates us	by	trivialities
	silences us	with	an unreasonable wisdom
	charms us	by	his subtlety and wit
	disgusts us	with	his coarse and bestial fantasies

As our brackets indicate, the series contains three antitheses, to express the mixed tortures and blessings that erupt from the Unconscious. These antitheses, however, are not rigidly antithetical. If they were, then the first pair of opposites would go something like this: "chills with an inhuman cruelty" and "warms with a divine mercy." But because a long series of such precise antitheses might be too symmetrical to hold our interest, McGlashan does not insist on being perfectly antithetical. And he gains variety by other means as well. He omits *us* from the first and second constructions, inserts another *he* in the third construction, and varies his prepositions, alternating *by* and *with* rather than keeping to one or the other. And, most important, he varies the length and structure of those phrases that follow the prepositions—moving from "an inhuman cruelty" to "a sheer grandeur of spiritual vision" and then to "trivialities," and so forth.

The final sentence in the passage contains another parallel series, a series of four nouns: strangeness, power, fascination, and unpredictability. Does this series, added to the previous one, give us too much parallelism? Does forceful repetition lapse into monotonous regularity? We think not—because this series greatly differs from the previous one in both pattern and pace. There we had six long phrases. Here we have merely four nouns.

The best modern prose, then, uses the forceful rhythm of parallelism but does not allow it to become tediously repetitive. Here is another passage that illustrates this point:

> Let us spell out the worst about this notorious mass-man and his mass-culture. He has a meager idea of the abundant life, confusing quantity with quality, size with greatness, comfort with culture, gadgetry with genius. He has as little appreciation of pure science as of the fine arts, and as little capacity for the discipline that both require; although he may stand in awe of them his real veneration goes to the engineers and inventors, the manufacturers of True Romances and Tin Pan Alley airs. He is frequently illiberal, suspicious of "radical" ideas, scornful of "visionary" ideals, hostile to "aliens"; in America he has developed a remarkable vocabulary of contempt that manages to embrace most of mankind—the nigger,

the mick, the chink, the wop, the kike, et cetera. He is the chief foe of the individualism he boasts of, a patron of standard brands in tastes and opinions as in material possessions, with a morbid fear of being thought queer or different from the Joneses; individuality to him is "personality," which may be acquired in six easy lessons or his money back, is then turned on to win friends and influence people, and is confirmed by the possession of "personalized" objects, which are distinguished only by having his initials on them. In short, he appears to be a spoiled child, fundamentally ungrateful to the scientists, political philosophers, social reformers, and religious idealists who have given him his unprecedented opportunities. He is therefore the natural prey of advertisers, politicians, millionaire publishers, and would-be dictators.

Herbert J. Muller [9]

Symmetry alternates with asymmetry. Regularity is tempered by variety. Even though Muller makes copious use of parallelism, and thereby strengthens his indictment of mass-man, the prose never sounds contrived and never becomes monotonous.

Exercises

I. Convert each of the following passages into a single sentence that uses parallel structure. Make the parallelism as closely balanced as possible. Rearrange ideas wherever you please, and delete unnecessary words.

1. Rocky was an excellent cook. He was also a charming host.
2. Scientists and mystics have ignored each other's field of knowledge. When considering each other's goals, they have shown only distrust.
3. The hero of *The Graduate* disrupts a marriage ceremony to steal the bride. And to beat away the crowd a huge cross is grabbed by him from the church altar.
4. She was a skilled accountant. As an investor, however, she was incompetent.
5. I disapprove of what you say. Your right to say it, however, is something that will be defended by me to the death. (Derived from a sentence by Voltaire.)
6. He loved to read the greatest works of the greatest writers. But

[9] From *The Uses of the Past: Profiles of Former Societies* by Herbert J. Muller. © 1952 by Oxford University Press, Inc. Reprinted by permission. *The Uses of the Past* (New York: Oxford University Press, 1952).

the kind of idle chatter that simpleminded talkers come up with earned only his scorn.

7. Senator Throckmorton is a friend to the employer. He is also a champion of the worker. Further, he is a veteran at cadging votes.

8. He wished to sell his stamp collection. Then, he hoped, he could retire to Switzerland. Once he was in Switzerland, he would write a newspaper column. It would be intended for people who felt lost. It would also serve those who were lonely.

9. She had never before seen so large a collection of such people. Fawning starlets made up a part of the collection. Also present were some opportunistic promoters. Further, she saw a number of vulgar, unscrupulous producers. Finally, the group contained some scheming swindlers.

10. So have I loitered my life away, reading books and doing other such things. I have looked at pictures. Sometimes plays have drawn me to them. I have done a good deal of hearing. Thinking is something else I have done. And I have written on what pleased me best. (Derived from a sentence by William Hazlitt.)

II. In the passage that follows, the parallelism is overly symmetrical and soon becomes monotonous. Enliven the passage by introducing greater variety. You need not destroy the parallelism. Simply make it less rigidly symmetrical.

If you like, you may fabricate new insights or information regarding Professor Simon.

Professor Simon is a demanding and rigorous instructor, and yet a gentle and sympathetic counselor. She is a detached, objective physicist, yet she craves the conversation of her students and the companionship of her colleagues. She is prim and austere, yet she sometimes tells a ribald joke and rouses raucous laughter. She can be rudely blunt, but is consistently candid. She is conservative in her politics but generous toward her neighbors. She is said to be deeply distrustful toward her fellow human beings, but she has been known to give a quarter of her salary to impoverished students.

III. Find the parallel structures in the passages listed below. Then evaluate each author's use of parallelism. Is it forceful? Is it too persistently symmetrical? Does it become monotonous? (On page 159 we mentioned that in our judgment Herbert J. Muller's extended use of parallels does not become over-symmetrical or monotonous. But we might have been wrong. Feel free to dispute our judgment.)

1. Germaine Greer on the modern ideal of feminine beauty (pp. 19-20)

2. Herbert J. Muller on "mass-man and his mass-culture" (pp. 158-59)

3. H. L. Mencken on the "incredibly obscure and malodorous style" of Thorstein Veblen (pp. 202-3)

4. James Thurber on the editorial expertise of Harold Ross (pp. 203-4)

5. Theodore Roosevelt on the "doctrine of the strenuous life" (pp. 218-19)

6. John F. Kennedy on the survival of liberty (p. 234)

IV. Go over one of your old essays to see how many of your sentences contained rhetorical parallelism. Then see whether you can reshape other sentences to achieve further parallelism. (But of course don't use so much parallelism that it becomes painfully conspicuous, and don't impose it on sentences in which it would not be appropriate.)

13

Sentence
Variety

Too much of anything—sex, money, playing a harp in heaven—can wind up being a bore. And too many sentences of the same size and structure can lead to boring prose, even when the message is far from boring:

I was in Soledad state prison. I fell in with a group of young blacks. They were like myself. They were in vociferous rebellion. They rebelled against the national situation as they perceived it. It was a continuation of slavery on a higher plane. We cursed everything American. We cursed baseball and hot dogs. We had no respect for politicians or preachers. We had no respect for lawyers. We had no respect for governors or Presidents. We had no respect for senators or congressmen. . . .

Compare this monotonous prose with the original from which it was derived—a passage in which Eldridge Cleaver tells of his bitterness when, in 1954, Americans debated whether black students should be integrated with white. Cleaver, at eighteen, had been sent to jail for possession of marijuana.

In Soledad state prison, I fell in with a group of young blacks who, like myself, were in vociferous rebellion against what we perceived as a continuation of slavery on a higher plane. We cursed everything American—including baseball and hot dogs. All respect we may have had for politicians, preachers, lawyers, governors, Presidents, senators, congressmen was utterly destroyed as we watched them

162

temporizing and compromising over right and wrong, over legality and illegality, over constitutionality and unconstitutionality. We knew that in the end what they were clashing over was us, what to do with the blacks, and whether or not to start treating us as human beings. I despised all of them.[1]

The power of this style comes largely from its emphatic variations. Cleaver uses both of the means by which you can vary, and invigorate, the rhythm of your prose. He varies his sentences both in *length* and in *structure*.

LENGTH

The average length of your sentences is probably somewhere between ten and twenty words. (Popular magazine articles average between fifteen and twenty words per sentence; literary and scholarly articles climb to an average somewhere between twenty and thirty words.) You can discover your average whenever you have time to do some counting. And whatever your average happens to be, you should try to vary from it occasionally. If your sentences average out at twenty words, inject some shorter sentences (maybe five or ten words long) and some longer ones (thirty, forty, or fifty words long). This simple strategy is one of the most effective for achieving a pleasurable and forceful variety in your sentences.

The passage by Eldridge Cleaver, though it averages roughly 23 words a sentence, is actually composed of two very short sentences and three long ones. (The sentence-by-sentence word count is 33, 9, 36, 30, and 5.) The passage is unusual in that it contains *no* medium-length sentences, only short ones and long ones. But this tactic seems appropriate here. Cleaver's long sentences are undeniably powerful, especially the third and fourth sentences because of their extended parallelism. His short sentences are powerful by virtue of their simple straightforwardness. And his alternation between short sentences and long ones heightens the power of *all* the sentences and thus helps to convey the intensity of his anger.

We should stress the value of the short sentence. Some writers less proficient than Cleaver shy away from the short sentence on the grounds that it seems amateurish; and so it does when it appears in a long, monotonous string of such sentences. But a short sentence that follows a long one, or several long ones, can be sharply emphatic. No strategy is more successful at emphasizing an important idea—as the Cleaver passage

[1] "On Becoming," *Soul on Ice* (New York: McGraw-Hill, 1968), p. 4.

illustrates: "We cursed everything American—including baseball and hot dogs." "I despised all of them."

STRUCTURE

Varying the length of your sentences is one means for achieving variety. The other is to vary the structure. Our language offers such a rich assortment of sentence structures that there is no excuse for sinking into a tediously repetitive style in which all the sentences seem to resemble one another. Further, a mastery of the various structures will enable the writer to express nuances of tone and meaning that would otherwise be outside his range of possibilities. Therefore the apprentice writer who wants to get beyond his apprenticeship would do well to practice diligently the structures set forth in the following pages.

Perhaps the best kind of practice is *imitation*. Passed down by the rhetoricians of classical Greece and Rome, this exercise retained its importance in the schools of the Renaissance (such as those that educated Shakespeare and Milton); and today it continues to figure in the education of the young in many British and Continental schools. Some aspiring writers resent the exercise because it calls for little originality in thought or expression; it involves only the imitation of somebody else's sentences. But writers who have worked with imitation long enough to let it produce its effects will testify that those effects are considerable. What begins as copying ends as something radically different; it ultimately frees the writer to express his thoughts with a greater subtlety and sophistication than he had known was possible.

Try the exercise for yourself, and see whether it enhances your skill. Suppose you are working with this sentence by Virginia Woolf:

> Most commonly we come to books with blurred and divided minds, asking of fiction that it shall be true, of poetry that it shall be false, of biography that it shall be flattering, of history that it shall enforce our own prejudices.[2]

You might begin by performing a rhetorical analysis, noting that the sentence opens with a generality and then adds four instances to explain the generality and support it with evidence. And if you happen to know one of the grammars of English, you can analyze the sentence grammatically, noting that it opens with an independent clause and then moves into a long modifier that starts with an *-ing* verb form and contains a series of subordinate clauses. But even without the advantage

---

[2] "How Should One Read a Book?" *The Second Common Reader* (New York: Harcourt, Brace and World Harvest Books, 1960), p. 235.

of a grammatical terminology, you can easily divide the sentence into its parts and then imitate each part. You can begin by imitating the opening words:

> Most commonly we come to books with blurred and divided minds . . .

> Usually we judge strangers by means of inflexible and indefensible stereotypes . . .

You can go on from there, part by part, until you come up with something like the following reconstruction—not a precise, word-for-word imitation, but one that comes close enough to be valuable to the imitator:

> Usually we judge strangers by means of inflexible and indefensible stereotypes, expecting of all teachers that they will be altruistic, of all business people that they will be opportunistic, of all advertising people that they will be liars, of all police that they will be inhumane.

Now, exactly how do you benefit by performing this kind of imitation? For one thing, you learn how to fashion certain valuable kinds of sentences—in this case, a particular variety of the so-called "loose sentence." Second, and more important, you develop a new versatility in your shaping of sentences—a new boldness in experimentation and a new facility in devising sentences with just the right rhythm and the best arrangement of words.

BEGINNINGS

One way to vary your sentences is to vary the beginnings. Most of your sentences will begin with an essential idea—an independent clause and its necessary modifiers. But occasionally you can begin with subordinate elements and save the independent clause for later.

In the next few pages we point out several of the subordinate elements with which you can begin your sentences. No doubt you use several of the elements in that way already, but you may find some that are new to you. Those new ones, of course, are precisely the ones you should practice whenever you can find some time for doing sentence imitations.[3] Subordinate clause:

---

[3] Most of the exemplary sentences in this chapter are repeated from our earlier chapter on subordination (Chapter 8), where we talked about the same sentence patterns but with a different purpose. That chapter serves as an introduction to this one. If you have doubts about whether you mastered it on your first reading, this would be a good time for review.

Just before the shaman goes into his trance, he raises his hands like a man preparing to dive into deep water.

While waiting for her first social security check, Mrs. Collins decided to earn some money by telling fortunes. [An elliptical clause: it omits the words *she was* between *while* and *waiting.*]

Prepositional phrase:

In the drive for greater income, the American blue-collar worker has fallen far behind the executive and the owner.

To many young people the ritual of keeping up with the Joneses seems a meaningless remnant from a false and outmoded religion.

Participial phrase:

Throwing her calculating machine out the window, she vowed never again to look at a column of figures.

Terrified by the possibility of failing the exam, Johnson became so nervous that he did indeed manage to fail.

Gerund phrase:

After deciding to educate their child at home, the Blanchards hired a lawyer to protect them against reprisals from the public school system.

Absolute phrase:

His confidence broken, he doubted whether he could ever again appear before an audience.

His head swimming with disjunctive syllogisms, he still couldn't believe that formal logic had any relation to real life.

Appositive noun:

A caustic and demanding *critic,* John Simon delights in tearing apart mediocre films.

Essentially a *figurehead* manipulated by generals and politicians, Emperor Hirohito could not prevent Japan from moving toward conflict with the Western democracies.

The *noose,* the *knife,* the *shotgun,* the telescopic *sight,* the magnum *revolver,* the gushing *blood,* the *face* contorted with pain, the *body* writhing in agony—these have become standard fare in the movies of violence.

Appositive adjective:

Always *resourceful,* he rigged up a quadraphonic system with speakers taken from junk-yard radios.

Silent, serene, oblivious to all their questions, the guru sat before them for the entire morning.

Adverb:

Slowly, cautiously, he tiptoed through the tulips.

The kind of sentence you have been looking at is one variety of the *periodic sentence,* a structure noted for its climactic ending. By offering the reader nothing but subordinate elements at the outset, you force him to wait expectantly, perhaps impatiently, for your main idea. Then he reaches the main idea at the very end of the sentence—an emphatic position even when it contains something less important than a main idea. To be sure, the climactic effect is slight if the introductory subordinate element is brief, as it is in most of the preceding sentences. The periodic structure displays its full power only when the introductory element is long enough to create a certain suspense in the reader's mind:

Although Joan exchanged cheerful greetings with the other secretaries, and though she nodded sympathetically at their grievances, chortled at their jokes, and listened patiently to their gossip, she detested every one of them.

While the alienated young people in America turned to the East in search of the equanimity of Taoism, the "self" of Hinduism, and the selflessness of Buddhism, the East turned to America in search of efficient technology and hard cash.

Be cautious with periodic sentences. One danger is that you may use too many of them, in which case your reader will become so accustomed to their powerful structure that they will lose all their power and seem painfully monotonous. Another danger is that you may use the periodic structure with the wrong kind of material and wind up with a bad case of anticlimax. Your patient reader, after the suspense of waiting for an important idea, will experience a terrible let-down:

Pale with terror, sweating feverishly, struggling to shape a grin but able to produce only a trembling simper, *he stood there.*

The only child of Jewish parents, neither of them wealthy, but both determined to give their son the best education Vienna could provide, *Sigmund Freud was born in 1856.*

In both sentences a big build-up leads to a little idea—as if a majestic march ushered in Elwood P. Gump, an inefficient dog-catcher from Middletown, Connecticut. Those sentences would be infinitely more effective if the subordinate elements were moved from the beginning to the end:

He stood there, pale with terror, sweating feverishly, struggling to shape a grin, but able to produce only a trembling simper.

Sigmund Freud was born in 1856, the only child of Jewish parents, neither of them wealthy, but both determined to give their son the best education Vienna could offer.

ENDINGS

Those last two sentences introduce the whole topic of subordinate elements that come *after* an independent clause rather than before. Some years ago, in the 1940s and 50s, teachers of composition had little to say about subordinate elements in the terminal position. If you needed to vary your sentences, you were told to do so by putting a subordinate element at the beginnings of a few sentences, not at the ends. But now, thanks largely to the efforts of the late Francis Christensen, the end of the sentence is getting more attention.[4]

In the next few pages we point out several of the subordinate elements that can come at the end of an independent clause or the end of a sentence.

Subordinate clause:

Ruth Jackson told us about the sordid aspects of the medical profession *after we had chosen her to be our family doctor.*

Subordinate clause introduced by a colon (or a dash):

We can draw only one conclusion from these laboratory tests: *Mr. Bentley's fondness for homemade wine has ruined his stomach.* (An effective way to emphasize the sentence-ending clause.)

Noun in apposition:

He learned how to fix cars from Miss Alice McMahon, *an elderly spinster.*

He values only one thing—*his new color television set.* (An excellent means for emphasizing the appositive noun.)

He learned how to fix cars from Miss Alice McMahon, *an elderly spinster* who used to spend all her spare time at the Ford garage.

She asked her friends if they knew a reliable mechanic, *a mechanic* who would do simple repairs without charging as if he had a Ph.D. in automotive engineering.

[4] Our entire discussion of sentence variety is indebted to the work of Professor Christensen, particularly his *Notes Toward a New Rhetoric* (New York: Harper & Row, 1967). Our discussion is also indebted to Virginia Tufte, *Grammar as Style* (New York: Holt, Rinehart and Winston, 1971).

The reward for his hard work seemed more like a punishment—
ruined eyesight, headaches, insomnia, and *loneliness.*

I can still remember his cruelty—*the snarling tone, the cutting words,
the savage eagerness* to scold and insult and condemn anyone who
disagreed with him on the smallest point.

Adjective in apposition:

The children finally came home, *exhausted* and *hungry.*

The guru sat before them for the entire morning—*silent, serene,
oblivious* to all their questions.

Mark is a gullible young man, *helpless* against the pronouncements
of every used-car salesman, politician, and latter-day prophet.

Participle:

The little boy hid way in the back of the closet, *trembling* at the
thought of being detected.

The job troubled him deeply, *forcing* him to meet people he didn't
like and *steering* him toward a future he detested.

Absolute phrase:

She slumped over the desk, *her thoughts leaping back to those days
at the beach.*

He waited impatiently, *his courage sinking fast, the old anxieties
returning, the twitch on his brow becoming just as violent as it used
to be.*

Several of these illustrations suggest how elaborate your sentence
endings can become, and Francis Christensen has quoted sentences
whose endings have an even greater complexity—this sentence by Hemingway, for instance:

George was coming down in the telemark position, kneeling, one leg
forward and bent, the other trailing, his sticks hanging like some
insect's thin legs, kicking up puffs of snow, and finally the whole
kneeling, trailing figure coming around in a beautiful right curve,
crouching, the legs shot forward and back, the body leaning out
against the swing, the sticks accenting the curve like points of light,
all in a wild cloud of snow.[5]

Christensen quotes student writers as well, to show that the extended
ending has exciting possibilities even in the hands of a novice. Here is

[5] From *In Our Time* by Ernest Hemingway, copyright 1925 Charles Scribner's
Sons. Reprinted by permission of Charles Scribner's Sons. Quoted by Christensen,
Notes, p. 8.

one such sentence [6] (in a format suggested by Christensen, but with a different set of grammatical labels):

> It was as though someone, somewhere, had touched a lever and shifted gears, and (independent clause)
> the hospital was set for night running, (independent clause)
> smooth and silent, (appositive adjectives)
> its normal clatter and hum muffled, (absolute phrase)
> the only sounds heard in the whitewalled room distant and unreal: (absolute phrase)
> a low hum of voices from the nurses' desk, (appositive noun)
> quickly stifled, (participle)
> the soft squish of rubber-soled shoes on the tiled corridor, (appositive noun)
> starched white cloth rustling against itself, (appositive noun)
> and, outside,
> the lonesome whine of wind in the country night (appositive noun)
> and
> the Kansas dust beating against the windows. (appositive noun)

Christensen advised all apprentice writers to compose sentence endings of like complexity. Granted, you could not use many such sentences in your essays. More than one to a page, perhaps more than one to an essay, could incite your reader to accuse you of rhetorical exhibitionism. Nevertheless your practice with those elaborate constructions would serve you well—would give you, Christensen believed, a "verbal virtuosity and syntactical ingenuity" that could be applied to all your sentences, whether they used extended endings or not. Speaking of his own students, he said, "I want them to become sentence acrobats, to dazzle by their syntactic dexterity." [7]

INTERRUPTIONS

We have pointed out that subordinate elements can appear before or after an independent clause. We now turn to their capacity for showing up in the *middle* of a clause. Usually, though not always, the interruption occurs between the subject and the verb. And usually, though not always, the interrupter will be a subordinate clause or an appositive phrase. In making this last statement, however, we are ignoring such small interrupters as *however, for example, on the other hand,* and *I believe*—interrupters you undoubtedly use already. In these pages

---

[6] *Notes*, pp. 11–12.
[7] *Notes*, pp. 14, 15.

we concentrate on interrupters less likely to be part of your standard repertoire.

Subordinate clause:

> This wildly ridiculous novel, *which was intended as a parody of pornographic literature,* became a best seller as soon as pornography addicts spotted the naked woman on the cover.

> This brief but important book by Edmund Wilson, *which charged our federal government with being both wasteful and oppressive,* attracted only a handful of readers and has now gone out of print.

Appositive noun:

> Macaulay Jones, a local *businessman,* was found to be the organizer of a state-wide ring of bicycle thieves.

> Because young people, especially *those* in minority groups, feel disconnected from the past, they question the value of studying history.

> *Forgive Us Our Sins,* a literary *sin* that should have led to everlasting damnation for the author, has just won the Robbins Prize for being the longest pornographic novel of the year.

> Several of the *New Yorker* humorists—*Robert Benchley, S. J. Perelman,* and *Woody Allen*—have excelled in the art of nonsense.

Appositive adjective:

> Those children—*selfish, deceitful,* and *sadistic*—were evidence of their parents' muddled sense of values.

> My teen-age son, *weary* after a long day at school, put on the earphones and sought relief in the world of Elton John.

Participle:

> Reginald, *convinced* of his greatness as a poet, stored all his sonnets in a safety deposit box.

> Reverend Cooper, *having failed* to win the argument by appealing to faith, decided he had better appeal to reason.

> The next customer, *trying* to show what a wise and knowing fellow he was, insisted on telling the waitress about his investments in gold and silver.

Absolute phrase:

> The robot, *his strength failing,* reached for a can of spinach.

Prepositional phrase:

> Then Mr. Maxwell, *with his customary indifference to popular opin-*

ion, asked the board to explain precisely why the high school needed a football team.

Sometimes, as we have intimated, the interruption does not occur between subject and verb, but elsewhere in the sentence:

This book was so entertaining, so informative and so agreeably written—*in contrast to what I remembered as the somewhat plushy overwriting of certain of the earlier books*—that I have gone on reading the further collections of historical essays and personal memoirs. . . .

Edmund Wilson [8]

If anyone thinks very intently on a single idea, with concentration and sustained attention, he will become conscious of a slight quiver or creeping feeling—*it has been compared to the creeping of an ant*—in the pineal gland.

Annie Besant [9]

Does the interrupter in that second sentence cause a loss in clarity? Does it sound awkward? Does it break up the normal flow of the sentence so badly that the flow is never quite restored? Possibly not—but those questions should be asked each time an interrupter jumps in and disturbs the normal word order. If the questions are not asked, we can wind up with sentences like this one:

The current inflation—brought on by such factors as the war in Viet Nam, the bloated federal budget, the devaluation of the dollar, the sale of wheat to Russia, the bad weather and the crop failures, and the soaring cost of energy—shows no signs of abating.

The interrupter makes that sentence unreasonably hard to follow. After slogging through the long interruption, the reader gets no special reward for the effort, no added eloquence to compensate for the loss in clarity. Here we offer a revision, for readers who don't like to fight their way through syntactical jungles with no hope of finding rhetorical treasure:

The current inflation has resulted from such factors as the war in Viet Nam, the bloated federal budget, the devaluation of the dollar, the sale of wheat to Russia, the bad weather and the crop failures, and the soaring cost of energy. And the inflation shows no signs of abating.

We add one further caution regarding interrupters, the same caution we have applied to subordinate beginnings and endings: Don't use

[8] "The James Branch Cabell Case Reopened," *The Bit Between My Teeth* (New York: Farrar, Straus and Giroux, 1965), p. 292.

[9] *Thought Power* (Wheaton, Illinois: Theosophical Publishing House, 1967), p. 37.

too many. Interrupters can add variety to your prose but excessive use of them will lead to a new kind of monotony:

> Radioactive lead, which occurs naturally in the environment and tends to settle on tobacco leaves, is probably the main cause of lung cancer in cigarette smokers. Tar and nicotine, although they contribute indirectly to the formation of cancer, are apparently not the primary cause. Dr. Edward Radford of Johns Hopkins, who will disclose further details in a paper to be delivered at the fifth International Congress of Radiation Research, has reported these findings.

The interruptions in the first two sentences are skillfully handled; the one in the third sentence creates a certain awkwardness because the concluding words in the sentence are not sufficiently impressive to follow so long a build-up. But the major failing in the passage is the lack of sentence variety: every main clause gets interrupted. Here we try to break up the tedium:

> Radioactive lead, which occurs naturally in the environment and tends to settle on tobacco leaves, is probably the main cause of lung cancer in cigarette smokers. Although tar and nicotine contribute indirectly to the formation of cancer, they are apparently not the primary cause. These are the findings of Dr. Edward Radford of Johns Hopkins, who will disclose further details in a paper to be delivered at the fifth International Congress of Radiation Research.

The first sentence keeps its interrupter; but the second moves the subordinate element to the beginning, and the third to the end—so that now the passage takes advantage of all three positions for subordinate elements.

And you, too, should try to take advantage of all three positions. You can practice by imitating the illustrative sentences in this chapter. Then you can move on to bolder experiments, with the goal of achieving "syntactic dexterity" and becoming one of Christensen's "sentence acrobats." Try some sentences in which the subordinate elements occupy two positions rather than one—like this sentence by Edmund Wilson:

> *As a child,* I imagined that a permanent antagonism existed between my father and me, *that I was always, in tastes and opinion, on the opposite side from him.*[10]

And try some sentences that take advantage of all three positions—like the sentence that follows:

[10] *A Piece of My Mind* (Garden City, New York: Doubleday Anchor Books, 1958), p. 154.

As they were passing a grassy knoll just before entering the wood, a pink-faced venerable man in a seer-sucker suit, with a shock of white hair and a tumefied purple nose resembling a huge raspberry, came striding toward them down the sloping field, a look of disgust contorting his features.

Vladimir Nabokov [11]

And then you can experiment with all sorts of sentences, with any fascinating patterns you happen to pick up in your reading of accomplished prosaists—Wilson or Nabokov or Woolf or Mencken or whomever. Here is the kind of sentence we have in mind, a magnificent 120-word bravura piece performed by H. L. Mencken, in which he explains why he chose to remain in the United States rather than take up residence in a more civilized society:

. . . here, more than anywhere else that I know of or have heard of, the daily panorama of human existence, of private and communal folly—the unending procession of governmental extortions and chicaneries, of commercial brigandages and throat-slittings, of theological buffooneries, of aesthetic ribaldries, of legal swindles and harlotries, of miscellaneous rogueries, villainies, imbecilities, grotesqueries, and extravagances—is so inordinately gross and preposterous, so perfectly brought up to the highest conceivable amperage, so steadily enriched with an almost fabulous daring and originality, that only the man who was born with a petrified diaphragm can fail to laugh himself to sleep every night, and to awake every morning with all the eager, unflagging expectation of a Sunday-school superintendent touring the Paris peep-shows.[12]

PARALLELISM

That sentence by Mencken leads us back to the subject of the previous chapter. Mencken's extended parallels serve as fresh evidence of the virtues of parallelism, another means by which you can vary your sentences. But since we have discussed those virtues so recently, there is no point in doing so here. Instead, we will merely offer some instances of effective parallelism—partly as a summary of our discussion in the last chapter, and partly as an addition to your stock of exemplary sentences, sentences that can serve as the basis for exercises in imitation.

[11] *Pnin* (New York: Doubleday & Company, Inc., 1964), p. 126.

[12] Copyright 1922 by Alfred A. Knopf, Inc., and renewed 1950 by H. L. Mencken. Reprinted from *Prejudices: A Selection* by H. L. Mencken, edited by James T. Farrell, by permission of Alfred A. Knopf, Inc. "On Being an American," *Prejudices: A Selection*, ed. James T. Farrell (New Yoork: Alfred A. Knopf Vintage Books, 1958), p. 92.

Two-part parallelism:

> Shakespeare's noblest characters express sentiments of *patriotic or personal* honor which to young modern ears sound *flamboyant or unconvincing.*
>
> Madeleine Doran [13]

> *Just when my husband granted that I was a person, just when he granted that I had the right to fulfill myself through a career,* I discovered that I detested him. [An example not only of parallelism but of the periodic sentence.]

Antithesis:

> We will have to repent in this generation *not merely for the vitriolic words and actions of the bad people, but for the appalling silence of the good people.*
>
> Martin Luther King, Jr.

> *To the mighty general war was a glorious enterprise; to the plodding foot soldier it was a grimy hardship.*

> I soon discovered *that the Land of the Redwoods could be as racist as the Land of Cotton, and that the Yankee police could be as bigoted as any good-ol'-boy Southern sheriff.*

> I learned *about the multiple orgasm but not about gonorrhea;* I learned *about the bites and scratches of lovemaking, but not about the oozing sores of syphillis.*

Triad:

> Many men have welcomed the women's liberation movement, with *its repudiation of sexual stereotypes, its demand for equal rights in employment, and its insistence on shared responsibilities in the home, the community, and the federal government.* [Note the triad within the last section of the larger triad.]

> The Puritan is simply one who, because of *physical cowardice, lack of imagination or religious superstition,* is unable to get any joy out of the satisfaction of his natural appetites.
>
> H. L. Mencken [14]

> Every man that has ever undertaken to instruct others can tell what slow advances he has been able to make, and how much patience it requires *to recall vagrant inattention, to stimulate sluggish indifference,* and *to rectify absurd misapprehension.*
>
> Samuel Johnson [15]

---

[13] *Something About Swans* (Madison: University of Wisconsin Press, 1973), p. 45.

[14] *Letters* (New York: Alfred A. Knopf, 1973), p. 278.

[15] *Life of Milton.*

Extended series:

> [The mass-man] appears to be a spoiled child, fundamentally un-grateful to the *scientists, political philosophers, social reformers, and religious idealists* who have given him his unprecedented oppor-tunities. He is therefore the natural prey of *advertisers, politicians, millionaire publishers, and would-be dictators.*
>
> Herbert J. Muller [16]

> I spent much of my time photographing the living things of the Mohave Desert: *cactus flowers in yellow bloom, an indigo bush with dark blue flowers, kangaroo rats hopping frantically over the sand, a vulture circling overhead, a rattlesnake basking in the sun.*

> At one moment [the Dreamer, the Unconscious,] chills by an inhuman cruelty, at another uplifts with a sheer grandeur of spiritual vision; he irritates us by trivialities, silences us with an unreasonable wis-dom, charms us by his subtlety and wit, and often enough disgusts us with his coarse and bestial fantasies.
>
> Alan McGlashan [17]

Parallelism is obviously much more than a technique for ensuring sentence variety. Having just read a dozen examples, you may have be-come a bit weary of parallelism for the moment, just as *any* reader does when *any* rhetorical weapon gets fired at him too persistently. But this weariness will pass. Don't let it prejudice you against so dependable a strategy—one of the simplest and yet surest means of enlivening your prose.

QUESTIONS AND COMMANDS

The typical sentence—the one you are now reading, for example—is declarative. It makes a statement. So one way to vary the rhythm of your prose is to depart from the normal declarative pattern and use a few interrogatives and imperatives—that is, ask a few questions and issue a few commands.

These devices will give your prose the diversity of lively conversa-tion. As a conversationalist you would certainly not confine yourself to declarative sentences. Even if your listener was a quiet person who gladly let you hold the floor, you would still utter occasional questions and com-mands to invite him into the conversation or make sure he was still listen-

[16] From *The Uses of the Past: Profiles of Former Societies* by Herbert J. Muller. © 1952 by Oxford University Press, Inc. Reprinted by permission.

[17] *The Savage and Beautiful Country* (Boston: Houghton Mifflin, 1967), p. 147.

ing. "Consider this idea," you might say, or, "What do you think of that possibility?" But when you become a writer, with only pen and paper for company, you are likely to forget your listeners—your prospective readers —and fall into a declarative frame of mind, making statement after statement in sentence after sentence, with never a thoughtful pause of interrogation or the urgent insistence of a command. And your readers will be all too willing to slip into passivity, until, perhaps, they slip off to sleep. Wake them up. Shake them out of their inattentiveness with a question or a command. Give them a taste of the lively interaction that makes good conversation so satisfying.

We add one qualification. These devices—the question and the command—become less appropriate, or downright inappropriate, when the prose is not meant to sound conversational. As you ascend the levels of style, rising to a high Middle Style or a High Style, your written "voice" will become increasingly impersonal, and thus you must become increasingly cautious in using such vestiges of conversational style as questions and commands.

The question is a handy device. If you find your tone becoming too rigidly declarative, you can easily temper it with a question or two. Suppose you had written the following passage:

> Recent television commercials suggest that men are expanding their definition of masculinity to include sensitivity and tenderness. But this changing image will probably not mean that men will totally abandon the traditional masculine values. Instead they will temper their rationality with emotion and their aggressiveness with compassion. They will not lose their strength as Samson did. Rather they will be gently strong like David—a warrior when necessary, but also the psalmist playing his harp.

This passage is acceptable as it stands, but if you had already written a page or two of declarative sentences and now felt the need for some variety, you could easily inject an interrogative change of pace:

> Recent television commercials suggest that men are expanding their definition of masculinity to include sensitivity and tenderness. *Does this changing image suggest that men will totally abandon the traditional masculine values?* Probably not. Instead they will temper their rationality with emotion and their aggressiveness with compassion. *Why must they lose their strength as Samson did?* Rather they can become gently strong like David—a warrior when necessary, but also the psalmist playing his harp.

Notice that the first question is answered by a sentence fragment: "Probably not." One advantage of the interrogative change of pace is that you can often follow it with a fragment—still another departure from the normal flow of declarative sentences.

The second question in that passage does not get an answer. Nor does it need one. Once the reader has read the question ("Why must they lose their strength as Samson did?"), he is able to answer it himself—with a definite "They don't have to." This technique—the question that implies its own answer—is traditionally labeled *the rhetorical question*. Here is another example:

> In San Francisco, during 1970 and 1971, 50 percent of all arrests were made in connection with victimless crimes. During the same period, the San Francisco police solved fewer than 13 percent of the city's serious crimes, the sorts of crimes that did involve victims. *Do we really want our police to spend their time arresting drunks and prostitutes rather than tracking down robbers and murderers?*

And the reader is expected to answer, "Of course not."

One very handy device is the question used as *transition*. For example, suppose you have just written three paragraphs about a change in the tax laws. When you begin the fourth paragraph, you ask, "And how did the ordinary American view this change? What was the response of the typical overworked, overtaxed member of the middle class?" Would your reader have any doubts as to the subject of the fourth paragraph?

Occasionally a question, or a series of questions, can introduce the subject of your entire essay. In the first few paragraphs you can ask the questions that your essay as a whole will try to answer:

> In Sunday school I learned that if I was assaulted, the proper Christian response was to "turn the other cheek." But is this advice wholesome? Does it benefit either the individual or society? Does my commitment to Christianity mean that I must expose myself unguarded to beach bullies who kick sand in my face or to chain-swinging motorcycle hoodlums? Must we, as Christians, renounce the right to preserve our dignity and our lives? Shouldn't we, instead, begin to fight back?

We turn now to the functions of the imperative sentence—the command. This device can serve some of the same purposes as the question: in particular, it can serve as a transition or an introduction to whatever is coming next. "Take a look at these examples," you might write, or, "Consider the consequences of this action"—and then, of course, you would supply the examples or describe the consequences. But a command can serve a variety of other purposes as well. It can remind the reader of a point established earlier ("Remember that this sort of opposition always drives the romantic hero to new heights of boldness"). It can state a point the reader has not yet encountered ("Keep in mind that at this time Craig had not yet seen the performances of the great Isadora Duncan"). It can give advice ("If you wish to understand the poetry of Wallace Stevens, be sure to read 'To the One of Fictive Music' and 'The Rock'"). And occasionally your commands will take the form of exhortations—advice charged with special urgency and intensity, as in this passage from Thoreau's *Walden:*

> However mean your life, *meet it and live it; do not shun it and call it hard names.* It is not so bad as you are. It looks poorest when you are richest. The fault-finder will find faults even in paradise. *Love your life, poor as it is.* You may perhaps have some pleasant, thrilling, glorious hours, even in a poor-house.

But we must offer our own exhortation regarding exhortations: Use them sparingly. Otherwise your prose will begin to sound preachy and self-righteous, as if to imply that you, and you alone, have arrived at moral and spiritual wisdom.

UNUSUAL SENTENCE PATTERNS

The strategies we have been discussing are the ones with which you can best give your sentences a varied and effective rhythm. Once you have mastered those strategies, you may wish to experiment with the more exotic sentence patterns to which we now turn—patterns which, precisely because they depart from the commonplace, can sometimes be especially forceful and elegant.

Consider *inversion:* a departure from the customary arrangement of words. Normally a sentence moves from subject to verb to complement:

> We did not really expect honesty in a public official.

Inversion can move the complement, or part of the complement, to the head of the sentence:

> *Honesty* we did not really expect in a public official, but we did expect a certain amount of discretion.

What do we accomplish by moving "honesty"? For one thing, the word gets greater emphasis than it did when buried in the middle of the sentence. Second, the inversion may promote greater continuity between sentences. If "honesty," either the word or the idea, was mentioned in a previous sentence, then the initial "honesty" in the present sentence will serve as an excellent transition. Third, of course, the inversion can contribute to a pleasing variety in sentence structure.

Another kind of inversion moves the verb, or part of the verb, to the front of the sentence.

Normal: Thus a thirty years' war *began* between Catholics and Protestants, a war that was to wipe out one-third of the German population.

Inverted: Thus *began* a thirty years' war between Catholics and Protestants, a war that . . . .

Normal: If you *had read* his dossier, you would have seen that he knows nothing at all about cryptography.

Inverted: *Had* you *read* his dossier, you would have seen . . . .

An especially elegant type of subject-verb inversion opens with a negative word, usually "nor."

Nor *is* Ju-ju the only organization intent on driving white settlers out of Africa.

Nowhere in Christian literature *can* we *find* a more intense yearning for liberation from the body and all its earthly trappings.

When using inverted sentences, keep in mind their tendency to sound awkward. As you reread your prose, consider whether the inverted sentences, in context, sound as graceful as you had hoped they would.

Another device worth using from time to time is a *that* clause as the subject of a sentence. This structure neatly compresses two sentences into one.

Two sentences:	*One sentence using a* that *clause:*
He failed to study. This was obvious to all his friends.	That he failed to study was obvious to all his friends.
She could no longer tell the difference between truth and falsehood. This became apparent to anyone who heard one of her long, confused stories about her arguments with her parents.	That she could no longer tell the difference between truth and falsehood became apparent to anyone who heard. . . .

Another device for occasional use is the one the classical rhetoricians labeled *anadiplosis*. This device—"dovetailing," as it is sometimes called—is a repetition of the last word of one sentence (or clause) as the first word of the next. Apart from its mild rhetorical effectiveness, the chief purpose of this dovetailing is to secure continuity between the two sentences (or clauses).

He talked at length about war games. "Games," however, seems an inappropriate term for strategies that lead to destruction and death.

A great many conservatives still yearn for isolationism, but isolationism in its traditional form is no longer possible.

Anadiplosis can be modified in several ways if the reiterated word threatens to sound clumsy or monotonous. (1) The repeated word can occur *near* the end of the first sentence rather than at the very end. (2) It can occur near the beginning of the second sentence rather than at the very beginning. (3) In its second occurrence, the repeated word can be converted into a synonym.

(1) Many absurd laws remain on the statute books, particularly in the *states* with sluggish governments. In one *state,* for instance, you are still prohibited from using another person's finger bowl.

(2) People who wish to preserve the illegality of "victimless crimes" insist that the victim in these cases is *"society."* What is *"society,"* however, but the sum of its *members?* And if these *members* are not injured, then how can "society" be injured?

(3) Recent events—the war in Viet Nam, the scandals of Watergate, the advent of Women's Liberation—have raised doubts about certain *traditional masculine virtues. Aggressiveness and competitiveness no* longer seem as valuable as they did ten or fifteen years ago.

Epanalepsis is another device that relies on repetition. It creates a striking effect by the simple expedient of using the same word or phrase at the beginning of a sentence and at the end.

An unreliable watch can make you unreliable. (From an advertisement.)

Jensen never considers anything but the safety and well-being of Jensen.

Greater centralization of government has always—in every culture, in every epoch—led to still greater centralization of government.

Antimetabole repeats words in reverse order:

Mankind must put an end to war—or war will put an end to mankind.
John F. Kennedy [18]

Pope Pius VI jeopardized his throne to preserve the Catholic faith; but Pius VII jeopardized the Catholic faith to preserve his throne.

Chiasmus is another kind of reversal. But instead of reversing words, it reverses grammatical elements:

He was kind to his enemies, but to his friends cruel.

[18] Speech at the United Nations, 1961.

A more ordinary rendering of this sentence would be:

He was kind to his enemies but cruel to his friends.

This version contains a forceful parallel structure. But possibly the version employing chiasmus is even more forceful—partly because that device is a striking departure from ordinary sentence structure, and partly because it moves the important word "cruel" to the emphatic position at the end of the sentence. Here are further examples of chiasmus:

He was wise and compassionate as a counselor, but as a teacher inefficient and ineffectual.

The student radicals of the 1960s prized moral consistency and tenacity above all else. Hence they felt a grudging respect for ultraconservatives and reactionaries, but for moderates and liberals nothing but contempt.

Another device worth trying occasionally is *ellipsis:* the omission of one or more words. For example:

One of the defendants was sentenced to 60 days; the other, to life imprisonment. [The second "was sentenced" is omitted.]

Youth is a blunder; manhood a struggle; old age a regret. (Benjamin Disraeli) [Two "is's" are omitted.]

Asyndeton also involves omission. It omits the conjunction that usually comes just before the last item in a parallel series. The effect is to put greater emphasis on that last item. In the following passage from Lincoln's Gettysburg Address, the "and" before the phrase "for the people" is omitted, so that the phrase gets even more emphasis than it otherwise would: ". . . we here highly resolve . . . that government of the people, by the people, for the people, shall not perish from the earth." And here is one further example:

The altar showed all the signs of being ready for a ceremonial hexing: three black candles dimly flickering, green smoke rising from a cauldron, the unmistakable odor of snake oil.

Finally, we come to the device known as *epanorthosis*, or "correction." By this means you can convey a sense of immediacy. The reader feels as if he is watching—almost participating—as you search for the right words to express your meaning. In the following sentences, both instances of epanorthosis are set off by dashes.

Primitive man can teach us lessons that are indispensable for our salvation. Thousands of years ago we forgot—*wanted* to forget—what he still knows.

. . . the prep school boys came from families who founded the country; hence they deserved—no, they earned—special rights to be in their clubs.

Thomas J. Cottle [19]

Perhaps we have made it sound as if you should plan in advance the grammatical and rhetorical structure of every sentence that you write—in this fashion: "I haven't used epanorthosis for a while; I'd better try one in the next sentence. And in the following sentence I'll use a sentence-ending absolute phrase and two participial phrases, to put together an impressive cumulative sentence. I'll follow that with a question and a pithy imperative. Then in the next sentence I'll insert an appositive series between the subject and the verb: I haven't used an appositive series in the last two pages, and haven't inserted an interrupting subordinate element between subject and verb since that splendid sentence in the next-to-last paragraph." The truth is that we don't know of a single writer who has worked in this way. Any writer who did would produce a hopelessly stilted and artificial prose that would be read by no one but a teacher paid to undertake such onerous work or a mother suffering from an especially bad case of motherly love. Not only would the writer's style be stilted, but his thinking would be superficial; he would be so preoccupied with grammatical problems that he wouldn't have any time left over for thinking about his subject matter.

We do recommend that you practice the various sentence patterns displayed in this chapter. We especially recommend that you practice imitation (see Exercises I and II on the following pages) and sentence combining (see Exercises III and IV). And we recommend that *after* you've done a piece of writing, you review it with a critical ear to find out whether the sentences have a pleasing and emphatic variety. If they don't, you can revise accordingly. But *while* you write, you would do better to ignore the subtleties of sentence rhythm and to concentrate on such larger problems as organization, reasoning, and clear expression.

Exercises

I. One purpose of this chapter has been to give you a brief handbook of sentence structures, a brief reference work to be consulted whenever you wish to reinforce your skill at using a variety of syntactical patterns. But your skill with those patterns will develop very slowly, or not at all, if you do nothing but review them passively. We recommend, again, that you practice *imitation*—that you create your own sentences modeled on the patterns you wish to master.

[19] "The Politics of Retrieval."

Reread the discussion of imitation on pages 164–65. Then imitate the following kinds of sentences. You can find an example of each kind of sentence—a model to imitate—by consulting the appropriate pages in the chapter.

1. Periodic sentences that begin with the following subordinate elements:
    a. subordinate clause (pp. 165-66)
    b. prepositional phrase (p. 166)
    c. participial phrase (p. 166)
    d. gerund phrase (p. 166)
    e. absolute phrase (p. 166)
    f. appositive noun (p. 166)
    g. appositive adjective (pp. 166-67)
    h. adverb (p. 167)
2. Loose (or cumulative) sentences that end with the following subordinate elements:
    a. subordinate clause (p. 168)
    b. subordinate clause introduced by a colon or a dash (p. 168)
    c. noun in apposition (pp. 168-69)
    d. adjective in apposition (p. 169)
    e. participle (p. 169)
    f. absolute phrase (p. 169)
3. Interrupted sentences that contain the following interrupters:
    a. subordinate clause (p. 171)
    b. appositive noun (p. 171)
    c. appositive adjective (p. 171)
    d. participle (p. 171)
    e. absolute phrase (p. 171)
    f. prepositional phrase (pp. 171-72)
4. Sentences in which subordinate elements appear at both the beginning and the end (p. 173)
5. Sentences in which subordinate elements occupy all three of the available positions—beginning, middle, and end (p. 174)
6. Parallelism
    a. two-part parallelism (p. 175)
    b. antithesis (p. 175)
    c. triad (p. 175)
    d. extended series (p. 176)
7. Questions
    a. a question that gets answered (p. 177)
    b. a rhetorical question (pp. 177-78)
    c. a question that might serve as a transition or as an introduction to the subject to be discussed next (pp. 178-79)

8. Commands

    a. a command that might serve as a transition or as an introduction to the subject to be discussed next (p. 178)
    b. a command that serves as a reminder of a point already established (pp. 178-79)
    c. a command that states a new point (p. 179)
    d. a command that advises or exhorts (p. 179)

II. The previous exercise asked you to imitate some of the most frequently used sentence patterns. Now you may wish to practice with other patterns that will not be used as often. Imitate the following patterns:

1. inversion (pp. 179-80)
2. *that* clause as subject of the sentence (p. 180)
3. anadiplosis (pp. 180-81)
4. epanalepsis (p. 181)
5. antimetabole (p. 181)
6. chiasmus (pp. 181-82)
7. ellipsis (p. 182)
8. asyndeton (p. 182)
9. epanorthosis (pp. 182-83)

III. One way of becoming adept at producing a rich variety of sentence structures is to practice sentence combining—to practice combining short sentences into longer ones. This kind of activity has long been recommended by rhetoricians and composition instructors, but its advantages have been recently, and persuasively, reaffirmed by the classroom experiments of John C. Mellon and Frank O'Hare.[19] This exercise and the next offer you a chance to do some sentence combining.

The following passages display a woeful sameness in the length and structure of their sentences. Rewrite one (or more) of the passages to achieve a greater diversity by combining these short sentences into various kinds of longer ones.

Don't be afraid to keep an occasional short sentence. The previous exercises have given you practice only with the *structure* of sentences, but don't forget that one of the easiest, surest means of gaining variety is to vary the *length*—to throw in an occasional short sentence when the surrounding sentences are fairly long.

[19] You might be interested in reading Mellon's *Transformational Sentence-Combining* (1969) and O'Hare's *Sentence Combining* (1973), both of which are available from the National Council of Teachers of English, 1111 Kenyon Road, Urbana, Illinois 61801.

These monotonous passages are derived from the first-rate prose of accomplished professionals: H. L. Mencken, James Thurber, and A. J. Liebling, in that order.

1. And so it went, alas, alas, in all his [Thorstein Veblen's] other volumes. A cent's worth of information was wrapped in a bale of polysyllables. In "The Higher Learning in America" the thing perhaps reached its damndest and worst. It was as if the practice of that style were a relentless disease. The style was incredibly obscure. It was incredibly malodorous. The disease was a sort of progressive intellectual diabetes. It was a leprosy of the horse sense. Words were flung upon words. Then all recollection that there must be a meaning in them was lost. All recollection that there must be a ground and excuse for them was lost. One wandered in a labyrinth. The labyrinth was made up of nouns, adjectives, verbs, and pronouns. It was also made up of adverbs, prepositions, conjunctions, and participles. Most of them were swollen. Nearly all of them were unable to walk. It was impossible to imagine worse English. It still is impossible to imagine worse English within the limits of intelligible grammar. It was clumsy and affected. It was opaque and bombastic. It was windy and empty. It was without grace. It was without distinction. It was often without the most elementary order. The professor got himself enmeshed in his gnarled sentences. He was like a bull trapped by barbed wire. His efforts to extricate himself were quite as furious as a bull's. They were also quite as spectacular. He heaved. He leaped. He writhed. At times he seemed to be at the point of yelling for the police. It was a picture to bemuse the vulgar. It was a picture to give the judicious grief.

2. Suppose you had a manuscript under Ross's scrutiny. This was like putting your car in the hands of a skilled mechanic. The mechanic was not an automotive engineer. He did not have a bachelor of science degree. But he was the kind of guy who knows what makes a motor go. He knows what makes it sputter. He knows what makes it wheeze. He knows what makes it sometimes come to a dead stop. He is a man with an ear for the loudest engine rattle. He also has an ear for the faintest body squeak. Consider the time when you first gazed upon an uncorrected proof. It was a proof of one of your stories or articles. You were appalled. Each margin had a thicket of queries. The thicket also contained complaints. One writer got a hundred and forty-four on one profile. It was as though you beheld the works of your car spread all over the garage floor. The job of getting the thing together again seemed impossible. It seemed impossible to make the thing work again. Then you realized what was happening. Ross was trying to convert your Model T or old Stutz Bearcat. He was trying to make it into a Cadillac or Rolls-Royce. He was at work with the tools of his unflagging perfectionism.

You exchanged growls or snarls. Then you set to work. You set out to join him in his enterprise.

3. A boxer must stand alone. He is like a writer. What happens if he loses? He cannot call an executive conference and throw off on a vice-president. He cannot throw off on the assistant sales manager. He is consequently resented by fractional characters. They cannot live outside an organization. A fighter's hostilities are not turned inward. A Sunday tennis player's hostilities are turned inward. A lady M.P.'s are turned inward. A fighter's hostilities come out naturally with his sweat. When his job is done he feels good. He has expressed himself. Chain-of-command types find this intolerable. They try to rationalize their envy. They do so by proclaiming solicitude for the fighter's health. What would happen, for example, if a boxer ever went as batty as Nijinsky? All the wowsers in the world would be screaming "Punch-drunk." Well, who hit Nijinsky? And why isn't there a campaign against ballet? It gives girls thick legs. Suppose a novelist who lived exclusively on apple-cores won the Nobel Prize. Vegetarians would raise a chorus. They would chorus that the repulsive nutriment had invigorated his brain. But the prize goes to Ernest Hemingway. Hemingway has been a not particularly evasive boxer for years. No one rises to point out that the percussion has apparently stimulated his intellection. Albert Camus is the French probable for the Nobel. He is an ex-boxer, too.

IV. The following passages all deserve to be studied so that you can see how the writers achieved such interesting variety in their sentences. Concentrate on one passage. A profitable and fairly painless way to study such prose is to mutilate it in precisely the same way as we mutilated the prose of Mencken, Thurber, and Liebling in the previous exercise. Cut every long or medium-length sentence into several shorter ones, aiming for sentences of ten words or less and certainly not allowing any sentence of more than fifteen words to escape your scissors. Aim for simple declarative sentences. You'll probably have to keep all questions and commands; you may even have to add a few new ones; but with a little luck and persistence you'll create a passage no more varied in its sentences than the typical product of a badly educated sixth-grader. After putting it aside for a day or two, revise it to restore all its original variety. Then compare your results with the professional passage that got you started.

1. Germaine Greer on the modern ideal of feminine beauty (pp. 19-20)

2. George Orwell on the language of politics (pp. 41-42)

3. Bernard Shaw on "the whole country as a big household" (pp. 191-92)

4. H. L. Mencken on California (p. 213)

5. Dwight Macdonald on the men of God who sell peace of mind (pp. 214-15)

6. Gore Vidal on drugs (pp. 230-31)

7. Hugh Kenner on why Johnny shouldn't go to college (p. 236)

8. Joyce Maynard on the goals of young people (pp. 236-37)

9. James Baldwin on the bitterness of his father (pp. 237-38)

10. Diana Trilling on Mar ',.1 Monroe (pp. 238-39)

V. Reexamine one of your recent essays—preferably one containing at least three or four pages, so that it can serve as a fair sample of your prose.

Read the essay slowly, paying close attention to the sound of its sentences. Do you find the sentences pleasantly and appropriately varied? Do you find any sections lacking in variety?

Examine the essay still more closely. See how many of the sentence patterns listed below do *not* appear. How do you interpret your findings? Did you not use those patterns because they were not appropriate or because they had not yet become a part of your rhetorical repertoire?

a. the periodic sentence

b. the loose (or cumulative) sentence

c. the interrupted sentence

d. the sentence in which subordinate elements appear at both the beginning and the end

e. two-part parallelism

f. antithesis

g. parallelism containing three parts or more

h. the question

i. the command

j. the short sentence surrounded by longer ones

Rewrite any sections of the essay that need greater sentence variety.

14

Figures of Speech

Perhaps you have believed that figures of speech belong strictly to poetry, that they have no useful purpose in expository prose. We hope to establish that such is not the case: that the most common figures of speech can play a valuable role in your prose—partly because they can add colorful ornamentation but also because, as Aristotle pointed out 2500 years ago, they can impart clarity, force, and elegance.

METAPHOR

The *metaphor* is probably the most useful figure, particularly if we allow the term to include the *simile*. The two figures do basically the same job. They each express a comparison between two things.

A simile indicates the comparison by supplying an appropriate word, usually *like* or *as*:

Life is *like* music; it must be composed by ear, feeling, and instinct, not by rule.

Samuel Butler[1]

I have squandered my life *as* a schoolboy squanders a tip.

Butler[2]

[1] *Note-Books* (New York: E. P. Dutton, 1917), p. 11.
[2] *Note-Books*, p. 13.

189

A metaphor offers no verbal signal of this kind. Sometimes it states its comparison as a simple equation:

> When I was a schoolboy at Shrewsbury, old Mrs. Brown used to keep a tray of spoiled tarts which she sold cheaper. They most of them looked pretty right till you handled them. *We are all spoiled tarts.*
>
> Butler [3]

At other times the metaphor states only one term of the comparison, leaving the other implicit. The following passage contains two of these "compressed" metaphors:

> If you have built *castles in the air,* your work need not be lost; that is where they should be. Now put the *foundations* under them.
>
> Henry David Thoreau [4]

Thoreau compares our dreams and ideals to "castles in the air," but he states only the second term in the comparison. His other metaphor works in the same way. He gives us only the word "foundations," and lets us deduce the unstated term in the comparison. What is the unstated term? What does Thoreau mean by asking us to build foundations? Probably that we should live the kind of life that will make our dreams a reality.

Although simile and metaphor are constructed differently, their task—the comparing of two things—is basically the same. Hereafter, then, we shall use the word *metaphor* to refer to both of these figures of speech.

And what are the functions of metaphor? What purposes can it help you to achieve? One purpose is clarity. Metaphor can sometimes achieve clarity when literal language has failed. An extreme instance is the metaphorical language of the mystics—St. John of the Cross, for instance, or William Law, or St. Theresa of Avila. In sixteenth-century Spain, St. Theresa set out to describe the mystical experience in terms that would be clear not only to theologians but to the general public. But ordinary, literal language would not serve the purpose; so she resorted to metaphor—referring to Christ as her "Divine Lover," to the early stages of mystical experience as a dalliance between lovers, and to the ultimate apprehension of God as an exquisite sexual climax or, sometimes, as a "rape of the soul."

You need not write about mystical experience to feel the need for a clarifying metaphor. George Orwell, in "Politics and the English Language," uses such a metaphor in explaining the circular process by which bad writing and bad thinking become mutually destructive.

---

[3] *Note-Books,* p. 9.
[4] *Walden,* Chapter 18 ("Conclusion").

Sloppy thinking, he says, will lead to sloppy writing, which in turn will lead to sloppier thinking, which in turn will lead to sloppier writing—and so on. To clarify this line of reasoning, Orwell offers the italicized metaphor:

> *A man make take to drink because he feels himself to be a failure, and then fail all the more completely because he drinks.* It is rather the same thing that is happening to the English language. It becomes ugly and inaccurate because our thoughts are foolish, but the slovenliness of our language makes it easier for us to have foolish thoughts.[5]

Orwell supplies a metaphor, then a literal explanation. Usually the order is reversed—first the explanation, then the metaphor. Alan Watts, in the passage that follows, gives literal explanation first, then metaphor, then a final sentence of explanation. Watts is explaining the abstruse Buddhist doctrine of *sunyata*.

> The doctrine . . . asserts only that there are no self-existent forms, for the more one concentrates upon any individual thing, the more it turns out to involve the whole universe. *The final Buddhist vision of the world . . . is symbolized as a vast network of jewels, like drops of dew upon a multidimensional spiderweb. Looking closely at any single jewel, one beholds in it the reflections of all the others.* . . . Any one form is inseparable from all other forms.[6]

The Orwell metaphor occupied one sentence; the Watts metaphor, two sentences. Now we ask you to examine an *extended metaphor*—or *analogy*—in which Bernard Shaw explains, and dramatizes, his vision of British society.

> Think of the whole country as a big household, and the whole nation as a big family, which is what they really are. What do we see? Half-fed, badly clothed, abominably housed children all over the place; and the money that should go to feed and clothe and house them properly being spent in millions on bottles of scent, pearl necklaces, pet dogs, racing motor cars, January strawberries that taste like corks, and all sorts of extravagances. One sister of the national family has a single pair of leaking boots that keep her sniffing all through the winter, and no handkerchief to wipe her nose with. Another has forty pairs of high-heeled shoes and dozens of handkerchiefs. A little brother is trying to grow up on a penn'orth of food

---

[5] Excerpted from "Politics and the English Language" in *Shooting An Elephant and Other Essays* by George Orwell; copyright, 1945, 1946, 1949, 1950, by Sonia Brownell Orwell; copyright 1973, 1974 by Sonia Orwell. Reprinted by permission of Harcourt Brace Jovanovich, Inc. and A. H. Heath & Co. Ltd., London.

[6] *Psychotherapy East and West* (New York: Ballantine Books, 1961), p. 82.

a day, and is breaking his mother's heart and wearing out her patience by asking continually for more, whilst a big brother, spending
five or six pounds on his dinner at a fashionable hotel, followed by
supper at a night club, is in the doctor's hands because he is eating
and drinking too much.[7]

This extended metaphor introduces the central thesis of Shaw's 500-page
Intelligent Woman's Guide: the belief that the members of a nation
should respect and assist one another just as if they were members of
one large family.

One purpose of metaphor, then, is to achieve clarity. Another is to
entertain: to give the reader pleasure. Earlier (in Chapter 4) we
pointed out the advantages of imagery: the liveliness, the vividness, the
excitement of experiencing things and people rather than merely abstractions and generalities. Metaphor can have the same advantages.
Orwell's notions about the intertwined degeneration of thought and
language become more impressive when joined to the image of the
man whose failure leads to drinking and whose drinking leads to more
abysmal failure. Watts's explanation of *sunyata* becomes charmingly
graphic when linked to the image of a vast net of jewels or a spiderweb
covered with drew drops. And Shaw's view of Britain's economic structure becomes touchingly dramatic when presented as the account of a
cruelly inequitable division of money within a single family. Let's look
at one further example. H. L. Mencken, a confirmed elitist, once defined
American democracy as that system of government in which the people
elect a Calvin Coolidge to the presidency when they have thousands
of more intelligent men to choose from. Not satisfied with expressing
his point literally, Mencken dramatized it figuratively:

It is as if a hungry man, set before a banquet prepared by master
cooks and covering a table an acre in area, should turn his back
upon the feast and stay his stomach by catching and eating flies.[8]

There again we see the pleasure to be derived from graphic metaphor,
a pleasure heightened in this case by Mencken's sense of the ridiculous.
Apprentice writers, too, can convey pleasure through metaphor. Up
to this point we have quoted only accomplished professional writers,

[7] *The Intelligent Woman's Guide to Socialism and Capitalism* (London: Con-
stable, 1932), p. 50. Reprinted by permission of The Society of Authors on behalf
of the Bernard Shaw Estate.
[8] From *Prejudices: A Selection*, by H. L. Mencken, edited by James T. Farrell.
Copyright 1926 by Alfred A. Knopf, Inc., and renewed 1954 by H. L. Mencken.
Reprinted by permission of Alfred A. Knopf, Inc.

but not to imply that the art of metaphor is reserved for the old pros.
Here are some examples from student writers:

> Gridley City is a concrete-and-neon atoll in a vast sea of peach trees.

> Professor Meyers somehow managed to combine the roles of solicitous guru and academic drill sergeant.

> The present style of marriage is a little like Russian roulette; and most of the time the chamber is loaded.

> These psychologists and mythologists tell us that Western civilization has reached a dead end. Our path has meandered through fields of glory only to terminate at the edge of a cliff. If we wish to save ourselves, we must retrace our steps.

Those last two passages originally served as essay conclusions. The concluding paragraph of an essay gives you an excellent chance to use metaphor. By doing so, you can restate an important idea in memorable form.

The metaphors presented thus far have all been at least a sentence long. Too many such metaphors and your prose would become too ornate, too richly decorated, to serve most purposes. If you were writing an intensely emotional prose (as James Agee did in certain sections of *Let Us Now Praise Famous Men*) or a free-wheeling, extravagant prose (as H. L. Mencken did in his writings on society and politics), then you might well stud your pages with shining jewels of metaphor; but more often you will aim for the moderate tone of the judicious thinker and reliable dispenser of information, in which case your sparkling metaphors would seem too gaudy. Compare the raucous, hard-hitting Mencken of *Prejudices* with the more scholarly Mencken of *Treatise on the Gods* or *The American Language*, and you will see a marked decline in the number and length of metaphors.

Consider the discretion with which Orwell uses metaphor in "Politics and the English Language." Though on some pages he uses three or four metaphors, he keeps them short to prevent them from becoming obtrusive. His one-sentence metaphor about the failure who turns to drink is the longest in the essay. The others—occupying only a half-sentence, a phrase, or a single word—are woven subtly into the fabric of the argument, clarifying ideas and adding pleasurable doses of concreteness, but never becoming ostentatious. Here are several that remain clear and effective apart from their context in the essay:

> [Modern] prose consists less and less of *words* chosen for the sake of their meaning, and more and more of *phrases tacked together like the sections of a prefabricated hen-house.*

. . . modern writing at its worst does not consist in picking out words for the sake of their meaning and inventing images in order to make the meaning clearer. It consists in *gumming together long strips of words* which have already been set in order by someone else, and making the results presentable by sheer humbug.

. . . the writer knows more or less what he wants to say, but an accumulation of *stale* phrases *chokes* him *like tea leaves blocking a sink.*

The *inflated* style is itself a kind of euphemism. A mass of Latin words *falls upon the facts like soft snow, blurring* the outlines and *covering up* all the details. The great *enemy* of clear language is insincerity. When there is a gap between one's real and one's declared aims, one turns as it were instinctively to long words and *exhausted* idioms, *like a cuttlefish squirting out ink.*

The debased language that I have been discussing is in some ways very convenient. Phrases like "a not unjustifiable assumption," "leaves much to be desired," "would serve no good purpose," "a consideration which we should do well to bear in mind," are a continuous temptation, *a packet of aspirins always at one's elbow.*

This *invasion* of one's mind by ready-made phrases . . . can only be prevented if one is constantly *on guard* against them, and every such phrase *anaesthetizes* a portion of one's brain.[9]

One-word metaphors can be particularly successful at enlivening your prose without becoming obtrusive. Take another look at the final sample from Orwell. He pictures an "invasion" of hackneyed phrases against which one must be "on guard"—as if the phrases, by threatening to attack the mind, could force the critical faculty to do round-the-clock sentry duty. How much energy the sentence loses if we lift out the metaphors: "This tendency of ready-made phrases to enter the mind in great numbers can only be prevented if one is constantly ready to keep them out." Notice, too, the impact of Orwell's saying that every ready-made phrase "anaesthetizes" a part of the brain, rather than literalizing the statement by saying that the phrase "renders a part of the thinking process inoperative."

One-word metaphors often take the form of verbs. Orwell, as we have seen, speaks of phrases that "anaesthetize" part of the brain. William Hazlitt, in his essay "On the Ignorance of the Learned," also

[9] Excerpted from "Politics and the English Language" in *Shooting An Elephant and Other Essays* by George Orwell; copyright, 1945, 1946, 1949, 1950 by Sonia Brownell Orwell; copyright 1973, 1974 by Sonia Orwell. Reprinted by permission of Harcourt Brace Jovanovich, Inc. and A. H. Heath & Co. Ltd., London. "Politics and the English Language," pp. 130, 134, 135, 136, 137.

makes good use of metaphorical verbs. He speaks of the scholarly mind as too often being "cramped" by custom and authority. The scholar, says Hazlitt, "clings to" books for his intellectual support. "He parrots those who have parroted others." Real objects, when "stripped of the disguises of words," will "stagger" his understanding. Further:

> He *stuffs* his head with authorities *built* on authorities, with quotations quoted from quotations, while he *locks up* his senses, his understanding, and his heart.

Verbs have rich metaphorical possibilities. You can have someone "elbow" his way through a crowd, "yawn" his way through a book, "hunger" for admiration, "intoxicate" himself with his own words, or "orchestrate" a conversation. Think of the metaphorical substitutes for the one verb "to talk." You can have a speaker gush, flow, or spout like running water; cackle, gabble, or cluck like a bird; bark or growl like a dog; orate, lecture, preach, or sermonize like someone talking from a podium or a pulpit; whimper or rhapsodize or explode or erupt or . . . The possibilities could continue for quite some time. Take advantage of such possibilities. Metaphorical verbs can add imagery and activity to your prose; and yet they are easily devised and can easily be kept from becoming obtrusive.

THE DANGERS OF METAPHOR

We have repeatedly warned against the overuse of metaphor. Lest our warning seem pointless, we now quote a passage in which the metaphors are so abundant that their relentless color and cleverness become too dazzling, and too distracting, for expository prose.

> Reverend Blessit of "His Place" on Sunset Strip in Los Angeles is a particularly flashy example of this Campus Crusade for Christ mentality, boutiqued over with paste-board psychedelic finish and restocked on the shelves as the Real Thing for the Youth Market, the Uncola of religious persuasion, bearing about as close a resemblance to anything revolutionary as those cleverly advertised, insipid little cheese-nothings, Screaming Yellow Zonkers, had to the nutrition revolution.
>
> This plasticine selling-of-the-revolution is operating on all levels now, and is particularly aimed at media-impressionable teeny- and micro-boppers. And it should be no surprise that the evangelism industry—which has used everything from Motown to motel-drawers in the past to push its product—should shift into the third-gear of its get-with-it campaign and begin strutting its stuff with a hippie-drug-cult border around it. . . . The marriage of Pop myths and

> evangelism is almost as perfect a union as the one between Holly-
> wood and establishment politics, both based on the manipulation of
> empty media myths to extort either souls or votes from the star-struck
> masses.
>
> James Nolan [10]

This is entertaining for the first sentence or two, but it soon becomes exhausting. And its tone is likely to arouse the reader's distrust. The tone surely does not suggest objectivity, sobriety, or judiciousness. Rather, we are led to suspect the writer of manic exhibitionism—of being more intent on sounding clever than on getting at the truth.

A second danger in using metaphors is that you may get enticed into using the old hackneyed ones: "busy as a bee," "sober as a judge," "packed like sardines," and the rest. If you wish to take advantage of the power of which metaphorical language is capable, be sure to devise your own brand-new metaphors. Huck Finn might have described his Pap's sickly complexion with some tired old phrase like "white as a sheet" or "pale as a ghost"; but Huck instinctively knew that no cliché would suffice.

> There warn't no color in his face, where his face showed; it was
> white; not like another man's white, but a white to make a body sick,
> a white to make a body's flesh crawl—a tree-toad white, a fish-belly
> white.

"Tree-toad white" doesn't carry much force today, now that so few of us get to see tree toads; but "fish-belly white"—the comparison of pallid skin to the slimy, gray-white belly of a fish—is likely to retain its power, is likely to "make a body's flesh crawl," for as long as the English language endures—unless "fish-belly white" happens to catch on in conversational English, gets worn out from overuse, and has to be labeled a cliché.

Another danger associated with metaphors is that they often sound nonsensical. For example:

> The real Count Dracula was a fifteenth-century Hungarian nobleman
> notorious for butchering thousands of peasants. He murdered them
> on the slightest pretext. Like a boiling lobster, the fertile plain of the
> Danube turned from dark green to blood red.

The writer strains too hard to be vivid, and the result is a violent yoking of dissimilar ideas: a comparison of the Danube plain to a lobster. Somehow the lobster seems comical.

---

[10] "Jesus Now: Hogwash and Holy Water," *Ramparts Magazine*, August 1971, pp. 22–23. © 1971 by Noah's Ark, Inc. (for *Ramparts Magazine*). Reprinted by permission.

A related danger is the *mixed metaphor,* the mixing of two incongruous comparisons. A notorious example originated with the American radio announcer who, after informing his listeners that World War II was officially over, declared joyously that "The Fascist octopus has finally sung his swan song!" Another marvelous example comes from the California state senator who charged that the intellectuals in our universities are "a bunch of termites relentlessly eating away the bedrock of our civilization." Not even intellectual termites can eat rock.

FURTHER POSSIBILITIES

Personification is actually one variety of metaphor, but it differs enough from other varieties to warrant a separate discussion. Personification compares the nonhuman to the human. It endows nonhuman entities with human characteristics. For example:

> The fossilized dinosaur egg reminded me that Nature is a gambler, a reckless improviser, and that most of her schemes have failed.

> The 1940s and 50s placed romantic love securely on the throne, making sentimentality an absolute ruler whom our popular novelists and playwrights did not dare to oppose.

Here personification turns Nature into a gambler who takes plenty of risks, and sentimental love into a tyrant who rules over popular taste. Personification also appears, in a more questionable form, in the following sentence:

> The Shadow side of the human race towers over us all, darkening the sky with its death-rays and its atom bombers.
>
> Erich Neumann [11]

This is daringly metaphorical. The "Shadow side" of human nature—its repressed emotions—becomes a dark giant towering over the earth. By using the word "towers," Neumann adds metaphor to metaphor: he turns the Shadow into a giant and then the giant into a tower. But somehow that doubling of metaphors does not seem illogical or "mixed," possibly because "tower" is almost a "dead metaphor," one that has lost much of its original force without becoming so objectionable as to be labeled a cliché. If we were to find fault with the sentence, we would do so on the grounds that the phrase "darkening the sky with its death-rays" seems to violate common sense. If rays can be seen at all, don't they

[11] *Depth Psychology and a New Ethic,* trans. Eugene Rolfe (New York: G. P. Putnam, 1969), pp. 19–20.

give off light rather than darkness? Perhaps Neumann means that the rays would block out the sun—but can rays be envisioned as doing that? The end of the sentence might come closer to being picturable if we revised it like this: "darkening the sky with its bombers and missiles and deadly gasses."

Synecdoche (si-nek'-du-key) substitutes a part for the whole, as when a farmer says he hired "seven hands" when he means seven workers. The Christian who prays "Give us this day our daily bread" would be disappointed if the Lord took the request literally, and the person who expresses gratitude for having "a roof over his head" would not be grateful if his walls were removed. But of course those phrases are figures of speech—instances of synecdoche in which "bread" stands for "food" and "roof" for "house."

Synecdoche is a valuable means of converting abstractions and generalities into concrete terms. Rather than writing "She is more likely to devote her law career to *working for large corporations* than *to working for political or social betterment*," you can replace those italicized abstractions with concrete instances—parts that represent the wholes. You might replace "large corporations" with one typical corporation, and replace "working for political or social betterment" with typical instances of such work. For example: "She is more likely to become an upper-echelon attorney at General Motors than a Nader's Raider or a storefront lawyer for people on welfare."

Here are further examples of this kind of conversion. In each pair of sentences, the first is needlessly abstract or general, and the second becomes more concrete by means of synecdoche:

It was a shoddy motel.
It was one of those motels where your room smells of mildew and you find two dead mice in the swimming pool.

When he was in high school, he always preferred intellectual activities to athletic or social ones.
When he was in high school, he always preferred Shakespeare or Rimbaud to football or dancing.

She has never done any serious reading.
Her reading has never gotten beyond the daily newspaper and the collected works of Harold Robbins.

Liberated women are rejecting most of the privileges traditionally associated with their sex and are engaging in aggressive activities once reserved for men.

[Liberated women] don't like to have men open letters, pay bills, or change their tires, and many of them are hardening their muscles and learning karate to defend themselves against muggers.

Caroline Bird [12]

An *allusion* is a reference to something other than the primary subject. The following examples from student essays are arranged in order of familiarity, beginning with the allusions most easily recognized.

In 1972 the Democrats nominated George McGovern, *the Barry Goldwater of the Left.*

This instructor was determined to respect *all* tastes. He would nod his approval even if a student confessed profound admiration for the artistry of *Clint Eastwood's spaghetti Westerns* or insisted that *Bob Dylan* was a greater poet than *Shakespeare* and that *Alice Cooper* had more to teach us than *Socrates* or *Jesus.*

During the late 1960s many students set aside academic pursuits for "rap sessions"; but once again *"the times they are a-changin'."*

In the animal kingdom *the meek* do not *inherit the earth.*

When I finally started dieting, I was too impatient in wishing that my *"too, too solid flesh would melt."*

The date was 1967. *Dionysus* had just invaded suburbia.

Sometimes an allusion can sum up a whole tangle of facts and attitudes. The reference to Barry Goldwater, in the first example, saved the writer a great deal of talk about landslide defeats, political idealism and extremism, and the various other elements common to the Far Left and the Far Right. In the third example the allusion to Bob Dylan's best-known lyric conjures up complex suggestions regarding the rise and decline of the counter-culture. And in the final example the allusion to Dionysus sums up in one word a sudden movement toward bright colors, spontaneity, drugs, sexual freedom, mysticism, and ecstasy—for better and worse. Further, the reference to Dionysus evokes a complex world-view that would take several pages to summarize. Allusions are at their best when they operate in this fashion: when they suggest a host of relevant associations and implications and thus produce an effect of concentrated richness.

A highly allusive style, then, can achieve a luxuriant texture, interwoven with strands from Russian literature, British history, comic books,

---

[12] © 1968, 1970, 1973 by Caroline Bird. From the book *Born Female*, published by David McKay Company, Inc. Reprinted by permission of the publisher. *Born Female*, revised edition (New York: David McKay, 1970), p. 243.

television commercials, the politics of ancient Rome, and so on. Gore Vidal, for one, achieves such luxuriance through the profusion and range of his allusions. In the following passage he alludes to subjects as diverse as anthropology, American Puritanism, Hebrew folklore, and current fashions in underwear.

> Though female nudes have been usually acceptable in our Puritan culture, until recently the male nude was unacceptable to the Patriarchs. After all, the male—any male—is a stand-in for God, and God wears a suit at all times, or at least jockey shorts. Now, thanks to Randy Lilith, the male can be shown entirely nude but, say the American censors, never with an erection. The holy of holies, the totem of our race, the symbol of the Patriarchs' victory over the Great Mother must be respected.[13]

Only a highly sophisticated audience could enjoy that stream of witty allusions. And this problem of audience is one that the user of allusions must constantly keep in mind. On the one hand, he must avoid the hackneyed allusions that would bore his audience: "the die is cast," "a Roman orgy," "to be or not to be," "met his Waterloo," and the rest. But on the other hand, he must not become so wide-ranging and recondite in his allusions as to puzzle his audience and convince them he is a pretentious pedant. Gore Vidal wrote that passage about nudes for the *New York Review of Books*, whose readers would have no trouble interpreting his allusions; but suppose he had written it for a publication of the American Chamber of Commerce or the Veterans of Foreign Wars. If it had gotten into print at all, it would have alienated most of its readers—for a variety of reasons, to be sure, but partly because of its erudite allusions.

One way to avoid seeming pretentious is to explain, unobtrusively, any allusion that might puzzle your readers:

> The inspiration for teaching girls to expect less than boys comes from a range of cultural sources, religious, literary, psychiatric, and pop. Even in the Bible, exceptional, independent women like Rebecca, Sarah, Deborah, or Ruth are practically "unknowns" compared with the infamous Eve or Delilah.
>
> Paula Stern [14]

> For centuries Western civilization has laughed at the poor Indian who sees gods in the clouds or hears them in the wind. But sud-

[13] Copyright © 1970, 1971 by Gore Vidal. Reprinted from *Homage To Daniel Shays: Collected Essays 1952–1972*, by Gore Vidal, by permission of Random House, Inc. "Women's Liberation Meets Miller-Mailer-Manson Man," *Homage to Daniel Shays* (New York: Random House, 1972), p. 401.

[14] "The Womanly Image," *Atlantic Monthly*, March 1970, p. 87. Copyright © 1970, by The Atlantic Monthly Company, Boston, Mass. Reprinted with permission.

denly some of our boldest thinkers—McGlashan, Jung, and Levi-Strauss, among others—have declared that the primitive savage can teach us lessons that may well be indispensable for the survival of the human race.

Any reader unfamiliar with the Biblical women mentioned in the first passage, or the "boldest thinkers" in the second, would still have no trouble following the authors' line of reasoning, so clearly are those references explained.

And another allusion in the second passage shows that one kind of out-of-the-way allusion needs no explanation whatever. Those phrases about the "poor Indian" are derived from Alexander Pope's *Essay on Man:*

Lo, the poor Indian! whose untutored mind
Sees God in clouds, or hears him in the wind. . . .

Readers who catch the reference will not only savor its implications but will enjoy having detected an esoteric allusion. And yet the writer takes no risk of puzzling or offending the rest of his readers, who will understand the passage easily enough, and will pass over the allusion without suspecting its presence.

Perhaps we should mention one additional figure. You will occasionally find use for *oxymoron,* the yoking of incongruous words. Asa Berger uses oxymoron in speaking of the "aggressive passivity" with which Dagwood Bumstead imposes his wishes on Blondie and his boss. A beginning teacher of our acquaintance used oxymoron when he spoke of the "awesome mediocrity" of his least enterprising students. And in the same way you might use oxymoron to characterize the "painful triumph" of a much-injured football team, the "calculated irrationality" with which some people win arguments, the "timid arrogance" of a petty bureaucrat, the "consistent inconsistency" of a wavering mind, or the "benevolent ruthlessness" of a Lenin. Note the flavor of irony in that phrase and in several of the others. You can find oxymoron used for the same effect in conversation, as when someone says, "Yes, you could call it a shocking movie—shockingly dull."

But oxymoron, like the other figures we've examined, should be used sparingly. "Nothing too much," the ancients used to say, applying this dictum to just about every branch of human activity, including the cultivation of an effective prose style. And to no other feature of style does the advice apply more readily than to the use of figurative language. Earlier epochs in the development of English prose welcomed a profusion of figures, such as could be found in the writings of Jeremy Taylor and Thomas Browne (seventeenth century) or Charles Lamb and Thomas De Quincey (early nineteenth century); but readers in our own century quickly become impatient with an ornately figurative style. The fancy figurations of a T. E. Lawrence may win our admiration for a while, but for the most part we prefer the plain but nutritious fare served up by an Orwell, an E. M. Forster, a Mary McCarthy, or an E. B. White. "Rich, ornate prose," as White has said, "is hard to digest, generally unwholesome, and sometimes nauseating." [15]

Exercises

I. Locate the figures of speech in the following passages. Identify each figure. Is it a metaphor, an instance of synecdoche, or what?

1. In the following excerpt from his *Preface to Shakespeare*, Samuel Johnson uses the word *quibble* to mean any toying or trifling with words: double-meanings, far-fetched metaphors, and the like. He has accused Shakespeare of indulging in such quibbles even at the cost of distracting his audience from scenes of tender love or high tragedy, and in the following passage he continues his attack on Shakespearian quibbles. We have modernized spelling and punctuation.

A quibble is to Shakespeare what luminous vapors are to the traveler: he follows it at all adventures; it is sure to lead him out of his way and sure to engulf him in the mire. It has some malignant power over his mind, and its fascinations are irresistible. Whatever be the dignity or profundity of his disquisition, whether he be enlarging knowledge or exalting affection, whether he be amusing attention with incidents or enchaining it in suspense, let but a quibble spring up before him and he leaves his work unfinished. A quibble is the golden apple for which he will always turn aside from his career or stoop from his elevation. A quibble, poor and barren as it is, gave him such delight that he was content to purchase it by the sacrifice of reason, propriety and truth. A quibble was to him the fatal Cleopatra for which he lost the world and was content to lose it.

Here H. L. Mencken denounces sociologist Thorstein Veblen for the "almost unbelievable tediousness and flatulence" of his prose: "his unprecedented talent for saying nothing in an august and heroic manner." Mencken has bombarded several passages from Veblen's *Theory of the Leisure Class*, and now continues his attack as follows.

And so it went, alas, alas, in all his other volumes—a cent's worth of information wrapped in a bale of polysyllables. In "The Higher

[15] William Strunk, Jr., and E. B. White, *The Elements of Style*, 2nd ed. (New York: Macmillan, 1972), p. 65.

Learning in America" the thing perhaps reached its damndest and worst. It was as if the practice of that incredibly obscure and malodorous style were a relentless disease, a sort of progressive intellectual diabetes, a leprosy of the horse sense. Words were flung upon words until all recollection that there must be a meaning in them, a ground and excuse for them, was lost. One wandered in a labyrinth of nouns, adjectives, verbs, pronouns, adverbs, prepositions, conjunctions and participles, most of them swollen and nearly all of them unable to walk. It was, and is, impossible to imagine worse English, within the limits of intelligible grammar. It was clumsy, affected, opaque, bombastic, windy, empty. It was without grace or distinction and it was often without the most elementary order. The professor got himself enmeshed in his gnarled sentences like a bull trapped by barbed wire, and his efforts to extricate himself were quite as furious and quite as spectacular. He heaved, he leaped, he writhed; at times he seemed to be at the point of yelling for the police. It was a picture to bemuse the vulgar and to give the judicious grief.[16]

Next James Thurber extols the intensity and the expertise of Harold Ross, the first editor of the *New Yorker*.

. . . there was more than clear concentration behind the scowl and the searchlight glare that he turned on manuscripts, proofs, and drawings. He had a sound sense, a unique, almost intuitive perception of what was wrong with something, incomplete or out of balance, understated or overemphasized. He reminded me of an army scout riding at the head of a troop of cavalry who suddenly raises his hand in a green and silent valley and says, "Indians," although to the ordinary eye and ear there is no faintest sign or sound of anything alarming. Some of us writers were devoted to him, a few disliked him heartily, others came out of his office after conferences as from a side show, a juggling act, or a dentist's office, but almost everybody would rather have had the benefit of his criticism than that of any other editor on earth. His opinions were voluble, stabbing, and grinding, but they succeeded somehow in refreshing your knowledge of yourself and renewing your interest in your work.

Having a manuscript under Ross's scrutiny was like putting your car in the hands of a skilled mechanic, not an automotive engineer with a bachelor of science degree, but a guy who knows what makes a motor go, and sputter, and wheeze, and sometimes come to a dead stop; a man with an ear for the faintest body squeak as well as the loudest engine rattle. When you first gazed, appalled, upon an uncorrected proof of one of your stories or articles, each margin had a thicket of queries and complaints—one writer got a hundred and forty-four on one profile. It was as though you beheld the works of your car spread all over the garage floor, and the job of getting the thing together again and making it work seemed impossible. Then you realized that Ross was trying to make your Model T or old Stutz Bearcat into a Cadillac or Rolls-Royce. He was at work with the tools of his unflagging perfectionism, and, after an exchange of growls or snarls, you set to work to join him in his enterprise.[17]

II. Compose metaphors (or similes) by completing the following expressions. For example:

As sober as *a preacher delivering a funeral sermon.*

Old age is like *ripples in a pond, repeating themselves until they disappear and the pond is motionless.*

Avoid clichés.

1. As fast as . . .
2. As slow as . . .
3. As lazy as . . .
4. As talkative as . . .
5. As shrewd as . . .
6. Anger is like . . .
7. Love is like . . .
8. Love that is not returned is like . . .
9. That book is like . . .
10. His hands are like . . .

III. Compose sentences that illustrate the following figures of speech. If you like, you may simply imitate the sentences enclosed in parentheses.

1. Simile (Life is like music; it must be composed by ear, feeling, and instinct, not by rule.)
2. Simile (The present style of marriage is a little like Russian roulette; and most of the time the chamber is loaded.)
3. Metaphor (Professor Meyers somehow managed to combine the roles of solicitous guru and academic drill sergeant.)
4. Metaphor (If you have built castles in the air, your work need not

be lost; that is where they should be. Now put the foundations under them.)

5. Metaphor as verb (Every ready-made phrase anaesthetizes a portion of one's brain.)

6. Metaphor as verb (She orchestrated the conversation as if she had known all of us for years.)

7. Personification (The fossilized dinosaur egg reminded me that Nature is a gambler, a reckless improviser, and that most of her schemes have failed.)

8. Personification (The Shadow side of the human race towers over us all, darkening the sky with its bombers and missiles and deadly gasses.)

9. Synecdoche (She is more likely to become an upper-echelon attorney at General Motors than a Nader's Raider or a storefront lawyer for people on welfare.)

10. Synecdoche (When he was in high school, he always preferred Shakespeare or Rimbaud to football or dancing.)

11. Allusion (The instructor would nod his approval even if a student insisted that Bob Dylan was a greater poet than Shakespeare and that Alice Cooper had more to teach us than Socrates or Jesus.)

12. Allusion (The date was 1967. Dionysus had just invaded suburbia.)

13. Oxymoron (Dagwood sometimes manages to bully his wife and even his boss through a kind of aggressive passivity.)

14. Oxymoron (He was polite and eager to please; but with the timid arrogance of a petty bureaucrat he refused to break, or even bend, the most trivial rules.)

IV. Review one of your earlier pieces of writing to see whether you can enliven it with figurative language, especially similes and metaphors.

15

Slanting

"I'm firm. You're stubborn. He's pigheaded." This line
from a parlor game shows how widely a set of synonyms can vary in
their connotations. The connotations can be favorable or unfavorable—
can praise or condemn. In many lists of synonyms you can find a neutral
word, a word that implies neither praise nor condemnation, but you can
just as easily, can *more* easily, find words whose connotations are com-
plimentary ("firm," "determined," "strong-willed") or insulting ("stubborn," "pigheaded," "dogmatic," "obstinate"). Thus you can refer to
someone's weight with a neutral word ("small," "large"), a complimen-
tary word ("slender," "sturdy"), or an insulting one ("thin," "scrawny,"
"cadaverous"; "fat," "blubbery," "overstuffed," "elephantine"). You can
express a neutral attitude toward a person's vocation by using terms such
as "governmental office worker," "teacher," "salesman," or "policeman";
you can imply a compliment by shifting to "civil servant," "educator,"
"sales representative," or "peace officer"; and you can sling an insult with
such terms as "bureaucrat," "pedant," "huckster," or "cop."

A passage loaded with either favorable or unfavorable connotations
is said to be *slanted*. If a writer is arguing in support of Senator Bilgepump, he can slant his argument, and take in many unsuspecting readers,
by using words whose connotations will cast a shimmering glow over the
senator's ideas and actions. And if a second writer wishes to debunk the
senator, he can load his prose with unfavorable connotations and turn
that shimmering glow into dust and ashes. What may surprise you is

how easily the same material can be slanted in either direction—how easily connotations can make the same ideas and events appear either glowing or ashen. This kind of wizardry, or black magic, is standard fare in the popular media.

A second means of slanting is the suppression of evidence: the omission of any facts that might weaken the writer's argument. Thus Senator Bilgepumps publicist, if he were sufficiently unscrupulous, would neglect to mention the senator's opposition to civil rights legislation, his tendency to spend money on weapons and big-business subsidies rather than education or food for the hungry, and his penchant for accepting extravagant gifts from special-interest groups. On the other hand, an unscrupulous *opponent* to Bilgepump would emphasize the senator's faults but fail to mention his courageous demand for fiscal responsibility in the federal government.

We will take a look at a few samples of slanted writing, but first we will examine a passage that comes fairly close to being neutral— "comes fairly close," we say, because no passage regarding people and beliefs can attain absolute neutrality.

Mrs. Henrietta Dunlap, representing the Taxpayers for Better Education, spoke last night before the board of education. She proposed that the board should discontinue all interscholastic athletics. In this way, she said, roughly $400,000 could be diverted to other, more valuable educational programs that need the money.

The interscholastic athletic program, Mrs. Dunlap said, serves three main purposes, but none of those purposes can justify the expenditure of $400,000. First, the more popular sports, especially football and basketball, provide entertainment for nonplaying students and the general public; but Mrs. Dunlap responded to that point by saying that the goal of the schools should be education, not entertainment. Second, the program lets many students get some after-school exercise; but Mrs. Dunlap asserted that the youngsters get plenty of exercise in their daily classes in physical education. Third, the program each year leads to college scholarships for some fifteen or twenty athletes; but Mrs. Dunlap suggested that these especially talented athletes could be identified and trained by other means—such as the public parks' leagues for young baseball players —and that in any case the scholarships do not compensate for the $400,000 spent each year on interscholastic athletics. That money, Mrs. Dunlap said, should be used to improve the education of all students, instead of being used to obtain scholarships for a comparatively small number of gifted athletes who may or may not be gifted as students.

At the end of Mrs. Dunlap's half-hour presentation, she was applauded by the citizens in attendance and by several members of the board. Thomas Nagel, the board chairman, thanked Mrs. Dunlap and invited her to attend a future board meeting for further discussion of the points she had raised.

This passage comes close to being neutral, as we have said, although perhaps its tone is slightly favorable toward Mrs. Dunlap and her anti-athleticism. But now let's examine a passage whose bias is not in doubt:

Mrs. Henrietta Dunlap represents the aptly named Taxpayers for Better Education, a group of citizens dedicated to improving the education of our youngsters without putting a greater burden on the long-suffering taxpayer. Last night Mrs. Dunlap appeared before
5   the board of education to enlighten them as to the wastefulness of interscholastic athletics. The musclebound athletic empire costs the public $400,000 every year. And that money is desperately needed by other programs, programs devoted to truly educational purposes and not the special interests of a few jocks, coaches, cheerleaders,
10 and pom-pom girls.
    What are the true purposes of this money-hungry empire? Well, it does give a few lucky jocks the chance to do some extra running and jumping after school lets out. But surely, as Mrs. Dunlap pointed out, they get abundant exercise in their regular physical education
15 classes, which meet *every* school day. Why should we give them extra fun and games at a cost of $400,000? We could just lend them a football or basketball and let them strut their stuff at the school playing fields or the public parks.
    Dogmatic defenders of interscholastic fun and games try to
20 argue that the whole scheme is worthwhile because it brings in some college scholarships. But how many? A paltry fifteen or twenty, often for blockheads who can barely memorize their football plays, let alone attempt the more civilized arts of reading and writing. And even those fifteen or twenty could be singled out for scholarships
25 through the public parks recreation system—by means of such splendid projects as Little League baseball, in which *all* boys and girls get to play, not just a few pampered hotshots.
    The interscholastic athletic nonsense has one other purpose, doesn't it? It entertains restless adolescents—of all ages—on Friday
30 nights and Saturday afternoons. But surely they can find their entertainment elsewhere—through television or movies or listening to records or talking with friends. Surely they can enjoy their lives without forcing the school system to dole out $400,000 for their benefit. The schools are supposed to provide education, not enter-
35 tainment.
    After Mrs. Dunlap had presented these insights, she received an ovation from citizens and board members alike. Thomas Nagel, the board chairman, expressed deep gratitude to Mrs. Dunlap and urged her to meet further with the board to discuss how the ideas
40 of the Taxpayers for Better Education might best be acted upon.

Perhaps this writer has suppressed some evidence, but most of the slanting is accomplished through connotations. All the friendly connotations are given to Mrs. Dunlap and all the hostile ones to the devotees of athletics. Mrs. Dunlap and her group are *dedicated* (line 2). She appears before the board not merely to offer them a few suggestions, but to *enlighten* them (5). She doesn't just state her ideas; she *points them out* (3–14), with the implication that they are obviously true. And later her ideas are termed *insights* (36), as if to imply that only someone as intelligent as Mrs. Dunlap could have discovered them. Meanwhile the high school athletes are labeled *jocks* (9, 12), *blockheads* (22), and *pampered hotshots* (27). Their fans are *restless adolescents of all ages* (29). And their athletic program is a *wasteful, money-hungry, muscle-bound empire* (5–6, 11), a little extra *running* and *jumping* (12–13), some highly expensive *fun and games* (16, 19), a *scheme* (20), and finally nothing but *nonsense* (28). And the passage contains a host of other words whose connotations throw a flattering light on Mrs. Dunlap and a gloomy darkness over interscholastic athletics.

Now let's move to a passage in which the slanting is reversed—in which the connotations praise athletics and damn Mrs. Dunlap:

Mrs. "Hen" Dunlap, of the so-called Taxpayers for Better Education, clucked away for quite some time last night before a patient board of education. The burden of her harangue was that the board should sacrifice all interscholastic athletics—should surrender football,
5   basketball, and all the rest—in order to pour more money into the various schemes these amateur educators would like to promote. Mrs. Dunlap, like a puritanical schoolmarm of old, blithely ignored the value of athletics as a source of pleasure for the whole family, whereby parents and youngsters can get together for a wholesome
10   afternoon at the stadium or evening at the gymnasium. Further, she lightly dismissed the very real value of athletics as a body-builder— a guarantee against breakdowns in the bodily functions, against ailments arising from stiff bones, weak muscles, and a sluggish heart. Finally, Mrs. Dunlap ruthlessly derided a most telling argument in
15   favor of high school athletics—that it provides college scholarships for a considerable number of gifted young people who might otherwise become dropouts: the Bill Russells and O. J. Simpsons of tomorrow.
       For the better part of an hour the board tolerated the blather-
20   ing of this self-appointed prophet for highbrow education. Then they courteously but firmly dismissed her, while her accomplices in the audience dutifully clapped their genteel hands—pale, flabby hands that have never become skilled in our time-honored American sports.

Suddenly Mrs. Dunlap has turned into a *clucking hen* (lines 1–2), a *puritanical schoolmarm* (7), and a *self-appointed prophet* (20). And obviously her thinking is demented. She *blithely ignores* one important point (7), *lightly dismisses* another (11), and *ruthlessly derides* a third (14). In short, she *blathers* (19–20). Meanwhile, interscholastic athletics have become *time-honored* American sports (23–24) that serve as a *guaranteed body-builder* (11), a *wholesome* influence on the *entire family* (8–10), and the salvation of innumerable young men who, instead of becoming high school dropouts, will become the *Bill Russells and O. J. Simpsons of tomorrow* (16–18).

Connotations are not the only means by which this writer slants his argument. He also suppresses evidence. Nowhere does he mention the $400,000 spent annually on interscholastic athletics. Nowhere does he tell exactly how many athletes (or how few) get college scholarships; he converts a mere fifteen or twenty into "a considerable number" (line 16). And nowhere does he mention that several members of the board applauded Mrs. Dunlap or that the chairman asked her to return for further discussion.

These omissions, and others, convince us that the writer is not to be trusted. He comes very close to being a liar. And thus he brings us to the question of how far a writer should go with this exciting but dangerous business of slanting. Exciting it is—because connotations, both positive and negative, charge the prose with emotion. Take another look at the neutral account of Mrs. Dunlap's talk and then at the slanted versions, and you will probably agree that slanting can be more exciting than neutrality. But more dangerous, too—dangerous because it can alienate all sensible readers. The neutral version of Mrs. Dunlap's talk might not arouse our emotions, but at least it wins our trust. It convinces us that the writer is trying to be as fair, as objective, as accurate, as his talents allow. But the writers of the slanted versions do *not* win our trust. Rather than aiming for fairness or accuracy, they seem to take pride in being biased. They brandish their bias like a club, as if to coerce the reader into agreement. The intelligent reader, however, will not be so easily coerced. He will distrust any writer who seems to be governed by prejudice rather than reason.

Does this mean you must always refrain from slanting? Not always —but often. Often you must remain neutral because your readers would become distrustful if you assumed any other stance. If you were a judge addressing the jury immediately before they left the courtroom to reach a verdict, you would certainly do your best to deliver an objective, impartial interpretation of the law, so that your several audiences—the jury, the contending parties, the lawyers, the higher courts, the general public —would see that you were guided by reason and a sense of justice, not by prejudice or emotion. And if you were a journalist writing a news story—rather than a feature writer or an editorialist—again you would assume the stance of neutral objectivity.

The neutral stance is often appropriate for the college writer, too. If you write a technical report—for a course in engineering or the physical sciences, let's say—your instructor will almost certainly expect you to remain strictly dispassionate. And the same expectation will govern much of your writing even in such subjects as history, government, philosophy, psychology, and literature. Yes, even in literature. If you write a bibliographical study of Edgar Allan Poe, trying to determine which of the unsigned articles in the *Southern Literary Messenger* were Poe's and which were not, you won't be likely to slant your argument with connotations, and you certainly won't suppress any evidence.

In other kinds of essays, however, you are entitled to inject more of your emotions. When a student interprets D. H. Lawrence's *Women in Love,* when a journalist writes editorials or feature articles rather than news stories, when a judge steps down from the bench and writes about social issues—at such times the writer does not have to remain strictly neutral.

But even then, we believe, he should refuse to suppress evidence. It's one thing to omit minor evidence of dubious value; but, as we have said, to omit important evidence because it might weaken the argument is not much different from lying. Does the writer have no moral objections to lying? Then at least he should avoid it on the grounds that he might get caught. Careful readers, even some who are not familiar with his subject matter, will catch him in his duplicity and become skeptical toward his entire argument. Consider once again the hypothetical reporter who (on page 209) suppressed various bits of evidence presented by Mrs. Dunlap: the annual cost of interscholastic athletics, the exact number of athletes who receive college scholarships, and so on. The readers who detected any one of his suppressions would suspect his entire article of being inaccurate, and a brief statement in the "letters from our readers" column could reveal his dishonesty for all to see.

For several reasons, then, both moral and prudent, we advise you not to suppress evidence. If the evidence against your thesis is so powerful that you are tempted to suppress some of it, you would do better not to tamper with the evidence but to revise the thesis. Perhaps it needs only minor qualifications; perhaps it needs major overhauling; but obviously in its present form it is no longer defensible. The general who sees his front lines being overrun and outflanked does not close his eyes to this disconcerting information. He retreats and retrenches, in hopes of establishing a stronger line of defense. And you as a writer should adopt a similar tactic if the evidence against your original position threatens to become overwhelming.

What if the opposing evidence is strong but not overwhelming—not strong enough to warrant a revision in your thesis? Then why not present the evidence? Let your readers know the most damaging things your opposition can say. Then you can repair the damage by presenting the much stronger evidence that supports your own position. This strategy can be remarkably persuasive. By stating the opposing evidence, you show how scrupulous and straightforward you are; you show your disdain for dishonesty. The reader will be favorably impressed—and then will be even more impressed when you demolish the opposition with your own irrefutable evidence.

So you should avoid suppressing evidence. But what about slanting by means of connotations? This device, we believe, is not only permissible but highly effective. It can charge your prose with the kind of excitement we mentioned earlier. Our only reservation about this practice is that your slanted connotations should rest on a solid argument. Otherwise the connotations would be just as irresponsible, and just as likely to alienate readers, as the suppression of evidence. But once you have offered plausible ideas and supported them with reliable evidence, you are certainly justified in enhancing your argument through connotations that make your own position even more attractive and the opposition even more repugnant. If your evidence has established that Mrs. Dunlap's ideas about education are hollow and the woman simply doesn't know what she's talking about, you might well be entitled to accuse her of clucking and blathering like an emptyheaded gossip. If your evidence has established that the interscholastic athletic program is truly a waste of the taxpayers' money, you might justifiably label it a musclebound, money-hungry empire and a nonsensical worship of fun and games.

Does this language sound too exaggerated—too heavily loaded with slanted connotations? Possibly it is. How far you go in that direction will depend on the expectations of your readers. Readers who don't insist on strict neutrality might still object if your connotations are drastically slanted. Has your evidence shown that one of your high school teachers was obsessed with trivia? Some readers would not be alarmed if you labeled that teacher "a fanatical pedant" or "a maniacal fussbudget." They would enjoy those extravagant adjectives—would recognize that "fanatical" and "maniacal" were deliberate hyperboles: overstatements for the sake of rhetorical effect, to be taken figuratively rather than literally. But other readers—college instructors, perhaps, or the readers of certain staid periodicals—would expect greater restraint and exactitude, in which case you might simply drop those adjectives and call the teacher a fussbudget or a pedant. The choice of language will depend on your purpose and your audience.

The following piece of slanting is too extreme in its use of connotations. Even if the underlying argument were a strong one, the connotations might seem excessively slanted. And the argument is far from strong. Its evidence is almost nonexistent. The author of the passage is that great master of exaggeration, H. L. Mencken. His subject is the California of the 1920s—Mencken's candidate for the title of least civilized state in the union.

[The old California] is simply extinct. What remains is an Alsatia of retired Ford agents and *crazy fat women*—a paradise of 100% *Americanism* and the *New Thought*. Its laws are the most *extravagant* and *idiotic* ever heard of in Christendom. Its public officers, and particularly its judges, are famous all over the world for their *imbecilities*. When one hears of it at all, one hears that some citizen has been *jailed* for reading the Constitution of the United States, or that some new *swami* in a yellow *bed-tick* has got all the realtors' wives of Los Angeles by the ears. When one hears of it further, it is only to learn that some obscure movie lady in Hollywood has murdered another lover. The State is run by its Chambers of Commerce, which is to say, by the worst variety of resident *shysters*. No civilized man ever seems to take any part in its public life. Not an idea comes out of it—that is, not an idea beyond the grasp of a Kiwanis Club secretary, a Christian Science *sorcerer*, or a *grand goblin* of the American Legion. Twice, of late, it has offered the country candidates for the presidency. One was the Hon. Hiram Johnson and the other was the Hon. William Gibbs McAdoo! . . .[1]

The italicized words are the ones with the most insulting connotations. And in the ensuing lines Mencken adds further insults: California, he charges, had been degraded in part by the incoming "hordes of morons," "hinds," and "vacuums" from Iowa, Nebraska, and "the other cow states."

Now, all this invective may be vastly entertaining, but it rests on the flimsiest sort of evidence. The passage remains unconvincing because insult after insult is left unsubstantiated. True, Mencken gives two names in support of his implied charge that California had offered only mediocre candidates for the presidency. And a second charge—that a citizen had been "jailed for reading the Constitution"—is explained, or partly explained, elsewhere in the essay. But none of the other accusations gets the slightest support from factual evidence. On faith alone we are

[1] From *Prejudices: A Selection*, by H. L. Mencken, edited by James T. Farrell. Copyright 1926 by Alfred A. Knopf, Inc. and renewed 1954 by H. L. Mencken. Reprinted by permission of Alfred A. Knopf, Inc. "The Champion," *Prejudices: A Selection*, ed. James T. Farrell (New York: Alfred A. Knopf Vintage Books, 1958), p. 211.

supposed to believe that the California of the 1920s was dominated by retired Ford agents, crazy fat women, idiotic laws, imbecilic judges, New Thought swamis, Christian Science sorcerers, and Chamber of Commerce shysters. Admittedly, the pleasure of reading Mencken comes largely from his grandiose insults, but usually his insults are kept in closer accord with his evidence. Perhaps Mencken would have agreed with us in denouncing this essay. In 1949, some twenty years after the essay first appeared, he didn't admire it enough to include it in his *Crestomathy,* a 600-page collection of his best writings.

The following passage by Dwight Macdonald does some of the same things as the Mencken passage. It attacks by throwing insults, and the insults are accomplished partly through connotations. But Macdonald's use of connotations is not as dangerous, as problematical, as Mencken's. For one thing, Macdonald doesn't slant his connotations as sharply as Mencken did; he indulges in no invective or name-calling. Second, Macdonald supports his insults with solid evidence, so that even his nastiest connotations seem justified.

Macdonald's subject is the how-to and self-help manuals that clutter up the bookstores these days, giving advice on just about every-thing—how to be sexy, how to be a church usher, how to rake in $100,000 during your coffee breaks, and so on. Macdonald particularly resents the "self-helps" that pretend to solve all emotional and spiritual problems by applying a little sure-fire know-how: "Everything that was once a matter for meditation and retreat into the wilderness has been reduced to the level of technique." And in the following passage he ridicules this tendency as it appears in the self-helps of Norman Vincent Peale.

> To provide a *semblance* of peace of mind, the *self-help* writer has two powerful *drugs* in his pharmacopoeia: psychology and religion. . . . The *big sales* are being *rung up* by the men of God. . . . The Reverend Dr. Peale, who is pastor of the Marble Collegiate Church, in New York City, first *hit the jackpot* with *A Guide to Confident Living* (1948) and now, with even more success, he has repeated the *mixture* as before in *The Power of Positive Thinking,* which starts out, "This is simply a practical, direct-action personal-improvement manual . . . a system of creative living based on spiritual tech-niques." *Big medicine,* that, every word of it, like the rest of the three-page introduction, which offers the diligent reader the rewards of both worlds—This and the Other—by means of the most power ful *incantations:* ". . . a practical method . . . successful living . . . peace of mind. . . . You will become a more popular, es teemed, and well-liked individual . . . scientific yet simple principle

of achievement, health, and happiness . . . new life, new power, increased efficiency, greater happiness . . . a happy, satisfying, and worthwhile life . . . applied Christianity; a simple yet scientific system of practical techniques, of successful living that works." It works, it's simple (yet scientific), its scientific (yet simple), it *guarantees* happiness & success & worthwhileness & peace & salvation, and, best of all, it has been *reduced* by the intellectual labors of Dr. Peale to a *system,* a *technique* (these words, or synonyms for them, appear twenty times in the three pages), that gets both God and Freud *on the job,* with "scientific counseling and . . . the application of religious faith." Let the *Gold Dust Twins do your work!* The actual text of Dr. Peale's book turns out to be a mite *disappointing*—proves, in fact, to be just the *usual collection* of real-life stories ("in a business office high above the city streets two men were having a serious conversation . . .") and exemplary instances ("The late Harlowe B. Andrews of Syracuse, New York, one of the best businessmen and competent spiritual experts I ever knew . . ."), *interlarded* with the *standard commonplaces* ("Most of our obstacles, as a matter of fact, are mental in character") and *spiced* with *religiosity* (Chapter 4: "Try Prayer Power"). Neither in title nor in content does Dr. Peale's book seem superior to dozens of its *competitors,* or even distinguishable from them. Why a hundred Americans should plunk down their two dollars and ninety-five cents for *The Power of Positive Thinking* for every two or three who purchase, say, *Peace and Power Within* or *You Can Master Life* is a mystery of *mass behavior* as puzzling as the periodic *suicides of lemmings* in the Arctic Ocean.[2]

We have quoted Macdonald at such great length partly to let you savor his wit, but mostly to show how thoroughly he substantiates his accusations. The amplitude of his evidence allows him to hurl some highly insulting connotations without fear of turning his readers against him. Mencken, in the passage lambasting California, lets his voice get louder and louder, as if he were shouting to a crowd and trying to whip up their emotions. He launches one wild insult after another, without pausing to add explanation or evidence. Macdonald's voice is quieter, subtler, more reflective. His insults are not as violent as Mencken's. His connotations are not as raucous or rambunctious. He goes at a slower pace so that he can add plenty of evidence. And ultimately his quiet reasoning is more persuasive than Mencken's bellowing.

[2] Copyright 1954 by Dwight Macdonald. Originally appeared in *The New Yorker.* Reprinted from *Against the American Grain,* by Dwight Macdonald, by permission of Random House, Inc. "Howtoism," *Against the American Grain* (New York: Random House, 1962), pp. 386–88.

Exercises

I. Each of the following exercises offers several roughly synonymous terms. Arrange each set of terms in a sequence that begins with the most laudatory and ends with the most derogatory. For example:

    a. stubborn
    b. firm
    c. pigheaded

The answer is: b, a, c.

The answers to several of the exercises are debatable, especially the answer to number 7.

1. a. sales agent
    b. salesman
    c. huckster
    d. sales representative
2. a. well-read person
    b. bookworm
    c. bookish person
    d. avid reader
3. a. politician
    b. national leader
    c. boss
    d. statesman
    e. politico
4. a. ambition
    b. aspiration
    c. greed
5. a. brave
    b. reckless
    c. courageous
    d. unflinching
    e. foolhardy
6. a. prudent
    b. cowardly
    c. unenterprising
    d. cautious
    e. judicious
7. a. leisurely
    b. lazy
    c. unhurried
    d. placid
    e. shiftless

f. sluggish

g. tranquil

II. The following passages are heavily slanted Choose two of them to work with. Rewrite those two in a neutral tone. Then rewrite one of them in a tone directly opposed to that of the original. In performing that second task, don't worry if you have to falsify or fabricate. Let yourself become as dishonest a slanter as any you might find in the mass media.

Here is the kind of passage you will be working on:

> As America steamed into its Industrial Age robber barons brainstormed more efficient ways of profiting from the natural resources of the land.
>
> Walt Shepperd [3]

Now here we offer a neutral version of that passage:

> As America entered its Industrial Age, business executives devised new ways of marketing the natural resources of the land.

And now we reverse the original slanting—so that Mr. Shepperd's robber barons wind up sounding like altruistic captains of industry:

> As America steamed into its Industrial Age, our most forward-looking business leaders labored to perfect new ways of finding, refining, and distributing the rich natural resources which the citizens of this country, and other countries, were eager to use.

> 1. [The modern liberated woman] is liberating herself not so much from sex, but from what goes with being a girl—all that sugar and spice and everything nice that sometimes seems especially attractive to frigid women. Because of the exploitation she sees associated with them, she has discarded all the little cues and clues and buttons and bows and smiles and wiles that invite a man to look her over. She wants, above all, freedom from the tyranny of being a girl. . . . Like the heroine of a recent Women's Lib play, she is likely to whack off her [hair], wear it scraggling around her face, witch-style, or conceal it under a tight bandana, nun-style. She wears no makeup, no frippery. A growing number of otherwise conventional young women refuse to squeeze themselves into brassieres, and they may, as the spirit moves, dispense also with shoes, stockings, and underwear of any kind.
>
> Caroline Bird [4]

---

[3] *Conjuring a Counter-Culture* (Paradise, Calif.: Dustbooks, 1973), p. 21.

[4] © 1968, 1970, 1973 by Caroline Bird. From the book *Born Female,* published by David McKay Company, Inc. Reprinted by permission of the publisher. *Born Female,* revised edition (New York: David McKay, 1970), p. 243.

2. [Eleaner Roosevelt's] life was crowded, restless, fearless. . . . She walked in the slums and ghettos of the world, not on a tour of inspection, nor as a condescending patron, but as one who could not feel complacent while others were hungry, and who could not find contentment while others were in distress. . . . But we dare not regard her as just a benign incarnation of good works. For she was not only a great woman and a great humanitarian, but a great democrat. . . . I mean that she had a lively and astute understanding of the nature of the democratic process. She was a master political strategist with a fine sense of humor. And, as she said, she loved a good fight.

Adlai Stevenson [5]

3. [The drug experience] weakens the aspects of personality which are socially patterned and reinforces those which are basically human. It takes the user out of his modern culture, for it makes him leave behind his culturally patterned priorities. That a young man is a Methodist, not a Baptist; American, not Mexican; rich, not poor— these cultural characteristics seem to have less relevance to what a person is feeling when he is high. . . . Drug-users view the psychedelic experience as the ammunition for their revolution against the "cool," detached, deferred-benefits personality and the mass society that cultivates it. They find that what they feel is another way of life, alien to modern Western culture and comparable to feelings in simpler cultures. They experience a style of living that is unified, not divided; involved, not detached; deeply emotional, not contrived.

Mark Gerzon [6]

4. . . . I wish to preach not the doctrine of ignoble ease but the doctrine of the strenuous life; the life of toil and effort; of labor and strife; to preach that highest form of success which comes not to the man who desires mere easy peace but to the man who does not shrink from danger, from hardship, or from bitter toil, and who out of these wins the splendid ultimate triumph.

The timid man, the lazy man, the man who distrusts his country, the over-civilized man, who has lost the great fighting masterful virtues, the ignorant man and the man of dull mind, whose soul is incapable of feeling the mighty lift that thrills "stern men with empire in their brain"—all these, of course, shrink from seeing the nation undertake its new duties; shrink from seeing us build a navy and army adequate to our needs; shrink from seeing us do our share of the world's work by bringing order out of chaos in the great, fair

[5] "Her Journeys Are Over," *Saturday Review*, 24 November 1962, p. 23.
[6] *The Whole World Is Watching* (New York: Paperback Library, 1969), p. 249.

tropic islands from which the valor of our soldiers and sailors has driven the Spanish flag.

Theodore Roosevelt [7]

5. Germaine Greer on the modern ideal of feminine beauty—but only the first paragraph (pp. 19-20)

6. Herbert J. Muller on "mass-man and his mass-culture" (pp. 158-59)

7. Bernard Shaw on "the whole country as a big household" (pp. 191-92)

8. James Nolan on the new "evangelism industry" (pp. 195-96)

9. H. L. Mencken on the "incredibly obscure and malodorous style" of Thorstein Veblen (pp. 202-3)

10. James Thurber on the editorial expertise of Harold Ross (pp. 203-4)

III. The following passage comes close to being neutral in characterizing "conventional people" and "deviants." Compose two slanted versions of the passage. In the first, sympathize with the deviants and condemn the conventional people. In the second, do exactly the opposite.

Perhaps the most fundamental and recurrent interpersonal problem of the deviant is that he or she faces the ever present danger of retribution from the people and the official agencies in the surrounding environment. Arrest and commitment of some kind are only the most extreme forms of this danger; they are the most spectacular but they really touch only a small fraction of deviants directly. Far more frequent and significant are the thousand and one daily discriminations and condemnations and hassles.

   Conventional people are hardly aware of the extent to which they continuously voice and act out their moral standards. But in the act of doing so they challenge, condemn, and ostracize those who are different. The habitual deviant faces some risk of job loss, of family crises, of "referral to counselling," and even of informal physical violence. These are real threats and not infrequent actualities. But these things are only the background to the daily realities of the disapproving frown and the quizzical look, the television comedian's joke, the shushed conversations which engender the sense that you are a stranger in a strange land.

J. L. Simmons [8]

[7] "The Doctrine of the Strenuous Life," *The Strenuous Life* (New York: Review of Reviews, 1900), pp. 3, 9.

[8] *Deviants* (Santa Barbara: Glendessary Press of Boyd & Fraser, 1969), p. 73.

IV. Search through your old essays until you find a passage (about 200 words long) that will give you a chance to use some slanted wording—a passage that praises its subject or censures it. Your job is to intensify the praise or the censure by adding words with laudatory or censorious connotations.

16

The Writer's Voice

Napoleon was asked to appoint a stranger to a position requiring intelligence, self-control, and a capacity for leadership. "Has he written anything?" the general asked. "Let me see his style." Perhaps the great man had too much confidence in his ability to detect the person through the style, but the fact remains that if you read with sensitivity, you can indeed form some notion of what kind of person the writer might be—prudent or impetuous, reasonable or emotional, gently judicious or scathingly satirical. You can almost hear the writer speaking— his tone of voice, his emphases, his slightest inflections—as if, rather than offering you merely words on paper, he were sitting across from you and telling you his thoughts.

The writer's voice, as this phenomenon has been called, is notoriously difficult to analyze; but it becomes somewhat more manageable if we divide it into two overlapping but distinguishable elements: *persona* and *tone.*

PERSONA

By *persona* we mean the writer's personal characteristics: beliefs, allegiances, prejudices, education, reading, experiences, emotional makeup, possibly even physical traits. You can learn some of this by reading a single page, but of course the more you read, the more you learn. If you read a single page by Edmund Wilson, for instance, you will at least recognize Wilson's extraordinary intelligence, simply by noting the range of his vocabulary, the complexity of his sentences, and the incisiveness of his ideas. But if you go on to read a great many of Wilson's pages, you learn about the diversity of his interests, which included such disparate subjects as the Dead Sea Scrolls, Ulysses S. Grant, Emily Post, and James Joyce; you learn about his extensive reading in the literatures of at least eight languages, both classical and modern; you learn about his contempt for the general run of college professors of literature; you learn about his early flirtation and later disenchantment with Marxism, and his antagonism toward the federal government—its wasteful and oppressive bureaucracy, its padded military budget, and its ineptitude in handling such urgent problems as the mediocrity of public education and the persistence of widespread hunger and bad housing. You learn about his growing distaste for modern American culture, which he believed to be dominated by vapid television, meretricious movies, and such lightweight intellects as Norman Mailer. You learn about his house in upstate New York, to which he retreated in his final years to achieve a stoic tranquility: "That the old life is passing away, that all around me are anarchy and what seems to me stupidity, does not move me much any more. I have learned to read the papers calmly and not to hate the fools I read about."[1]

And yet Wilson does not reveal the whole of his personality. No writer does—for reasons to be examined in a moment. You could read Wilson's published writings in their entirety (more than twenty volumes) and yet never suspect that this scrupulous scholar and painstaking stylist was "a short, overweight man in floppy dark clothes, wearing a floppy hat and carrying a floppy suitcase."[2] Perhaps you would guess that he sometimes delivered his opinions with bludgeon-like bluntness (he once told a movie critic, "I always stay away from the movies you recommend"[3]); but even if you had read Wilson's essays on magicians, you probably wouldn't guess that this cranky, cantankerous old man of American letters delighted in doing magic tricks for children, or that while he chatted with friends about the Dead Sea Scrolls, the evolution of Marxism, or the meaning of *Finnegans Wake*, he would exercise his magician's skill with a pack of cards, which he rippled and flashed, collapsed and collected, without ever losing his train of thought.[4]

The persona reflected in the writings, then, is not the entire personality of the writer. Hence our use of the word *persona* rather than *personality* or *person*. *Persona* is the Latin for *mask*, particularly the

[1] Wilson, *Upstate* (New York: Farrar, Straus and Giroux, 1971), p. 386.
[2] "Edmund Wilson," *The New Yorker* (24 June 1972), p. 96.
[3] "Edmund Wilson," p. 96.
[4] Eleanor Perényi, "Wilson," *Esquire* (July 1963), p. 83.

theatrical mask worn in Greek and Roman drama to signify various kinds of characters—tragic or comic, dignified or vulgar, arrogant or peace-loving. Now, in a sense the writer dons a mask when he expresses himself on paper—however paradoxical that assertion may seem. He doesn't reveal his entire personality. He reveals only those features of his personality that seem appropriate to the writing he is doing at that moment. Out of the chaotic complexity of his actual personality he shapes the persona best suited to his present task. If that task happens to be a scholarly study of Jane Austen, the persona will be scholarly—no matter how passionate and anti-academic the writer may sometimes feel. He will ignore those features of his personality that don't fit, simply because his readers—college students and professors, most likely—would distrust a writer who didn't seem scholarly enough to have valuable ideas about Jane Austen. His persona will not display his passion for his new lover, or his irritation with his bawling three-year-old and whining eight-year-old, or the fierce competitiveness he exhibits during Saturday-morning football. He won't use the four-letter words or the exaggerations that he might disgorge while sharing beers with his fishing buddies. None of these traits would suit the persona he has created for his essay on Austen: the persona of a sophisticated reader—intelligent, judicious, refined, devoted to literature and high culture in general. But if the same writer—by some freakish accident—happens to write a defense of sexual liberation and experimentation, he will have to create a new persona. He might then reveal his irritability, his competitiveness, his beer-drinking language, and of course his passion for his new lover, as well as some other sides of his personality that were best left hidden when he assumed his scholarly persona. But his new persona will have other things to hide—including, perhaps, his fondness for reading Jane Austen, Charles Lamb, Max Beerbohm, and other literary figures for whom sexual experimentation would have been anathema.

The writer who deals with a great variety of subjects may have to develop a variety of personas—or *personae*, to use the Latin plural. Ezra Pound acknowledged this multiplicity of artistic selves when he gave the title *Personae* to his collected early poems, in which he assumed a variety of guises: the witty dissector of personal foibles, the brooding critic of society at large, the Chinese woman yearning for her husband, the Roman poet who preferred making love to making war, and so on. H. L. Mencken showed a similar skill in varying his personae:

In the heyday of *The American Mercury* and in his "Prejudices," H. L. Mencken showed himself a master of protest, dealing with Dr. Coolidge, the Bible Belt, the Sahara of the Bozart, mountebanks, and charlatans, and lashing out against hocus-pocus. In "The American Language" he showed an occasional flash of humor, but for the most part he wrote with smooth regard for reader and subject, and he respected the dignity of both. He was not the same Mencken. And in his reminiscent book, "Happy Days," being the recounting of his Baltimore childhood, his prose was properly benign, his mood mellow, and his style quiet. There was no need to whambang. In "The American Language" he was a scholar and he wrote in an appropriate manner. In his "Prejudices" he was the Bad Boy of Baltimore, in "Happy Days" an old man recalling. In each case he adapted his writing to the requirements of the job.

Charles W. Ferguson [5]

The same thing is true of other writers of prose—James Agee, for example, whose tender, compassionate persona in *Let Us Now Praise Famous Men* differs sharply from the witty, sardonic Agee who wrote movie reviews and the fun-loving Agee who wrote the screenplay for *The African Queen.*

So don't feel that you have to confine yourself to a single persona for all your writing. It's true that within any one piece of writing you won't be likely to shift from one persona to another; you won't be a Jane Austen scholar on your first page and a beer-drinking libertine on the next, lest you confuse your readers and lose their confidence. But each time you do a new piece of writing, you are entitled to use whatever new persona is suited to the new occasion. Consider your subject, your audience, and your purpose; then emphasize those features of your personality and experience that seem most likely to fit the circumstances.

Does it sound as if we want you to be deceptive and hypocritical? That's not at all what we mean. We mean simply that you should be as flexible in your writing as in your speaking. You use one style of speaking for your father, another for your sister, another for the friend you've known for the last ten years, another for the lover you met six months ago, another for a college professor, another for an employer. You use one style in class, another at a party, and another for a job interview. The same flexibility should be exercised in your writing. There, too, you should present the features of your personality best suited to the occasion.

TONE

The *tone* of a passage is the *emotion* reflected in that passage. Tone is usually thought of as the sum of two of the writer's attitudes.

[5] *Say It with Words* (New York: Alfred A. Knopf, 1959).

The first is his *attitude toward his subject:* the emotions he feels toward whatever he's writing about. Obviously such emotions can be infinitely diverse—can range from hatred to love, from sorrow to joy, from lugubrious despair to ecstatic affirmation. And the emotions can vary widely within a single piece of writing—even within a single paragraph. As the writer moves from one phase of the subject to another, his emotions will change accordingly. If in one passage, for instance, he describes a favorite teacher, then the prose will reflect admiration, affection, gratitude, and nostalgia. But if in the next passage he describes the very *worst* of his teachers, his emotions may change to anger and bitterness.

The second ingredient in tone is *the writer's attitude toward his audience.* This attitude shouldn't vary as much as his attitude toward his subject. In fact, readers have every right to be disconcerted if they find the writer friendly on one page and then impersonal, insolent, or condescending on the next; and the writer should avoid such surprises unless he has some sensible way of fitting them into his larger rhetorical scheme.

The writer's attitude toward his reader can take a variety of forms, but usually the crucial factor is his degree of friendliness. Where does his tone fall on the scale that starts with *chummy* and ends with *aloof?* Chatty and intimate? Reserved and impersonal? Or does the tone fall somewhere between the extremes by being relaxed and friendly?

A writer's position on that scale will often depend on the level of style. High Style tends to be impersonal. It usually contains few *I*'s or *you*'s, and its sophisticated wording and elaborate sentences are reminiscent of the learned journal, the professorial lecture, and the ceremonial speech. Low Style tends to be chummy. It often abounds in *I*'s and *you*'s, and its easy little sentences, together with its colloquial and sometimes slovenly wording, can make it sound like casual chatter over cocktails. Middle Style tends to be relaxed and friendly. It uses occasional *I*'s and *you*'s and occasional contractions and colloquialisms. Its words are accurate without being unusual. And its sentences, though longer than those of Low Style, are never hard to follow. Middle Style evokes the image of an amiable, intelligent person addressing a small group of friends, or people who might easily become his friends. He is neither aloof nor chummy. He doesn't pose as a visiting lecturer on esoteric subjects, but neither does he pretend to be your long-lost pal.

Tone, then, reflects the writer's attitude toward subject and audience. To illustrate these points, let's examine two passages whose tones are sharply different. (Both passages, as it happens, come from the same page of a daily newspaper—the front page of the *Sacramento Bee* for August 27, 1974.)

How would you characterize the tone of this first passage?

The 1974 California State Fair is five days old and toddling right along at Cal Expo. Tonight, on the jingle-jangle, "get 'em while they're hot" flood-lit grounds, you can take your pick. . . . And to-morrow—there's even more going on. Including——pssssssst! You like gossip? Rona, Rona Barrett, the noted Hollywood tongue-wagger, is going to be telling all at the Women's Day Luncheon. . . .

Nancy Skelton, "Swinging Fair"

First, how would you describe Skelton's attitude toward her subject— toward the fair? Excited? Enthusiastic? Cheerful? Playful? Whimsical? *All* those words might be applied; and maybe you can add some others. Second, what is Skelton's attitude toward her readers? *Chummy* might be an accurate adjective. Skelton assumes the role of an old pal who doesn't hesitate to use *you*'s, contractions, colloquialisms, sentence frag- ments, and even a "pssssssst." And she offers lots of friendly advice: you can take your pick of tonight's activities; there's even more going on tomorrow; and if you have a weakness for gossip, be sure to hear tongue- wagging Rona Barrett.

Just below that article on the fair appeared a memorial tribute to Charles A. Lindbergh—and a sharp contrast in tone:

From a distance some said the plane looked like a lone eagle as it swooped in from the west toward Mather Field. The silver-gray monoplane streaked over the field, less than 100 feet off the ground, and then banked and swooped in again. Lindy had come to Sacra- mento and the city was agog for the arrival of one of the greatest heroes of American aviation. Charles A. Lindbergh, who died yester- day at the age of 72 in an isolated cottage on a Hawaii beach, landed the Spirit of St. Louis in Sacramento on Saturday, Sept. 17, 1927, four months after he became the first man to fly the Atlantic alone.

Steve Duscha, "Capitol Was Agog for Hero Lindy's '27 Visit"

The writer's attitude toward his subject? Though the article was oc- casioned by Lindbergh's death, the tone is not especially sorrowful—ex- cept, perhaps, in that one reference to an isolated cottage. Instead, the dominant emotion seems to be a nostalgic admiration, almost a reverence, for the Lindbergh of the 1920s. This emotion is pointed up by several phrases: "a lone eagle," "one of the greatest heroes of American aviation," and "the first man to fly the Atlantic alone." Even the gracefully soaring sentences help to convey the writer's admiration. How different the tone would have been if Duscha's sentences had been as short and quick as those with which Skelton conveyed her excitement over the California State Fair.

And Duscha's attitude toward his readers? Clearly it is much less intimate than Skelton's. Here we find no *you's* to snag the reader's attention, no contractions, no colloquialisms, no sentence fragments. Duscha's style is somewhere in the upper ranges of Middle, verging on High, and his attitude toward the reader might be characterized as impersonal—all of which is appropriate in a tribute to the recently dead.

Before leaving the subject of tone, we should say a few words about the entertaining tonal variation known as *irony*. Irony is fun to write. And it can also be fun to read—if the reader sees exactly what sorts of tricks the writer is up to. In using irony, the writer says something he doesn't mean. Sometimes he says the exact opposite of what he means. "That was a bright idea," you remark to your friend, and the acid in your voice implies that you are being ironic. "Women are not human. They lie when they say that they have human needs," writes Dorothy Sayers, and all but the dullest readers know that she, too, has become angrily ironic.[6] Dwight Macdonald, in a passage quoted in full in the last chapter, uses irony to attack the self-help manuals that promise to renovate your mind through some simple but infallible system. Macdonald quotes the Reverend Dr. Norman Vincent Peale, who professes to make both God and Freud your spiritual counselors and to give you "a simple yet scientific system of practical techniques, of successful living that works." Then Macdonald comments:

> It works, it's simple (yet scientific), it's scientific (yet simple), it guarantees happiness & success & worthwhileness & peace & salvation, and, best of all, it has been reduced by the intellectual labors of Dr. Peale to a system, a technique . . . that gets both God and Freud on the job, with "scientific counseling and . . . the application of religious faith." Let the Gold Dust Twins do your work![7]

Macdonald doesn't mean a word of this, but sometimes an ironist comes slightly closer to saying what he means. Perhaps he uses *ironic understatement*, as a student did a few years ago when she wrote that "The Nixon administration has not been notably successful in achieving a reputation for candor and clean government." Or perhaps the writer uses *ironic overstatement*, as Gore Vidal did in talking about our national forgetfulness: "our country has always existed in a kind of time-vacuum:

---

6 "The Human Not Quite Human," *Masculine/Feminine*, Betty and Theodore Roszak, eds. (New York: Harper and Row, 1969), p. 121.

7 Copyright 1954 by Dwight Macdonald. Originally appeared in *The New Yorker*. Reprinted from *Against The American Grain*, by Dwight Macdonald, by permission of Random House, Inc. "Howtoism," *Against the American Grain* (New York: Random House, 1962), p. 387.

we have no public memory of anything that happened before last Tuesday." [8]

Germaine Greer, in the following passage, spices her irony with silly clichés—which she then debunks:

> I cannot claim to be fully emancipated from the dream that some enormous man, say six foot six, heavily shouldered and so forth to match, will crush me to his tweeds, look down into my eyes and leave the taste of heaven or the scorch of his passion on my waiting lips. For three weeks I was married to him.[9]

Greer's final sentence gives the irony away, just in case anybody had been taking it seriously. The danger in using irony is that your reader might not know when to take you literally and when to relax and enjoy your double-meanings. This confusion occurs most easily if you slip in and out of irony without giving any hint that you're doing so. Yvor Winters, one of the great literary critics of the century, once made the mistake of pinning the following ironic statement to the tail end of a serious paragraph: "We have, in other words, a rather fine poem about nothing." [10] Many readers took this to mean that the poem in question did a good job of revealing the nothingness, the meaningless void, underlying all reality. What Winters actually meant was much less metaphysical: that although the poem was skillfully executed, it rested on some undiscoverable and probably nonexistent meaning, and was therefore unsuccessful. But Winters' own meaning was so well hidden that it, too, seemed undiscoverable or nonexistent to a great many readers. Such are the dangers of irony. But the risk is worth taking, we believe, because the reward—the pleasure for both writer and reader—is likely to be substantial.

HEARING VOICES

The writer's voice, then, is a mixture of two things—or three, if you prefer to look at it that way. First, the *persona*: the writer's personality, or rather those features of it that he exhibits in a given piece of writing. Second, the *tone*, which in turn may be divided into (1) the writer's attitude toward his audience and (2) his attitude toward the subject.

[9] Germaine Greer, *The Female Eunuch* (New York: McGraw-Hill, 1971), pp. 52–53. (London: MacGibbon & Kee Ltd.)
[10] *In Defense of Reason* (Denver: Alan Swallow, 1947), p. 48.

When you analyze a writer's voice, you will sometimes find it difficult to make sharp distinctions between persona and tone. The two things frequently overlap. But analysis is easier if you begin by keeping them separate, bearing in mind that like so many of the rhetorician's useful but artificial distinctions, the separation is likely to break down.

Let's try analyzing two passages from two of the best American essayists of the last 25 years: Edmund Wilson and Gore Vidal.

First Wilson:

> When I wrote a review last November of Pasternak's *Doctor Zhivago,* I was aware that the main theme of the book was death and resurrection, which was constantly turning up in the images, the situations and the religious references, but I was only just becoming aware that the characters, all of whom were named—as was customary in Russia under the old régime—after saints of the Orthodox calendar, were partly to be understood in terms of the legends of these saints. The more one studies *Doctor Zhivago,* the more one comes to realize that it is studded with symbols and significant puns, that there is something in it of *Finnegans Wake,* and something of the cabalistic *Zohar,* which discovers a whole system of hidden meanings in the text of the Hebrew Bible. . . . The more one reads *Doctor Zhivago,* the more one becomes convinced that it is really pervaded by a poetic symbolism, and from the moment one begins to get the sense of this, the story gains another dimension.
> . . . Symbols and parallels do . . . exist in *Zhivago.* They are deliberate and very important: the whole story is organized around them; they lie at the center of the meaning of the book; and once we have become aware of them, we see it composed as a harmony.
> . . . *Doctor Zhivago* is not at all old-fashioned: in spite of some echoes of the Tolstoyan tone in certain of the military scenes, there is no point in comparing it with *War and Peace.* It is a modern poetic novel by a writer who has read Proust, Joyce and Faulkner, and who, like Virginia Woolf or the Lawrence Durrell of the Alexandria series, has gone on from his predecessors to invent in this genre a variation of his own.[11]

Persona. Immediately upon entering Wilson's first sentence, with its precise and yet intricate syntax, we know we are in the hands of a sophisticated writer. And soon we discover that he has read *Zhivago* in the original Russian, has looked into the legends surrounding the Russian saints, and even knows something about the Jewish mystical work, the *Zohar;* and he talks about major figures in modern literature—Proust, Faulkner, Woolf, and the rest—as familiarly as teenagers talk about old

[11] "Legend and Symbol in *Doctor Zhivago,*" *The Bit Between My Teeth* (New York: Farrar, Straus and Giroux, 1965), pp. 447, 469.

cars and new movies. What's just as surprising is that this remarkable scholar can admit that he sometimes makes a mistake. Wilson readily confesses that when he first wrote about *Zhivago* ("last November"), he had not fully appreciated it—had failed to recognize the depth and complexity of its symbolism. Here we have a scholar whose bold erudition is tempered by humility.

Tone: attitude toward audience. The passage comes very close to the High Style, but even its longest sentences are not hard to follow and even its most erudite words are not esoteric. (Wilson has long been praised—and, by some, condemned—for being one of those rare literary critics who feel no need for the perplexing jargon of the various schools of criticism.) The formal *one's* in the second and third sentences might easily have made the prose impersonal, but they are counteracted by the personal *I's* in the first sentence and by the openness, the honest self-revelation, in Wilson's admission that he didn't always understand *Zhivago* as well as he does now. In short, the style reaches toward High, but still keeps the ease and personal warmth of Middle.

Tone: attitude toward subject. Perhaps the warmth we've just mentioned didn't arise so much from Wilson's attitude toward his audience as from his feelings toward his subject—namely, his discovery of new depths of meaning in *Doctor Zhivago*. How can we characterize those feelings? Wilson, we might say, is *enthusiastic* about his own process of discovery, and *respectful*, or even *reverential*, toward *Doctor Zhivago* as a work of art and Boris Pasternak as an artist.

Now let's listen to a strikingly different voice—that of Gore Vidal:

> It is possible to stop most drug addiction in the United States within a very short itme. Simply make all drugs available and sell them at cost. Label each drug with a precise description of what effect—good and bad—the drug will have on the taker. This will require heroic honesty. Don't say that marijuana is addictive or dangerous when it is neither, as millions of people know—unlike "speed," which kills most unpleasantly, or heroin, which is addictive and difficult to kick.
>
> For the record, I have tried—once—almost every drug and liked none, disproving the popular Fu Manchu theory that a single whiff of opium will enslave the mind. Nevertheless many drugs are bad for certain people to take and they should be told why in a sensible way.
>
> Along with exhortation and warning, it might be good for our citizens to recall (or learn for the first time) that the United States was the creation of men who believed that each man has the right to do what he wants with his own life as long as he does not interfere with his neighbor's pursuit of happiness (that his neighbor's idea of happiness is persecuting others does confuse matters a bit).

This is a startling notion to the current generation of Americans. They reflect a system of public education which has made the Bill of Rights, literally, unacceptable to a majority of high school graduates (see the annual Purdue reports) who now form the "silent majority"—a phrase which that underestimated wit Richard Nixon took from Homer who used it to describe the dead.

Now one can hear the warning rumble begin: if everyone is allowed to take drugs everyone will and the GNP will decrease, the Commies will stop us from making everyone free, and we shall end up a race of Zombies, passively murmuring "groovie" to one another. Alarming thought. Yet it seems most unlikely that any reasonably sane person will become a drug addict if he knows in advance what addiction is going to be like.[12]

Persona. What a delightful voice to listen to! This is clearly an intelligent man, yet one who refuses to be stuffy or stand-offish. For one thing, he is honest about himself; he readily tells us something that might get him into trouble: that he has tried almost every kind of drug, *pro*scribed as well as *pre*scribed. (If the same thing were true of you, you might confess it to friends and relatives, and even casual acquaintances, but would you publish it in the *New York Times*, where this essay originally appeared?) Second, this writer enjoys making his writing enjoyable. He has a lively sense of humor—as in his lambasting of the "popular Fu Manchu theory" regarding opium, his characterization of Richard Nixon as an "underestimated wit," and his portrait of a drugged America: "a race of Zombies, passively murmuring 'groovie' to one another." Further, he has a lively way with ideas, particularly ideas opposed to the commonplace, ideas that swim against the American mainstream: all drugs should be legalized; marijuana is neither dangerous nor addictive; the public schools have taught Americans to disbelieve the Bill of Rights; etc.

Tone: attitude toward audience. The style sounds very much like lively conversation among intelligent people. It conveys the image of a friendly speaker who has no use for falseness or affectation, but prefers to express himself honestly and take his listeners into his confidence. The style has this effect partly because Vidal tells us frankly about his experiments with drugs and because he amiably assumes that we can appreciate his touches of irony—such as his mention of the "heroic honesty" required to tell the simple truth and his assertion that Nixon is an "underestimated wit." But the easy friendliness of Vidal's tone is also the result of his adherence to the Middle Style, which, as we have said, avoids both the impersonality of High Style and the chumminess of Low, and achieves instead a pleasant cordiality. Vidal's style sits right in the middle of Middle, with only occasional excursions into High and Low. (The traces of High are, possibly, the word *exhortation* and, certainly, the lengthy sentences in the third and fourth paragraphs and the impersonal *one* in the last paragraph. The traces of Low are the personal *I*, the contraction *don't*, the colloquialisms *speed, kick, Commies,* and *groovie,* and the sentence fragment "Alarming thought" in the final paragraph.)

Tone: attitude toward subject. Notice the variations. No single adjective could sum up Vidal's attitude toward his subject, because his attitude varies as he moves from one phase of the subject to another. Vidal's tone might be labeled *serious,* or even *urgent,* in those passages in which he issues his recommendations for solving the drug problem. But when he shifts his attention to the American people and their alleged obtuseness in handling such matters, his tone becomes *sardonic, condescending,* and sometimes downright *insulting.* In the opening paragraph, where Vidal introduces his proposed solution, we hear only the note of urgency. But the second paragraph offers a mixture of two tones: condescension toward "the popular Fu Manchu theory that a single whiff of opium will enslave the mind," and then, in the second sentence, a renewed sense of urgency as Vidal returns to his recommended solution. The third and fourth paragraphs ridicule American ignorance and the American penchant for meddling in other people's affairs; and in those paragraphs Vidal's tone is one of unmitigated insult. The tone of insult continues into the final paragraph, where Vidal offers a tongue-in-cheek summary of popular platitudes. But in the final sentence he returns to his own proposal for handling drugs, and there he again takes on the seriousness of a man with a cause.

We recommend that you practice this kind of analysis whenever you particularly admire a writer's style—whenever you are deeply stirred or lightly entertained by the voice of a Dwight Macdonald, a Germaine Greer, an Edmund Wilson, or a Gore Vidal. Characterize the author's persona and tone, and then examine the style to find out exactly how it implies that particular persona and that particular tone. Consider the style in all its details. Consider the wording, for one thing. To what extent is the wording formal or colloquial, clear or cloudy, specific or general, figurative or unadorned? And consider the sentences: their length and complexity, their tight conciseness or looser chattiness, their tendency to present subordinate elements before, during, or after the main clause; their use of various coordinate structures and subordinate ones; their use of parallelism and active voice and transitional markers. . . . And so on and so forth.

By analyzing a writer's voice in this way you not only review all your knowledge about prose style, but you get a chance to pick up some new insights and strategies. A second benefit is that you become more skillful at projecting your own voice and at varying your voice to suit a diversity of topics and audiences.

Don't underestimate the importance of voice. Max Beerbohm once praised the writings of James McNeill Whistler on the grounds that "every sentence is ringing with a clear vocal cadence." "That vocal quality," Beerbohm continued, "is the chief test of good writing." [13] Perhaps Beerbohm exaggerated, but his insistence on finding a distinct vocal quality in prose seems increasingly pertinent now that so many of the statements issued by government, business, and the learned professions are as destitute of vocal quality—as dry, dreary, and impersonal, as deficient in rhythm and vitality—as if the writers had done their very best not to sound like human beings.

Exercises

I. These exercises offer you practice in varying your "voice" Do whichever two or three exercises you feel most comfortable with.

1. You are a middle-class worker—let's say a carpenter—and you are writing a letter to be printed in a highly respected newspaper: the *New York Times,* perhaps, or the *Christian Science Monitor.* The ideas you wish to convey are stated in the following excerpt from an interview recorded in Myron Brenton's *The American Male:*

> I can't think of one man I know who's working nine to five and satisfied with that. No matter how high you get, you're always holding on to some part-time work. The guys in my neighborhood—firemen, policemen, accountants—they're all working overtime. They've got something going in every direction. My father worked hard, he put in a good day, and that was it. Now you have a house and mortgage payments and your repairs and all the expenses for the kids. I mean, these are sort of basic; you can't get out of them no matter how you cut things. And then there's college. Even if you're earning fifteen thousand dollars a year, you can't relax. You've got to hustle.[14]

---

[13] "Whistler's Writing," *The Incomparable Max* (New York: Dodd, Mead, 1962), p. 149.

[14] *The American Male* (Greenwich, Conn.: Fawcett Premier Books, 1970), pp. 20–21.

2. You are a highly urbane professor of English at a major university, and you are writing an essay for the kind of well-educated audience that reads *Harper's* or the *Atlantic Monthly*. The ideas you wish to communicate were stated in the previous exercise—in the interview about the middle-class need to hustle.

3. You edit a newspaper in a small New England town that prides itself on its citizens' clear thinking and sound judgment. The community strongly favors individual freedom and the preservation of human rights, but tends to be isolationist in its stance toward the rest of the world. You are writing an editorial endorsing the following ideas from John F. Kennedy's Inaugural Address:

> . . . Man holds in his mortal hands the power to abolish all forms of human poverty and all forms of human life. And yet the same revolutionary belief for which our forebears fought is still at issue around the globe, the belief that the rights of man come not from the generosity of the state but from the hand of God.
>
> We dare not forget today that we are the heirs of that first revolution. Let the word go forth from this time and place, to friend and foe alike, that the torch has been passed to a new generation of Americans, born in this century, tempered by war, disciplined by a hard and bitter peace, proud of our ancient heritage, and unwilling to witness or permit the slow undoing of those human rights to which this nation has always been committed, and to which we are committed today at home and around the world.
>
> Let every nation know, whether it wishes us well or ill, that we shall pay any price, bear any burden, meet any hardship, support any friend, oppose any foe to assure the survival and the success of liberty.

4. You are a blue-collar worker delivering a harangue at a union meeting. You wish to convince your fellow workers to go out on strike. You are angry about the sorry plight of blue-collar workers, and you become impatient with anyone who hesitates to strike. Part of your speech is devoted to the following ideas:

> The worker is becoming the "forgotten American." On the most immediate level, that of job satisfaction, the worker is acutely aware of the declining status of manual labor. . . . Consequently the blue-collar worker increasingly feels that his work has no status in the eyes of society, the media, or even his own children.
>
> Moreover, this loss of status is an accurate reflection of economic reality. Automation has carved deep into the ranks of blue-collar jobs. . . . The much-vaunted material progress made by workers is in many ways illusory. Most often overlooked is the critical fact that blue-collar workers have actually lost the economic mo-

mentum they reached in the early postwar years. From the rapid gains of wartime, workers have again fallen behind managers and professionals in their drive to increase income. Price increases have cut sharply into blue-collar buying power: in the past five years, because of inflation workers have actually lost ground in terms of real purchasing power (measured in 1957–59 dollars), from a high of $88.06 per week in 1965 down to $85.35 five years later. Added to this are the especially rapid rises in the cost of necessities that hit the lower middle class the hardest: between 1958 and 1968, according to the *Wall Street Journal,* daily hospital care went up 101%; auto insurance 44%; physicians' fees 38%; property insurance 36%.

Richard Parker [15]

5. You are the new President of the United States delivering your inaugural address. You wish to express most forcefully the ideas stated by Richard Parker in the previous exercise, so that you can gain support for programs designed to better the lot of blue-collar workers. At the same time you wish to preserve a dignity and decorum appropriate to the occasion.

6. You are a sophisticated journalist writing for a sophisticated audience, the kind of audience that might read the *New Yorker* or *Harper's* or the *Atlantic Monthly.* Although you like to engage in witticism and irony, you are basically a serious writer with a keen dislike for all forms of injustice and foul play. You wish to express substantially the views stated by J. L. Simmons on page 219 (in the passage from *Deviants*), but you favor the "deviant," as opposed to "conventional people," much more vigorously than Simmons does in that passage. Further, you like to spice your prose with a good many more specifics than Simmons offers.

7. You are a college student writing a letter to a close friend who still lives in your old hometown. Liberalized by your education, you have come to agree with the ideas stated by J. L. Simmons on page 219; and though you were once the most conventional of "conventional people," your sympathy now goes out to "deviants"—the mavericks who get snubbed at your college or those who get badgered and bullied in your hometown. The person to whom you are writing is a high school senior—sensitive and intelligent but not entirely free of the illiberal values sometimes inculcated by a small rural community.

8. You are writing for a conservative Protestant magazine whose subscribers, in a recent poll, chose Norman Vincent Peale as the religious

[15] *The Myth of the Middle Class* (New York: Harper and Row, 1972), pp. 139–40.

writer who, apart from Biblical authors, had most strongly influenced their lives. You do not admire Dr. Peale's writings—for reasons similar to those offered by Dwight Macdonald on pages 214–15. You wish to explain your reasons in a manner that won't offend your readers and might possibly cause a few of them to doubt whether Dr. Peale is truly a great spiritual counselor.

9. You are addressing the local chapter of the Daughters of the American Revolution. You try to explain the ideas stated by Caroline Bird on page 217 in such a way that the Daughters will listen patiently, take in your meaning, and perhaps in the future be more sympathetic toward the woman who discards "all the little cues and clues and buttons and bows and smiles and wiles that invite a man to look her over."

II. Analyze the "voice" of *two* of the following passages. First characterize the writer's *persona*, then the *tone*, which you should treat as the sum of two things: attitude toward audience and attitude toward subject.

1. Johnny goes by the official title of "student." Yet Johnny's is the face every professor would prefer to see anywhere but in his classroom, where it blocks with its dreary smile, or its stoical yawn, the educational process on which we are proud to spend annually billions of dollars. By his sheer inert numbers he is making the common pursuit of professors and students—real students—impossible.

No one, least of all his professor, wills Johnny an injustice. Even the dean of students, whose lot he renders abysmal, finds it impossible not to like him, though some miraculous multiplication of loafers and fish sends Johnnies in an endless column trooping past the dean's receptionist, to stammer out their tale of dragging grades and just not digging the stuff.

Johnnies by the thousand, by the hundred thousand, clutter up every college in the land, where they long ago acquired a numerical majority. If you have a teenager in your home, thinking of college, the chances are you have Johnny. On behalf of my 400,000 colleagues in the academic profession, I'd be grateful if you'd keep him home.

Hugh Kenner [16]

2. [For some young people today] the best thing to be . . . isn't go-getting or up-and-coming, but cool. Broad social conscience has been replaced by personal responsibility, and if they plan at all, their plans will be to get away. The new movement is away from the old group forms of moratorium crowds and huge rock concerts and communes. Young doctors who once joined the Peace Corps are

[16] "Don't Send Johnny to College," *Saturday Evening Post,* 14 November 1964, p. 12.

turning more and more to small-town private practices, Harvard scholars are dropping out to study auto mechanics or farming. Everybody wants to buy land in Oregon and Vermont. If we have any ambition at all now, it is not so much the drive to get ahead as it is the drive to get away.

When my friends and I were little, we had big plans. I would be a famous actress and singer, dancing on the side. I would paint my own sets and compose my own music, writing the script and the lyrics and reviewing the performance for the New York *Times.* I would marry and have three children (they don't allow us dreams like that any more) and we would live, rich and famous (donating lots to charity, of course, and periodically adopting orphans), in a house we designed ourselves. When I was older I had visions of good works. I saw myself in South American rain forests and African deserts, feeding the hungry and healing the sick with an obsessive selflessness, I see now, that was as selfish, in the end, as my first plans for stardom.

Now my goal is simpler. I want to be happy. And I want comfort—nice clothes, a nice house, good music and good food, and the feeling that I'm doing some little thing that matters. I'll vote and I'll give to charity, but I won't give myself. I feel a sudden desire to buy land—not a lot, not as a business investment, but just a small plot of earth so that whatever they do to the country I'll have a place where I can go—a kind of fallout shelter, I guess. As some people prepare for their old age, so I prepare for my twenties. A little house, a comfortable chair, peace and quiet—retirement sounds tempting.

Joyce Maynard [17]

3. [My father] could be chilling in the pulpit and indescribably cruel in his personal life and he was certainly the most bitter man I have ever met. . . . He claimed to be proud of his blackness but it had also been the cause of much humiliation and it had fixed bleak boundaries to his life. He was not a young man when we were growing up and he had already suffered many kinds of ruin; in his outrageously demanding and protective way he loved his children, who were black like him and menaced, like him; and all these things sometimes showed in his face when he tried, never to my knowledge with any success, to establish contact with any of us. When he took one of his children on his knee to play, the child always became fretful and began to cry; when he tried to help one of us with our homework the absolutely unabating tension which emanated from him caused our minds and our tongues to become paralyzed, so that he, scarcely knowing why, flew into a rage and the child, not knowing why, was punished. If it ever entered his head to bring a surprise

[17] Excerpt from *Looking Back* by Joyce Maynard. © 1972, 1973 by Joyce Maynard. Reprinted by permission of Doubleday & Company, Inc. *Looking Back* (Garden City, New York: Doubleday, 1973), pp. 155–57.

home for his children, it was, almost unfailingly, the wrong surprise and even the big watermelons he often brought home on his back in the summertime led to the most appalling scenes. I do not remember, in all those years, that one of his children was ever glad to see him come home. From what I was able to gather of his early life, it seemed that this inability to establish contact with other people had always marked him and had been one of the things which had driven him out of New Orleans. There was something in him, therefore, groping and tentative, which was never expressed and which was buried with him. One saw it most clearly when he was facing new people and hoping to impress them. But he never did, not for long. We went from church to smaller and more improbable church, he found himself in less and less demand as a minister, and by the time he died none of his friends had come to see him for a long time. He had lived and died in an intolerable bitterness of spirit and it frightened me, as we drove him to the graveyard through those unquiet, ruined streets, to see how powerful and overflowing this bitterness could be and to realize that this bitterness now was mine.

When he died I had been away from home for a little over a year. In that year I had had time to become aware of the meaning of all my father's bitter warnings, had discovered the secret of his proudly pursed lips and rigid carriage: I had discovered the weight of white people in the world. I saw that this had been for my ancestors and now would be for me an awful thing to live with and that the bitterness which had helped to kill my father could also kill me.

James Baldwin [18]

4. [Marilyn Monroe] was already an established star before I knew her as anything except the latest pin-up girl. There is always this shield of irony some of us raise between ourselves and any object of popular adulation, and I had made my dull point of snubbing her pictures. Then one evening I chanced on a television trailer for *Bus Stop,* and there she was. I'm not even sure I knew whom I was seeing on the screen, but a light had gone on in the room. Where everything had been gray there was all at once an illumination, a glow of something beyond the ordinarily human. It was a remarkable moment, of a kind I don't recall having had with any other actress, and it has its place with certain rare, cherished experiences of art such as my youthful remembrance of Pavlova, the most perfect of performing artists, whose control of her body was like a radiance, or even the quite recent experience of seeing some photographs of Nijinsky in motion. Marilyn Monroe was in motion, too, which is important, since no still picture could quite catch her electric quality; in posed pictures the redundancy of flesh was what first

imposed itself, dimming one's perception of its peculiar aliveness, of the translucence that infused body with spirit. In a moment's flash of light, the ironies with which I had resisted this sex idol, this object of undifferentiating public taste, dropped from me never to be restored.

Diana Trilling [19]

5. A boxer, like a writer, must stand alone. If he loses he cannot call an executive conference and throw off on a vice president or the assistant sales manager. He is consequently resented by fractional characters who cannot live outside an organization. A fighter's hostilities are not turned inward, like a Sunday tennis player's or a lady M.P.'s. They come out naturally with his sweat, and when his job is done he feels good because he has expressed himself. Chain-of-command types, to whom this is intolerable, try to rationalize their envy by proclaiming solicitude for the fighter's health. If a boxer, for example, ever went as batty as Nijinsky, all the wowsers in the world would be screaming "Punch-drunk." Well, who hit Nijinsky? And why isn't there a campaign against ballet? It gives girls thick legs. If a novelist who lived exclusively on apple-cores won the Nobel Prize, vegetarians would chorus that the repulsive nutriment had invigorated his brain. But when the prize goes to Ernest Hemingway, who has been a not particularly evasive boxer for years, no one rises to point out that the percussion has apparently stimulated his intellection. Albert Camus, the French probable for the Nobel, is an ex-boxer, too.

I was in the Neutral Corner saloon in New York a year or so ago when a resonant old gentleman, wiry, straight, and white-haired, walked in and invited the proprietors to his ninetieth birthday party, in another saloon. The shortly-to-be nonagenarian wore no glasses, his hands were shapely, his forearms hard, and every hair looked as if, in the old water-front phrase, it had been drove in with a nail. On the card of invitation he laid on the bar was printed:

Billy Ray
Last Surviving Bare Knuckle Fighter

The last bare-knuckle fight in which the world heavyweight championship changed hands was in 1882.

Mr. Ray would not let anybody else in the Neutral buy a drink. As I shared his bounty I thought of all his contemporary lawn-tennis players, laid away with their thromboses, and the golfers hoisted out of sand pits after suffering coronary occlusions. If they had turned in time to a more wholesome sport, I reflected, they might still be hanging on as board chairmen and senior editors instead of having their names on memorial pews. I asked Mr. Ray how many

[19] "The Death of Marilyn Monroe," *Claremont Essays* (New York: Harcourt, Brace and World, 1964), pp. 231–32.

fights he had had and he said, "A hundert forty. The last one was with gloves. I thought the game was getting soft, so I retired."

A. J. Liebling [20]

6. Germaine Greer on the modern ideal of feminine beauty (pp. 219-20)

7. George Orwell on the language of politics (pp. 41-42)

8. X. J. Kennedy on King Kong (p. 49)

9. Max Beerbohm on systematic philosophers (p. 139)

10. Herbert J. Muller on "mass-man and his mass-culture" (pp. 158-59)

11. Bernard Shaw on "the whole country as a big household" (pp. 191-92)

12. H. L. Mencken on the "incredibly obscure and malodorous style" of Thorstein Veblen (pp. 202-3)

13. James Thurber on the editorial expertise of Harold Ross (pp. 203-4)

14. Dwight Macdonald on the men of God who sell peace of mind (pp. 214-15)

III. Analyze your own "voice," or rather the voice you spoke in *one* of your old pieces of writing. Describe your *persona* and then your *tone* (toward both audience and subject). And then you might consider the following questions and any others that seem pertinent: (1) Was the voice appropriate to the occasion? (2) Was it an interesting voice to listen to? (3) Did it represent a large part of your personality?

[20] *The Sweet Science* (New York: Viking Press, 1956).

Suggestions for Further Reading

If you wish to continue your study of prose style, the readings listed here will amply reward your efforts. We recommend that you begin with the four anthologies marked with asterisks. They will acquaint you with the central issues in the study of style. Moreover, they offer selected portions of other books on this list, and they contain the essays listed here as well as others of great value.

Monroe C. Beardsley. "Style and Good Style." *Reflections on High School English: NDEA Institute Lectures 1965.* Ed. Gary Tate. Tulsa: University of Tulsa, 1966. Pages 91–105. Reprinted in *Contemporary Essays on Style*, ed. Love and Payne.

Marjorie Boulton. *The Anatomy of Prose.* London: Routledge and Kegan Paul, 1954. Hardbound and paperbound.

Francis Christensen. "A Generative Rhetoric of the Sentence." *Notes Toward a New Rhetoric: Six Essays for Teachers.* New York: Harper and Row, 1967. Pages 1–22. Reprinted in *Contemporary Essays on Style*, ed. Love and Payne.

Edward P. J. Corbett. *Classical Rhetoric for the Modern Student.* 2nd ed. New York: Oxford University Press, 1971. See section IV ("Style"), pp. 414–593.

Edward P. J. Corbett. "A Method of Analyzing Prose Style with a Demonstration Analysis of Swift's *A Modest Proposal.*" *Reflections on High School English: NDEA Institute Lectures 1965.* Ed. Gary

Tate. Tulsa: University of Tulsa, 1966. Pages 106–24. Reprinted in *Contemporary Essays on Style*, ed. Love and Payne.

* J. V. Cunningham, editor. *The Problem of Style*. Greenwich, Conn.: Fawcett, 1966. Paperbound.

Bonamy Dobrée. *Modern Prose Style*. 2nd ed. New York: Oxford University Press, 1964.

Richard M. Eastman. *Style: Writing as the Discovery of Outlook*. New York: Oxford University Press, 1970. Paperbound.

Walker Gibson. *Tough, Sweet and Stuffy: An Essay on Modern American Prose Styles*. Bloomington: Indiana University Press, 1966. Hardbound and paperbound.

* Donald Hall, editor. *The Modern Stylists: Writers on the Art of Writing*. New York: The Free Press, 1968. Hardbound and paperbound.

* Glen A. Love and Michael Payne, editors. *Contemporary Essays on Style: Rhetoric, Linguistics and Criticism*. Glenview, Illinois: Scott, Foresman, 1968. Paperbound.

J. Middleton Murry. *The Problem of Style*. London: Oxford University Press, 1960. Paperbound.

George Orwell. "Politics and the English Language." *Collected Essays, Journalism and Letters*. New York: Harcourt, Brace and World, 1968, IV, 127–40. Reprinted in *The Modern Stylists*, ed. Hall, and *Modern Essays on Writing and Style*, ed. Wermuth.

Walter Raleigh. *Style*. London: Edward Arnold, 1897.

Herbert Read. *English Prose Style*. Boston: Beacon Press, 1955. Paperbound.

James R. Sutherland. *On English Prose*. Toronto: University of Toronto Press, 1957. Paperbound.

Virginia Tufte. *Grammar as Style*. New York: Holt, Rinehart and Winston, 1971. Hardbound and paperbound.

Rulon Wells. "Nominal and Verbal Style." *Style in Language*. Ed. Thomas Sebeok. Cambridge: MIT Press, 1960. Reprinted in *The Problem of Style*, ed. Cunningham, and *Modern Essays on Writing and Style*, ed. Wermuth.

* Paul C. Wermuth, editor. *Modern Essays on Writing and Style*. 2nd ed. New York: Holt, Rinehart and Winston, 1969. Paperbound.

John B. Williams. *Style and Grammar: A Writer's Handbook of Transformations*. New York: Dodd, Mead, 1973. Paperbound.

Index of Topics

Index of Authors